The African American
Experience in Crime Fiction

The African American Experience in Crime Fiction

A Critical Study

ROBERT E. CRAFTON

McFarland & Company, Inc., Publishers
Jefferson, North Carolina

LIBRARY OF CONGRESS CATALOGUING-IN-PUBLICATION DATA

Crafton, Robert E., 1953– author.
The African American experience in crime fiction : a critical study / Robert E. Crafton.
      p.   cm.
Includes bibliographical references and index.

ISBN 978-0-7864-9938-0 (softcover : acid free paper) ∞
ISBN 978-1-4766-2129-6 (ebook)

1. American fiction—African American authors—History and criticism.
2. Detective and mystery stories, American—History and criticism.
3. Urban fiction, American—History and criticism.
4. African Americans in literature.   5. Crime in literature.
6. Crime writing.   I. Title.

PS374.N4C73 2015   813.009'896073—dc23   2015017988

BRITISH LIBRARY CATALOGUING DATA ARE AVAILABLE

© 2015 Robert E. Crafton. All rights reserved

No part of this book may be reproduced or transmitted in any form or by any means, electronic or mechanical, including photocopying or recording, or by any information storage and retrieval system, without permission in writing from the publisher.

On the cover: Harlem neighborhood in New York City (Thinkstock)

Printed in the United States of America

*McFarland & Company, Inc., Publishers
Box 611, Jefferson, North Carolina 28640
www.mcfarlandpub.com*

Table of Contents

Preface: Putting Things in Perspective   1

1. High Anxiety   7
2. A More Perfect Union: Pauline Hopkins, *Hagar's Daughter* and the Struggle for Equality   21
3. "A Mystery Tale of Dark Harlem": Rounding Up the Usual Suspects   53
4. *Plus ça change*: Chester Himes's Harlem Domestic Series   77
5. *Entr'Acte*: A Postmodernist Interlude   104
6. Falling into History: Easy Rawlins and the Arc of African American Experience   135
7. Our Kind of People: Stephen L. Carter and the Mysteries of the Black Bourgeoisie   160
8. Detecting Difference?   178

Chapter Notes   191
Works Cited   195
Index   201

Preface: Putting Things in Perspective

I first started reading detective fiction in the mid–1990s, not long after hearing Lucha Corpi read from *Cactus Blood*, the second of her Gloria Damasco books, at the National Council of Teachers of English annual convention. At that time I was engaged in co-teaching a multicultural literature course entitled "New Voices for All Ages," a course offered in a midwestern university's MAT program for teachers seeking to advance their careers and education. That multiethnic American authors could still be classified as "new voices"—and that much of the course was devoted to introducing (mostly white) teachers from all grade levels to a body of literature and histories and ethnic experiences with which they were almost wholly unfamiliar—suggest just how little minority authors and experiences had been integrated into the schools and into mainstream American culture forty years after *Brown v. Board* had begun the long process of integrating American education.

Our purpose in the course was to move these teachers beyond the typical heroes-and-holidays curriculum, beyond dutiful attention to black history during the month of February, to a position where they were capable of evaluating the depiction of minority peoples in picture books, young adult literature, and adult literature and of integrating this body of literature into the classes they taught. And to create this critical perspective, we needed to place these books in a historical and cultural context, a framework most of these teachers lacked. As young teachers, most in their mid- to late twenties, they had been born in the late 1960s and attended school in the last quarter of the twentieth century, a period when school systems were actively seeking ways to integrate otherwise segregated schools. While some progress was apparent in magnet schools and programs promoting inter-district transfers, textbooks and instruction, especially in language arts and American history classes, hadn't fully caught up.

Of the histories of America's multiethnic peoples, the students were all but ignorant. Even today, many first-year college students, at least those in my composition courses, know little about the Trail of Tears, about the Sand Creek and Wounded Knee massacres, about boarding schools like the Carlisle Indian Industrial School where the stated aim was to acculturate native children to white society, to "kill the Indian but save the man." Few know much about the internment of Americans of Japanese descent during World War II, about the contributions of Chinese immigrant labor to the construction of the transcontinental railroad, or about Angel Island—Ellis Island they tend to know about—or about immigration policies limiting the numbers of Asian peoples applying for entry into the United States.

Booker T. Washington and Martin Luther King, Jr., they have certainly heard of and studied in their history books, but Malcolm X they know mostly from Spike Lee's movie, and W.E.B. Dubois they have never heard of. Nor do they know anything about eugenics and its role in shaping laws and social policies in the opening decades of the twentieth century, though all of them know about Nazi atrocities committed to advance the superior genetic heritage of the Aryan race. Given the inadequacies of the textbooks they use and even of the standards of learning governing history instruction in many states, few students, whether in 1995 or today, recognize or know much about the historical events that have shaped the lives and experiences of America's minority populations. Of their vernacular experiences and the distinct ways of knowing, the alternate epistemologies that operate within minority communities, they are equally ignorant. This limited understanding of history and culture, still evident today, was the immediate barrier that we confronted in trying to teach multiethnic American literature to elementary, middle and high school teachers in 1995.

So Lucha Corpi's reading from *Cactus Blood* proved something of a revelation. In the course of a few pages, and in a pop culture form, the murder mystery, she had managed to digest a world of experience, the action and investigation in this book looking back to the Mexican farm workers strike and grape boycott. Here were the history, the vernacular experiences, and the alternate ways of knowing, the basic cultural contexts my students lacked, and in a more fully imagined form than they had ever encountered in the textbook literature. The murder mystery effectively mediated between pop cultural forms and minority experiences, providing a point of entry into the study of multiethnic American literature. In 1993, however, the available body of literature, the number of mystery novels centered in minority communities, was quite limited; critical studies of this material were practically nonexistent. Still, authors like Corpi and Walter Mosley, along with a growing number of series by lesbian authors, in addition to the commercially successful if controversial example of Tony Hillerman's long-running Leaphorn and Chee books, suggested the possibilities and possible viability of this subdivision of detective fiction.

While inducing even dedicated teachers to spend their summers immersed in the scholarly literature addressing minority history and culture might prove difficult, suggesting that they read *Devil in a Blue Dress* or *Eulogy for a Brown Angel* seemed more likely to succeed. This body of material might still seem sub-literary, not necessarily the kind of work covered in survey courses or even in courses devoted to African American or Latino/a literature. On the other hand, the popular nature of this genre proved it an important and viable topic of study to cultural studies.

In the last fifteen or so years, the landscape has changed markedly, at least with regard to detective fiction written by multiethnic American authors and its critical study. In 1995, locating mystery novels that centered on minority peoples and experiences required real effort, and the fruits of those investigations, as often as not, yielded books by Euro-American authors writing about Navaho or Cherokee or Japanese American characters, not all that different from the Charlie Chan novels and movies of an earlier generation. The best of these books, Hillerman's, for instance, were based on long experience with and careful research into the peoples and places represented in their pages. That such books proved to be the subject of controversy—Sherman Alexie includes a less than flattering portrayal of a Hillerman-like mystery author in *Indian Killer* and some of his short stories, for instance—was also the case.

These books may have avoided the stereotypical representations of Earl Derr Biggers's Charlie Chan, but their commercial exploitation of these materials, if nothing else, always proved to be an issue. Having established that such books had a market, however, numerous authors, some with well-established literary credentials, entered the field. Today there are dozens of series in print representing a kaleidoscope of peoples and experiences. Some of these books, as always, are formulaic potboilers intended simply to make money; others, by contrast, are remarkably more sophisticated literary efforts that engage and often revise the genre, re-examining the assumptions built into the form, one traditionally associated with pop cultural senses of justice and populated by racist and sexist stereotypes. At the same time that they revise the genre, these authors also engage and rewrite the historical narrative. A growing body of critical literature has taken up this material as the subject of its study. And some mystery authors, Walter Mosley, for instance, have been included in literary anthologies like the highly canonical *Norton Anthol-*

ogy of African-American Literature, transcending the ghetto of so-called "genre fiction."

The study that follows will track the emergence of the murder mystery in African American literature, from the earliest years of the twentieth century through the first decade of the twenty-first. The study looks at representative authors, some well known, some deserving to be better known, beginning with Pauline Hopkins's *Hagar's Daughter*, currently identified as the first mystery novel published by an African American author, though a novel that appeared only in serial form in the periodical literature, not in book form. The study then moves to Rudolph Fisher's *The Conjure-Man Dies*, the first mystery novel by an African American author to be published as a book. The study concludes at the far end of the century and beginning of the twenty-first century with the works of Walter Mosley, both the Easy Rawlings and Leonid McGill series, and Stephen L. Carter's mysteries.

Situated squarely in the middle of this investigation is the work of Chester Himes and the Harlem Domestic series, the first commercially viable series, if not, perhaps, one that is fully successful aesthetically. The study will look particularly at the relatively obscure *Plan B*, a book Himes wrote and then abandoned, an alternate ending to the series which Himes wrote prior to writing and publishing *Blind Man with a Pistol*, the last of the Coffin Ed Johnson and Gravedigger Jones books. *Plan B* was published for the first time in France in 1983, the year before Himes died; the first American edition appeared in 1993, published by the University Press of Mississippi.

Also occupying this middle ground and marking something of a transition from genre to literary fiction is a consideration of Ishmael Reed's two novels featuring PaPa LaBas, *Mumbo Jumbo* and *The Last Days of Louisiana Red*, post-modernist anti-detective novels, both published in the 1970s, and of Colson Whitehead's *The Intuitionist* (1999), which advances the post-modernist novel into what Ramon Sandivar has described as "post-racial" territory. While *Mumbo Jumbo* earned a position as one of the paradigmatic works of African American literature in Henry Louis Gates, Jr.'s, *The Signifying Monkey*, first published in 1989, I suspect that were that book being written today, *The Intuitionist* might replace it.

Each of the books and/or series of books included in this study will be considered as a historical artifact, an expression of the prevailing anxieties of these authors with regard to the social systems—legal, medical, educational, literary and cultural—that historically have determined the prevailing attitudes and prejudices toward African Americans.

The study itself has evolved over a period of time, from 2007 to 2014, the initial research and first chapters written during a sabbatical leave during the spring and summer of 2007; subsequent chapters were written over the next few years, mostly during the summer, as time permitted. I have tried to position this study in the opening and closing chapters by examining the prevailing anxieties of 2007 and 2014, respectively, at least as they were recorded in popular culture in general, especially as reflected in primetime television series where police procedurals and crime dramas continue to occupy a large part of the programming. The discussion of *Monk* and *24* may seem an odd place to begin, even if *24* did manage to elect an African American president (and then a woman) well in advance of Barack Obama's ascent into that office. Both series have since concluded, but both, each something of a cultural phenomenon in its own right, clearly establish a baseline experience, a subject position, a point of comparison for this study.

That the rather quirky and sometimes psychic detectives popular during the middle years of the decade have largely closed down shop while the forensic specialists have expanded seems somehow telling. What hasn't changed much, perhaps, is the prevailing notion that "it's a jungle out there," as Adrian Monk might put it. What is interesting is the degree to which the contemporary authors considered in this study seem to share or redefine the sources of our cultural anxieties. On some levels, Stephen L. Carter's and Walter Mosley's concerns will be very different; the conservative Yale law professor's patrician characters couldn't be more different from the "darker race" populating Mosley's books. On other levels, their concerns will be similar, reflecting, to some degree, the now historical trauma induced by Al Qaeda's September 11, 2001, attacks and the wars, only recently "concluded," against terror in Iraq and in Afghanistan, the longest running wars in United States history.

The opening of the canon during the last quarter of the twentieth century to include works by women and minority authors and the ascent of cultural and new historical critical models no longer require critics to justify the study of what was once considered sub-literary genre fiction, a vernacular literature that, however popular, was not worthy of scholarly consideration. (The same charge might have been made against Charles Dickens in the closing years of the nineteenth and opening decades of the twentieth century.) While formulaic and a touch didactic at times, the structures of thought and the interpolated lectures clearly serve thematic and rhetorical purposes, no more nor less than the mechanical devices employed in any body of fiction, in the works of a Dickens or a Twain, for instance. Such elements suggest a self-consciousness, an explicit awareness of generic conventions and the constructedness of these fictions; in turn, they identify the implied audience for and purposes of these books.

On the other hand, these books' individual engagement with constitutional law or early twentieth-century theories of endocrinology or contemporary rap music's allusions to the Illuminati, while sometimes subtle or seemingly off-hand, anchor these books to their historical moment and the prevailing anxieties of these times. Dr. Archer's understanding of blood types (and his seemingly unusual preference for a rather early and mostly outmoded system of labeling different types of blood) in *The Conjure-Man Dies* or the otherwise very proper and very patrician Lemaster Carlyles's secret passion for gangsta rap in *New England White* seem, on careful consideration, more than mere quirks of character. The fine details will often prove as interesting and informative as the broad designs.

1

High Anxiety

> Detective fiction has always been intensely responsive to, and reflective of, the needs of its own times. Detective fiction is almost obsessively *au courant*.... It is unsurprising, then, that contemporary detective fiction ... touches time and again on contemporary American fears.
> —Kaufman and Kay 226

Prime Suspects: Contemporary Crime Fiction and Its Depiction on Television, Spring 2007

As a genre, detective fiction has always been built on contradictory impulses. Historically, it links to gothic literature, the commission of a crime, the play of irrational impulses, the existence of unexplained evil—and the thrill of fear it all engenders—one element in its making, while the protagonist, our knight errant, represents something of a romance figure who works to repair this rift in the social fabric. As a work of "genre fiction," it is a rule-governed system, an ideal construction in line with its romance roots. On the other hand, the work itself, examining social values and intimately tied to place and time and to social systems largely devoted to the maintenance of order, the narrative obsessed with methods and motives where the means through which the crime is accomplished must prove as plausible as the underlying impulses that led to its commission in the first place, depends on the elements of realistic fiction to frame the drama. And the drama itself, playing out according to these rules of engagement, of the generic contract the author enters into with his or her readers, proves satisfyingly conservative, as critics of the genre always point out, the rift in the social order, the product of evil impulses and/or sociopathy—the act of a morally and psychologically disordered personality—repaired by the operations of the (more than) rational detective. Order is restored, the forces of evil contained, (social) justice done. That is, until the craziness breaks out all over again in the next installment of these typically serialized adventures.

But the work is not, need not always involve an act of social reproduction, though reproducing/restoring social order seems to be the immediate result of most "golden age" mysteries, where the crime is an anomaly in village life, the evil act an aberration (Rzepka 153). In the noir constructions of "hard boiled" fiction, the systems themselves have been corrupted. In this case, the detective can hope, at best, to achieve a momentary stay against the pervasive confusion and corruption of the prevailing social systems. The achievement of justice here, however provisional, can only suggest the possibilities, perhaps the fantasy, of social reconstruction. In either case, the work, whether golden age or hard boiled, reflects and responds to the anxieties of the moment, as Kaufman and Kay suggest, the golden age mysteries, for instance, an antidote to the greater disruption of the First World War, an attempt to restore some semblance of order, a sense of business as usual, in the face of so much and so many lost, while the hard-boiled mystery confronts the rise of gangsterism and political corruption under prohibition and economic depression (Rzepka 184–85).

The mixed messages common to crime fiction are immediately illustrated on primetime television where the programming, particularly on the traditional networks, seems to be dominated by police procedurals, from the long-running *Law and Order* franchise, represented in the 2006–07 season in three variations,[1] to the *CSI* shows, also unfolding in three separate venues, to a number of variations on these themes, including other forensic investigators (*Crossing Jordan, Bones, NCIS*), psychological profilers (*Criminal Minds*), shows focusing largely on specific kinds of cases (unresolved investigations in *Cold Case,* domestic crimes in *Close to Home,* missing persons in *Without a Trace*), series built around oddly-gifted, idiosyncratic characters (the obsessive-compulsive Adrian Monk; the former child prodigy now professor of mathematics Charles Epps in *Numb3rs*; the psychic soccer mom Alison Dubois in *Medium*; and even a wizard, Harry Dresden, in *The Dresden Files,* who, like Monk, appears on a cable channel, not quite ready, evidently, for prime-time coverage)—among many other offerings, including several set in law offices and/or the offices of public prosecutors. The general interests and trends in these shows attest to the commercial viability of this programming, to a seemingly obsessive sense, as Monk suspects, that "it's a jungle out there," to a social order under siege where justice will generally prevail, but often in imperfect and certainly impermanent ways.

And always according to the narrative conventions and generic constructions of the mystery novel. *Monk,* for instance, stands in a direct line of descent from the gifted Holmes, with his own quirks and history of substance abuse, and from Miss Marple and Hercule Poirot, sharing their powers of observation and ratiocination along with the classic elements of their plots. Recent shows, for instance, have played variations on the locked-room/country-house puzzles of the golden age and involved the intentional use of a red herring plot to sidetrack the investigation.[2] These are classic puzzle pieces, solved by a gifted detective with uncanny powers, who, in spite of his talents, cannot solve the murder of his wife, an investigative reporter killed by a car bomb, an event that has unleashed all of the demons of his obsessive-compulsive nature, all seemingly held in check while his wife was alive. This is engaging if lightweight fare, the plots both overly elaborate and underdeveloped,[3] the characters cartoonish, the whole thing played for comedy, though in the midst of Monk's own unrelieved nightmare. Monk's dysfunctional nature both renders him unfit for employment and the only one capable of solving the crime. His obsessions and phobias and compulsions, his vain attempts to create order in a disordered world, invariably reveal the one clue necessary—a loafer missing from the closet—to unravel the riddle of the case, that is, when you add in his extensive knowledge of criminology and forensic science. *Monk* is clearly a throwback, recalling the traditions of the golden age mystery, though updated, set in a world where post-traumatic stress disorder is pervasive. The disorder and confusion are everywhere, except, perhaps, inside Adrian Monk's apartment where, quite sadly, everything is in its place.

But other contradictions immediately appear in the current offerings, where the powers of science and mathematics, the later-day descendants of Holmesian observation and ratiocination, the forces of reason that guide investigations in shows like *CSI* and *Numb3rs*, are counter-balanced by the other-worldly, paranormal powers of *Medium*, a reference to the gothic roots of the form. It's all Darwin versus intelligent design. On *CSI* and *Numb3rs*, random acts of violence, often propelled by greedy self interest, prove to be describable, predictable, statistically probable events; in the case of *Criminal Minds*, even the utter irrationality of serial killers succumbs to reasoned analysis, psychology allowing the investigators to develop remarkably accurate profiles of the "un-sub" making it possible for them to predict where and when the perpetrator will next strike. The boy geniuses Charlie Epps (*Numb3rs*) and Spenser Reid (*Criminal Minds*) may each find life itself a bit of a challenge, but data sets, further refined by each subsequent crime, ultimately yield to statistical and/or psychological analysis.

On the other hand, science and mathematics and psychology can only ever, it seems, take us so far. Some mysteries remain, solvable only by those in touch with higher powers. Alison Dubois's visions and premonitions, something in her genes, some ability she has inherited and which she, in turn, has passed to her daughter, clearly attest to the existence of things unseen, to the reality of the spirit and, perhaps, of a superior power, something more than meets the eye. There exists in nature an irreducible and unexplainable complexity, something that can only be accounted for by powers beyond those that manifest themselves in the mechanical systems of empirical science. *Medium* asks a great deal of its audience, more than the willing suspension of disbelief typically required in any of these shows. That the show has survived[4] suggests a willingness to believe as much in psychics as in psychology, much as significant segments of the population in the United States profess belief in the literal truth of the biblical accounts of the creation and early history of this world regardless of the empirical evidence offered by carbon dating, geology, fossil records, and the like. It is a mystery.[5]

In general, these alternative approaches to solving crimes, both deeply rooted in the genre, on one level represent alternative epistemologies, different ways of knowing and being in the world, and, on another level, represent the inherent contradictions prevailing in public life where we seem to be capable of holding and operating within two incompatible belief systems simultaneously. We are always of two minds. Our officially secular democracy, built on the division of church and state, has been reborn in every administration since Gerald Ford's; professed and practicing atheists are essentially unelectable. While we officially profess a belief in science and the statistical significance required in scientific systems, a belief that numbers mean something, the one form of proof that the patterns observed do rise above the operations of chance, an equally large number of people officially believe in the existence of some other-worldly, extraterrestrial intelligence, some ideal form that can only be intuited, never known empirically, that plays a greater or lesser role in human affairs, and which regularly transgresses the laws of physics, at least as science currently understands those laws. Nothing is left to chance; everything is subject to the operations of chance. In the end, neither prospect is particularly comforting.

In this regard, Adrian Monk seems something of a post-modernist everyman, an image of the anxiety that is contemporary existence. Deprived of the one thing in his life that grounded him, that gave meaning and structure to his life, the one thing he adored, he is reduced to creating a mechanical order, entropy held at bay by his obsessive tidying, straightening, cleaning up, his efforts never fully equal to the task. It is a blessing and a curse, as he periodically remarks in the course of the show, but so is Alison Dubois's psychic ability a blessing and a curse, an inherent contradiction. She would, in the end, so much prefer to be normal.

These shows often seem to play out the debate, in one way or another, over Darwin and intelligent design, of the ends of law and justice, of the limits of empirical knowledge and logical systems versus the evidence of intuition and gut instinct. Charlie Epps, for instance, is constantly exploring the limits of his logic systems, even in minor ways, learning that in poker, a game that should be playable by the numbers, he has to play the opponent, not the cards, or that in golf, a thorough understanding of physics will never ensure success. The wholes always exceed the sums of their parts, a discovery that results in some fresh anxiety, a small reminder that the laws meant to ensure order and the principles of justice are never identical.

Problems exist here on two levels, that terms like *normal* and *justice* are used as though they are self-evident, and that the codes of law are adequate to the production of justice. Clearly, there is no such thing as justice, no objectifiable, physical measure to which we can all point, some higher standard which our legal systems only ever imperfectly represent. Justice is socially constructed, a product of what we say it is, however imperfect, which always proves a point of conflict in contemporary mysteries, where the systems themselves have always been corrupted, on the one hand, and where a body of people, on the other, believe that they know better, that they are in touch with, that their actions are justified by a higher authority. Such is the case most clearly in *24*, which is rife with contradictions, a perfect embodiment of the anxieties that have emerged in public life since terrorists brought down the World Trade Center and the United States entered Afghanistan and Iraq in an effort to root out terrorism and disarm the weapons of mass destruction aimed at the United States. *24*, which ran from November 6, 2001, through May 24, 2010, a total of eight seasons, 193 separate shows, was reportedly a favorite among hard-line supporters of Bush administration policy and military action, those who felt that the "American way of life" is under siege and must be protected by any means necessary, even if it means the transgression of our own constitutionally-sanctioned civil and legal rights. Joel Surnow, the creator of the show, for instance, is a self-described "right-wing nut job" (Mayer 68). In this scenario, Jack Bauer is a necessary weapon in the war on terror. His tendency to overstep the law, to ignore direct orders, to even, at times, temporarily resign from government service is justified by the need to be able to pursue that course of action which the exigencies of events demand but which cannot otherwise be officially sanctioned. He just knows better.

But if the body-politic is under siege from some infectious agent, the metaphoric threat literalized in some seasons by terror plots involving the release of biological agents in shopping malls and upscale hotels, the dangers are always compounded by internal corruption, a kind of auto-immune disease where the defense mechanisms pose as much if not more of a problem to the body politic than do the external threats. It is hard at moments like these not to believe that the show is being written by a left-wing nut job. Corporate self-interests, some controlled by the Bauer family, bear as much responsibility for the threats we face as do the terrorists. Corporate actions, in fact, have put weapons in the hands of the terrorists, while in Washington, even presidential assassination is deemed permissible if Wayne Palmer's defense of civil liberties and his attempts to resolve situations diplomatically prevent the deployment of the military forces and actions that hardliners believe to be the only viable response to these threats. (Vice presidents always prove to be particularly villainous in these scenarios.) Representatives of the military have even voiced their alarm over the show's frequent recourse to torture to extract information from terrorists. The show has been implicated in shifting attitudes among West Point cadets toward torture; these same attitudes have also turned up in Iraq and seem to be implicated in field operations there (Mayer 72). The show has proven to be particularly popular both at the military academy and in the field.

The show, in all these ways, seems to descend directly from the hard-boiled traditions of the 1930s, transmitted through the spy dramas of the Cold War '50s, all of the problems compounded by contemporary concerns, the hegemonic systems at work so complex, the webs of intrigue so tightly woven that no escape is ever possible. The show is an anxious response to contemporary life, that anxiety transferred directly to the viewer through the show's real-time format, Jack Bauer always facing the threat of a ticking time bomb. In that regard, *24* is either the best show on television, or the worst— the best, because it more fully exploits the potential of the medium to create a visceral response in the audience than does any other show on television, the worst, because it exploits our anxieties more fully than any other show on television. Much like the news coverage of the 9/11 attacks on the World Trade Center, we can only sit in terror, watching the buildings repeatedly collapse, the dramatic footage capable only of traumatizing the viewer, not of explaining the complex political, economic, theological, and psychological forces that coalesced in that moment.

The concerns of these shows, the police procedurals and the loosely-related espionage thriller, are obsessively *au courant*, reflecting anxieties that seem particularly post-modernist, and as post-modernist, particularly white, male, securely middle class. Whiteness at the end of the twentieth century seems to be a post-modernist condition, a world of collapsing binaries, of abstract and arbitrary systems of meaning, a world we know through the numbers. This anxiety can result in a nostalgia for the ways things were, which always seems to translate into white, male, middle class, heterosexual, Christian, in a rear-guard action to preserve patterns of power and privilege, in the expression of belief in increasingly dogmatic forms of faith. At this moment, we are fortifying our border with Mexico in a war against illegal immigration, entertaining marriage amendments that will limit the rights and privileges of marriage to heterosexual couples, and entertaining legislation to undo affirmative action and bilingual language programs in our schools at the same time that we lament the lack of progress being made in closing the achievement gap. This lack of academic achievement has led to the creation of curriculum standards state by state and assessment routines that only seem to frustrate, not facilitate educational reform in poorer schools and in school districts that are becoming increasingly segregated, not less so. We all have reason to feel anxious.

In a world so constituted, we can only ever contain the crime, not prevent it. Given the pervasiveness of crime on primetime programming, we are clearly under siege, at war, both at home and abroad. The only possible response is to arrest and prosecute the offenders, that is if they live long enough to make it into court. Such attitudes seem to echo the policies of containment that result in our typically spending more money to incarcerate criminals, a group of people disproportionately poor, under-educated, and drawn from racial minorities, than we spend on our public school systems. The problems do seem systemic, where inadequate social and medical services (limited prenatal care, the uneven distribution of medical resources) can never offset the environmental challenges and insults in inner-city neighborhoods, where old and deteriorating housing contribute to lead poisoning and where poor air quality links directly to asthma, conditions which result in physical and cognitive disadvantages that are only aggravated, not ameliorated, by the inadequacy of the educational services offered in urban schools. We all live in New Orleans all the time, with Katrina headed our way, and we all know how that story turned out.

A Minority Response

The anxieties that emerge in these primetime dramas seem, by and large, to express concerns most clearly aligned with majority values, typically white, middle class, heterosexual, Christian, generally conservative, though quick to decry racism, sexism, and homophobia where they appear, usually among bigots whose extremist beliefs pose their own threat to the social order. For the most part, we have placed our faith in detection, prosecution, and punishment, not in prevention, investing in prisons, not social and educational programs. Though the casts of these shows are generally multiethnic and as likely to include women as men among their central characters, and while the shows will often consider the underlying tensions that still characterize questions of race and gender, the subject position, the prevailing ethos, along with the anxieties outlined above, are white. For members of minority groups, the concerns will be different.

In this regard, one of the most notable trends in contemporary detective fiction is the development of minority subject positions and subjectivities in a genre that, if not exclusively written by white, male, heterosexual authors, at least seems to privilege that position. Women authors have always played a prominent role in the mystery genre, though most commentaries point to the appearances of authors like Muller, Paretsky and Grafton in the 1970s as initiating the first truly feminist revision of the form. African American authors, most notably Pauline Hopkins and John Edward Bruce, writing in the black periodicals at the beginning of the twentieth century, Rudolph Fisher, writing during the Harlem Renaissance, and Chester Himes, in the 1950s and '60s, have published in this form, though their works seem exceptional, as do the anti-novels produced by Ishmael Reed and Clarence Major in the '70s. Starting in the late 1980s, early '90s, however, a number of African American, Latino/a, gay and lesbian, Asian American and Native American authors have moved into the field. In some cases, the authors involved are established "literary" figures who have crossed over into genre fiction, authors like Rudolfo Anaya and Lucha Corpi. In many other cases, the authors are solely associated with the mystery genre. In either case, their work has begun to attract attention and to generate a significant body of criticism. These critical investigations typically consider how minority authors, entering into a genre that is largely perceived as conservative in nature, one that sees any threats to the prevailing social order typically repaired, the order re-inscribed in the course of the novel's investigations, adapt, resist, reformulate, or subvert these conservative tendencies. Opinions will vary on the success of these attempts.

Three recent studies—Maureen T. Reddy's *Traces, Codes and Clues: Reading Race in Crime Fiction* (2003), Ralph E. Rodriguez's *Brown Gumshoes: Detective Fiction and the Search for the Chicano/a Identity* (2005), and Phyllis M. Betz's *Lesbian Detective Fiction: Woman as Author, Subject, and Reader* (2006)—along with somewhat earlier works, e.g., Stephen F. Soitos's *The Blues Detective: A Study of African American Detective Fiction* (1996), illustrate the range of opinions on this question. Of the three recent studies, only Betz seems to feel that lesbian authors have succeeded in co-opting the form, of using the generic elements in genre fiction, the "popular" nature of this pop culture form, to "normalize," to render generic, to popularize a subject position that is often taken as aberrant and unpopular:

> Commentators on popular culture and literature describe a complex relationship between the production and consumption of genre fiction. Tied from the beginning to technological advances in publication and distribution systems, situated in an urban environment, and directed to a diverse, often segregated readership, popular fiction has the task of bridging such differences, at least temporarily [2].

Reddy cites Scott McCracken in support of this position, that "[p]opular fiction ... mediates social conflict" (qtd. in Betz 2).

As a popular art form genre fiction is rooted in populist movements which, in turn, are tied to innovations in production and to a growing reading public. Pulp fiction is a case in point, one that is certainly implicated in the growth of the hard-boiled novel. In addition, the formulaic nature of popular forms, that they often work on a theme-and-variations basis, the rule-governed form providing the "theme" on which the author plays variations, provides an opening for the incorporation of novel material. The formulas provide a high degree of comfort, an implicit contract between author and audience, while the variations played on those themes allow the author to incorporate potentially disruptive materials into the narrative. Betz writes:

> This ability of popular genres to address and accept change brings us full circle to the purpose and value of such literature. The normalizing function of the reliance on formula and repetition gives popular fiction the ability to contain the potentially dangerous shifts in the modern world. By relying on the reader's familiarity with form while simultaneously allowing for adaptation, popular fiction facilitates a balancing of old and new. The safety of genre conventions permits the introduction of difference because, as readers, we trust that the author will still meet our reading expectations [8].

In this case, lesbians and lesbian interests can be integrated directly into the popular formulas of detective fiction, thereby rendering as "normal" relationships and perspectives often seen as abnormal. The conventional constructions of the genre effectively "normalize," render conventional, an unconventional subject position.

The "populist" nature of pop culture, however, does not necessarily guarantee a socially progressive politics or a popular appeal. The lesbian mysteries have perhaps succeeded in the ways that Betz describes but only because innovations in publishing have allowed small presses operating in niche markets to address interests and audiences the larger publishing houses do not serve. Lesbian detective fiction is still, by and large, a niche market, the books found more often in the gay and lesbian sections of bookstores than among the mysteries. Written for a lesbian audience by lesbian authors who publish on lesbian presses, these books have not typically generated the interest and commercial successes of Muller's, Grafton's and Paretsky's works.

That said, Betz has a point, and her claims do seem to echo Soitos's analysis of African American detective fiction. Soitos argues that African American detective fiction turns on four tropes: the inclusion of an African American detective, double-consciousness detection, the use of black vernaculars, and hoodoo. Each of these elements represents a variation on a generic theme, centering the narrative on a character, an epistemology, and a cultural context that describes an alternate universe, perhaps, but one which is internally consistent, coherent, and recognizable. The differences are really a matter of degree, not kind. The African American detective may speak a different dialect, but the distinction is dialectal, typically a version of the hard-boiled language characteristic of the genre, albeit one that is inflected by geographical location, socio-economic circumstance, historical experience, etc., again, a variation on a theme. A realistic form always grounded in the specifics of time and place, detective fiction operates inside the vernacular culture, within the languages, music, culinary habits, and modes of dress prevailing within that society, a point which is just as true of African American detective fiction, of what Soitos terms "the blues detective," as it is of other variants within the genre. And the action of the book, the investigator's movement through this field, represents an epistemological act, the marshaling of evidence, the interrogation of suspects and assumptions describing the ways in which we know the world. The African American's double consciousness, his or her recognition of the competing constructions which describe African American experience, again represent a recognizable variation on the mystery novel's themes. The presence and preservation of the conventions can, as Betz claims, normalize a subject position different from that typical in the genre.

Reddy and Rodriquez, however, are not so certain that the substitution of African American or Latino/a characters and interests is enough to subvert the value systems prevailing in detective fiction, value systems which often perpetuate rather than reconstruct the dominant social order. What we often seem to get in African American or Latino/a detective fiction is a dialectal variation where what we need is a new language. If nothing else, commercial pressures, the need to sell books beyond the niche market, require compromises that blunt the effect.

For Reddy, the problem emerges in the ideological predisposition of the hard-boiled novel, an ideology that proves to be essentially racist. "Hard-boiled ideology," she writes," is an exaggerated version—but only a very slightly exaggerated version—of mainstream American ideology, particularly as that ideology was propounded in the years between the world wars" (9). Emerging between the wars, hard-boiled fiction cannot help but reflect the racial tensions of the period: "Hard-boiled fiction's rise, then, coincides neatly with widespread anxiety about race and about the difficulties of maintaining the whiteness of the United States" (19). A case in point is William Wu's claim that the Yellow Peril theme, prevalent in American literature from 1850 to 1940, reached its height in the pulp fiction of the 1930s. In this context, the internment of Japanese Americans during the Second World War seems the logical conclusion of such attitudes, but other indicators exist as well. The period in question also coincides with the promulgation of eugenics theory and the development of social policies justified by eugenics—laws against miscegenation, laws permitting the mandatory sterilization of the mentally deficient, laws limiting immigration—and with The Great Migration, the movement of African Americans out of the Deep South which began during the First World War. The racist attitudes and anxieties characteristic of the period are clearly inscribed in hard-boiled fiction, "the ideology and the fiction inseparable" (Reddy 35).

The hard-boiled novel's racism is inescapable:

> It is not possible to read that fiction "innocently"; either one engages in the bonding ritual, whether consciously or not, or one critiques it, refuses it, places oneself (or is placed) outside it. White/male/heterosexual bonding is not incidental to the reading of hard-boiled fiction but absolutely constitutive of its pleasures. Readers who speak of the "guilty pleasure" of reading crime fiction generally mean the pleasure of reading less-than-literary fiction, but the far guiltier pleasure is indeed participation in a ritual that helps to perpetuate racism, sexism, and heterosexism [Reddy 38].

While women authors of detective fiction have been successful in creating a viable counter-tradition, male writers—Reddy cites Walter Mosley and Dale Furutani as examples—have not.

At least part of the problem seems to be that the very elements Reddy identifies as problematic—the failure, for instance, of the fiction to see whiteness as a cultural construct, accepting it as a given, as the default setting in the program—is also a defining characteristic of whiteness as a construct. The "colorlessness" of whiteness compared to the "colored" perspectives of African or Asian or indigenous populations and their admixtures (e.g., mestizo/Chicano/Latino/a); the rootlessness of white experience vs. the rootedness of others; the failure of self-realization that results from these attitudes—all seem defining properties of whiteness as an ethnic construction. At some levels, the problem seems to be linguistic, that to be a white male means inhabiting a symbolic order that is non-referential, empty, arbitrary, abstract, wholly conventional, not natural in construction, one where statistical means of accounting mean something. In this regard, it seems telling that Gloria Damasco, Lucha Corpi's detective, is a trained speech therapist, as is the spouse of Chang-rae Lee's protagonist in *Native Speaker*. The generic assumptions, the racist constructions can only be located if we step outside of the language and the systems they describe. The problem is analogous to that in history, where the study, shaped by certain paradigms/ideological constructions, results in a master narrative where certain elements remain invisible, anomalous data, "noise." Only a shift in the paradigms can bring the invisible into view.

Reddy may be right that many writers of crime fiction have not been perfectly successful in challenging the white, male, heterosexist assumptions of the genre. On the other hand, a number of authors have begun to revise the forms and formulas that crime fiction depends on. This revisionary movement must take place on several levels. As a form dependent on the conventions of social realism, the work set into a recognizable cultural and historical context, the author must engage the historical constructions and consciousness prevailing in popular culture, telling a different story. In many cases, the defining events that describe minority experience in the United States are still inadequately represented in state curriculum guidelines and certainly inadequately imagined in textbooks. Concepts like Manifest Destiny, the genocidal intent of the Indian wars, the policies of forced assimilation ("kill the Indian but save the man"), incidents like the Trail of Tears, the Sand Creek Massacre (including the killing of children, justified because "nits cause lice"), Wounded Knee, the internment of Japanese Americans (including, in at least one case, a group of orphans)—the list is a long one—are left unexplored. Detective fiction can engage the historical consciousness—certainly as Mosley does in the Easy Rawlins series, tracing the arc of the African American experience from the end of the Second World War through the mid-'60s, or as Corpi does, her stories referencing the Mexican Farm Workers Strikes, or as Naomi Hirahara does in her Mas Arai mysteries with their references to the internment of Americans of Japanese descent—and often in more vital ways than the official accounts offered in history texts can or will do. Establishing this kind of historical context, evoking the vernacular experiences of a particular group, will "normalize" that experience, often a problem the incorporation of so-called multiethnic subjects and literature into a curriculum poses, where these materials are treated as exotic or exceptional. As Betz suggests, the pop culture form will formalize relationships, showing these experiences to be just as conventional as those that characterize majority culture.

Along with the ability to tell an alternate history, multiethnic mysteries can also explore alternative epistemologies, different ways of knowing and being in the world. On one level, the double-consciousness that Soitos describes as one of the defining tropes of the Blues Detective represents one part of that alternative epistemology, one that is equally true of many of the detectives featured in multiethnic crime fiction. On a deeper level, the hoodoo traditions in African American experience or the mystical elements in Latino/a perspectives that emerge in magic realism describe paradigms or belief structures that contrast with the rational, statistical systems of knowing the world that prevail in European-American discourse. The detective's movement between and through these alternative systems, code switching between them much as a bilingual or bi-dialectal speaker will code switch between the two linguistic systems, dramatizes the different ways of knowing the world.

For readers of conventional mystery novels, the incorporation of these more "magical" elements into the novel can be uncomfortable, disrupting generic expectations. Anaya's Sonny Baca and his investigation of Don Eliseo's traditional belief systems, compounded of Catholic and native elements, is a case in point. These kinds of materials subvert the terms of the implicit contract the reader expects, but so will other elements that appear in some of these books, most notably, for instance, the lack of closure in Sherman Alexie's *Indian Killer*. We expect the novel to reveal the identity of the killer; we expect the investigation will result in the apprehension and punishment of the perpetrator of the crimes here committed. The novel's failure to identify the killer violates these conventions, and these violations of the conventions, in turn, reveal the conventionality of the structure, the rules that govern the depiction of character and conflict, the act of detection, and concepts of justice. The reader, whether willingly or not, becomes doubly conscious of the conventions of the genre and the conventionality of the social structures described in these pages, resulting in the sensations of guilt, perhaps, accompanying the pleasure we derive from these books.

In many ways, then, these books represent an "achieved anxiety," to borrow an old phrase from Harold Bloom. They speak simultaneously to the authors' and the readers' anxieties, jointly projected in these books. Reddy, for instance, argues that a white reader of *Devil in a Blue Dress* ought to find the experience deeply disquieting and speculates that the historical positioning of the story, that setting the story over half a century ago in the years immediately following the Second World War deprives it of that power, insulating the reader from the full impact of its accusations (96). Reading the book in the context of the series which begins in *Gone Fishin* and tentatively ended in *Blond Faith*, however, provides a different reaction, one that does prove to be deeply disquieting, and probably disquieting, I suspect, for all its readers, whether white or black, male or female. Like watching *24*, it's very hard to feel good about any of this. Which, in the end—and the stories never quite end—seems to be the point.

2

A More Perfect Union
Pauline Hopkins, Hagar's Daughter *and the Struggle for Equality*

Hagar's Daughter, published in the *Colored American Magazine* in monthly installments between March 1901 and March 1902, is certainly an odd work. Currently identified as the first murder mystery written by an African American author, the work is something of a hybrid, a genre work, clearly, which does feature a murder and a detective, but one in which the mystery element plays a supporting role, not appearing until the final third of the book. The first two-thirds of *Hagar's Daughter* is more aptly described as romance fiction, with love and marriage the central concerns of the plot. The plot is driven by concealed identities and dramatic revelations and by a ten-year gap and a series of fantastic coincidences, the story told in a prose heavily populated by adjectives and adverbs, the work, in many ways, quite conventional in construction. It is, like the magazine in which it was published, an attempt to create a popular literature for African American readers, a small but untapped and unserved market, a work written by an African American author for African American readers. The serialized novel and the magazine in which it appeared represent groundbreaking work.

What may seem initially odd, however, is that the primary characters are all white, or at least seem to be, with the African American characters largely consigned to supporting roles, domestic servants/slaves in the earlier section, domestic servants, cleaning ladies and washerwomen in the latter stages of the book. Because of their long service to the families who employ them and because of the access their positions give them to domestic affairs and after-hours' activities, these characters are critical to the solution of the crime, the restoration of justice largely a product of their efforts. That the people who benefit from their efforts are not wholly worthy of these efforts, their sometimes liberal support for African Americans of a piece with their support of the ASPCA and abused animals—as proves to be the case with the young, Harvard-educated Cuthbert Sumner—is also clear. The African American characters tend to be character types who play stereotypical roles and whose attitudes remain recognizable even today in characters satirized in *Boondocks*. The story does, as the subtitle suggests, provide a portrayal of "Southern caste prejudice," though the prejudice proves to be shared even by the liberal figures from Massachusetts. The attitudes described here are pervasive. Though now free men and women—free to pursue college educations, as does the brother of Venus, whose domestic service in Senator Bowen's household allows her to support her brother's efforts at the same time that it provides her with the inside knowledge needed to solve the case; free to hold mortgages, as does Venus's mother, Marthy—their lives have not necessarily improved. The terms of the mortgage, with the principal coming due, prove oppressive, one form of slavery replaced by another. These are anxious moments, made more anxious still by how little attitudes have changed following the Civil War and the emancipation of the slaves.

The Story

The story that Hopkins tells is nothing if not convoluted, driven by remarkable (which is to say, utterly unrealistic) coincidences, and dependent on most of the central characters in the first part of the narrative reappearing in the second in disguise, a tool as overworked here as amnesia proves to be in contemporary crime fiction. It also straddles the Civil War. The story opens in 1860–61, just on the eve of the Civil War; the book's first chapter is set in Charleston, South Carolina, where the Confederate States of America is in the process of being born in response to Lincoln's election. Included among the parties here convened, an assembly likened to the infernal congress convened at the end of Book I in *Paradise Lost* (ll. 752–757), are St. Clair Enson, the younger, impecunious, and disreputable brother of Ellis Enson, the honorable master of a Southern Maryland plantation, and Walker, a St. Louis slave dealer. St. Clair and Walker join forces and immediately head for Maryland, where St. Clair hopes to avail himself of his brother's charity. Ellis, then age 40, has recently wed Hagar Sargeant, the eighteen-year-old daughter of and only heir to the adjoining estate, who has herself recently returned from boarding school and who, a year following her marriage to Ellis, bears him a daughter. An almost Edenic sense of happiness prevails on the combined estates which the entrance of the fallen brother will disrupt.

The story, in this case, is Hagar's. Years earlier, the Sargeants, facing financial difficulties, had rented the estate and moved to St. Louis where they had, over a period of years, repaired their failing fortune. The formerly childless couple return to Maryland with a daughter, then approximately six years of age, Hagar. Now twenty, Hagar would have been born in St. Louis in 1840–41, prior to the Sargeants' return in 1846–47. The narrative is less than specific on these points, but her marriage at eighteen, the celebration of her anniversary and birth of her daughter, all placed in relationship to the story's opening in the fall of 1860, clearly define the timeline. What is left unsaid until St. Clair and Walker appear is that Hagar is not the Sargeants' biological daughter. Rather, in spite of her light complexion, she is the mixed-race daughter of slaves, "lent" (52) by Walker to her parents when he was unable to find a buyer for her because of her light complexion. She remains Walker's property, as does the child. The otherwise honorable Ellis hesitates, at first deciding that he must give up Hagar:

> I have thought the matter over and much as I wish it might be otherwise, much as I would sacrifice for you, I feel it my duty as a Southern gentleman, the representative of a proud old family, to think of others beside myself and not allow my own inclinations to darken the escutcheon of a good old name. I cannot, I dare not, and the law forbids me to acknowledge as my wife a woman in whose veins courses a drop of the accursed blood of the Negro slave [59].

Several pages later, the author provides commentary:

> Here was a woman raised as one of a superior race, refined, cultured, possessed of all the Christian virtues, who would have remained in this social sphere all her life, beloved and respected by her descendants, her blood mingling with the best blood of the country if untoward circumstances had not exposed her ancestry. But the one drop of black blood neutralized all her virtues, and she became an unclean thing. Can anything more unjust be imagined in a republican form of government whose excuse for existence is the upbuilding of mankind! [62].

Ellis does repent of his decision, and he decides to relinquish the estate to St. Clair and to take Hagar and child to Europe where they can live free of the prevailing prejudices, but before he can put the plan into effect, a body, apparently that of Ellis, seemingly a suicide, appears, and Hagar and daughter are seized by Walker, who immediately attempts to sell them in the Washington, D.C., slave market along with the rest of the slaves from the estate. Hagar escapes her fate by leaping into the Potomac, her daughter in her arms, the two of them presumed to have drowned. When the story resumes ten years later, a seemingly new cast of characters takes the stage, the action now set in Washington, D.C., as the government settles into business as usual following the war. A few characters reappear, most notably the former slaves from the Enson-Sargeant estates, including Aunt Henny Sargeant, her daughter Marthy, who is married to St. Clair's former slave Isaac, and their children, Venus and her brother.

The story that follows, however, proves that people are not always who they appear to be. General Benson, an official in the Treasury Department, proves to be St. Clair in disguise; he has recreated himself following his conviction *in absentia* in the Lincoln assassination conspiracy and a sojourn in Europe. He is in league with Major Madison, the former Walker, and his daughter Aurelia, a mixed-race woman passing as white, who have all set their sights on the fortunes of Senator Bowen of California, newly come to Washington, with his second wife, the former Hagar, and his daughter from his first marriage, Jewel. The plot turns on separating Jewel from her fiancé, Cuthbert Sumner, Benson's under secretary, who had earlier been involved with Aurelia, so that General Benson can marry Jewel. The plan nearly succeeds until the general's stenographer, his former mistress and the mother of his young illegitimate son, threatens to reveal Benson's secret unless he marries her. He kills her, frames Sumner for the murder, and presses his suit for Jewel's hand.

It is, finally, at this point, that the murder mystery is initiated. With Sumner accused of murder, Jewel contracts the services of a government investigator, Chief Henson, the former Ellis Enson, and, in a show of good faith, marries Sumner, who is in jail awaiting trial. The Senator dies under somewhat mysterious circumstances, leaving behind a revised will naming the general as Jewel's guardian. Jewel disappears, as does Aunt Henny, who is now employed as a cleaning woman at the Treasury Department. Henson will succeed, with information and investigative assistance from Venus, and with the additional assistance of a disabled African American Civil War veteran, in rescuing Jewel and Aunt Henny, whose testimony is instrumental in exonerating Sumner and leading to the unmasking and arrest of Benson and Madison. In the process, Ellis/Henson and the widow Bowen/Hagar are reunited, though her mixed heritage is again discovered, much to the horror of her stepson-in-law. The story's final surprise, however, occurs at this point as Hagar discovers certain tokens among her husband's possessions that reveal that Jewel is her daughter, rescued from the Potomac by Bowen, then an oysterman, prior to his relocation to California during the gold rush. Sumner is doubly disconcerted to learn that his wife is also of mixed blood. Though he hesitates to own her, he, too, will quickly decide, as Ellis did years before, that he cannot give her up, though not before Ellis, Hagar, and Jewel depart for Europe. A year later, seeking to be reconciled with Jewel, Sumner discovers that she has died of Roman fever and is now buried on the Maryland estate where the story began and where Ellis and Hagar have taken up residence. He ponders his fate:

Cuthbert Sumner questioned wherein he had sinned and why he was so severely punished.

Then it was borne in upon him: The sin is the nation's. It must be washed out. The plans of the Father are not changed in the nineteenth century; they are shown us in different forms. The idolatry of the Moloch of Slavery must be purged from the land and his actual sinlessness was but a meet offering to appease the wrath of a righteous God [283–84].

The story is not exactly subtle, the plot almost artless in its repeated and exaggerated use of motifs, of disguise and discovery, of concealed identities and the tokens that reveal who these characters really are, of the parallel plots of Ellis's and Sumner's reactions to their wives' mixed blood. The formulaic nature of the work, the heavy dependence on the most artificial conventions of popular fiction, the didactic tone of the piece, often conveyed through authorial intrusions into the narrative, all position *Hagar's Daughter* inside the traditions of genre fiction.

Engaging History

Everything in the story turns on questions of marriage, on St. Clair/Benson's attempts to subvert marriage contracts, first his brother's and then Sumner's, which stand between him and the property and wealth he desires, and, more importantly, on the issues that surround the marriage of mixed-race women to white men. Ellis's dilemma is two-fold, a combination of social convention and legal concerns. Societal standards recognize Hagar as "negro," the one drop of negro blood determining her racial classification, and as such, she is not an appropriate mate for Ellis Enson; Maryland law, in fact, forbids the intermarriage of whites and blacks, as the quote above acknowledges. His marriage to Hagar is null and void. By contrast, Sumner's concerns demonstrate the limits of his liberal sentiments, though his qualms will, again, be founded in a complex web of social, civil, and scientific concerns. When Aurelia's mixed-race status is revealed, Sumner is horrified to have been earlier engaged to such a woman and immensely relieved to have escaped (158–60). When his mother-in-law's racial heritage is discovered, he is again horrified and immediately determines that his wife can have no further dealings with her stepmother, the woman who raised her; he regrets the necessity of this action but sees "separation"—his word—as the only possible solution (265). Jewel, it must be noted, is also disconcerted by this discovery. When Jewel is revealed to be Hagar's biological daughter, Sumner endures twenty-four hours of mental torment before his "good angel" prevails and he finds his love stronger than both social convention (282) and his own intellectual objections to polluting the blood line through amalgamation ("Ought we not, as Anglo-Saxons, keep the fountain head of of [sic] our racial stream as unpoluted [sic] as possible?" Sumner asks Ellis Enson following the discovery of Hagar's origins [271].) According African Americans equal rights before the law is one thing; these are issues that Sumner seems to have examined at Harvard and about which he published an essay in a local paper, establishing his liberal credentials (265). Intermixing with African Americans socially was, however, a totally different matter: "he had never considered for one moment the remote contingency of actual social contact with this unfortunate people" (265). Though "born with a noble nature," "his faults were those caused by environment and tradition" (265).

The role that marriage plays in the narrative is further framed, somewhat artificially, by a scene in Chapter 1, set in the Charleston slave market where Walker is introduced and where he is in the process of selling wives apart from their husbands, and by the final paragraphs in the novel, when Sumner finds that Ellis and Hagar have brought St. Clair's illegitimate son to live with them on the ancestral estate. In the first instance, among the potential buyers in the market is a "noted divine, who was considered deeply religious" (9), who in the course of the conversation lectures Walker on his need to find religion:

> Religion is a good thing to live by, and we'll want it when we die. And a man in your business of buying and selling slaves needs religion more than anybody else, for it makes you treat your people well. Now there's Mr. Haskins—he's a slave-trader like yourself. Well, I converted him. Before he got religion he was one of the worst men to his niggers I ever saw; his heart was as hard as a stone. But religion has made his heart as soft as a piece of cotton. Before I converted him he would sell husbands from their wives and delight in doing it; but now he won't sell a man from his wife if he can get anyone to buy them together [12].

The devaluation of marriage noted here contributes directly to the conclusion of the book and the moral it draws, not, it would seem, the most obvious conclusion to be drawn nor a thought that would necessarily be foremost in Sumner's mind, having just discovered his wife's grave:

> Cuthbert watched him [St. Clair's child] with knitted brows. In him was embodied, a different form, a lesson of the degradation of slavery. Cursed be the practices which pollute the soul, and deaden all our moral senses to the reception of the true doctrine of Divinity.
>
> The holy institution of marriage ignored the life of the slave, breed [sic] indifference in the masters to the enormity of illicit connections, with the result that the sacred family relation is weakened and finally ignored in many cases [284].

Though somewhat obscured by editorial problems, the sense seems to be that the practices of slavery were injurious to both master and slave, that the master, not recognizing the sanctity of marriage among his slaves (and, perhaps, forcing his sexual attentions on them), found his own sense of marriage devalued, thus leading to St. Clair's illicit affair with his stenographer and its issue in the child Sumner here contemplates. Sumner, now a changed man, "views life and eternity with different eyes and thoughts from what he did before he knew he had wedded Hagar's daughter" (284), proving nobler than even he knew himself to be. Still, the final lines belong to Longfellow, the refrain from "My Lost Youth": "A boy's will is the wind's will,/And the thoughts of youth are long, long thoughts."

These materials, the slave-market scene in Chapter I and the moral it leads to in the final paragraphs of the book, seem digressions, unnecessary to the expository purposes of the opening movement in the first case and off-point emotionally, if nothing else, in the book's final moment. Sumner, seeking to reconcile himself with his wife after an emotionally turbulent year, a separation that he might have avoided had he not hesitated at the critical moment, has just discovered his wife's grave. Ellis Enson, having not acted quickly enough following the discovery of Hagar's heritage in the early pages of the novel, had lost her, a mistake he does not repeat in the end. He and Hagar and Jewel had already departed for the continent when Sumner, twenty-four hours after learning of Jewel's mixed blood, reconciles himself to her heritage and moves to reclaim her. The lesson seems to have little to do with the ways that slavery has led to a devaluation of marriage. But this framing element does position the story within a broader context, one which is largely unstated but which explains the urgency of the story that Hopkins is telling. The opening narrative, set on the eve of the Civil War but with roots in St. Louis in 1846–7 when Walker "lends" Hagar to the childless Sargeants, corresponds to Dred Scott's initiating of those suits that result ten years later in the infamous Dred Scott Decision, a decision which, in turn, provides a decided push toward war. The issues raised in the Scott Decision, addressed variously by The Emancipation Proclamation, the passage of the Thirteenth and Fourteenth Amendments, and by the war itself, are far from settled at the turn of the century, as the 1896 decision in *Plessy v. Ferguson* demonstrates. The action and composition of the book are framed by these two decisions. Where *Scott* declared whites and blacks separate because inherently unequal, *Plessy* permits separation even though whites and blacks are equal in the eyes of the law. In both cases, marriage laws are cited as justification for the rulings. In the case of the latter decision, the precedent the ruling establishes will find "scientific" reinforcement in eugenics, which arising in the final decades of the nineteenth century, will become a determining force in social policy in the opening decades of the twentieth. These are anxious moments, and it is that anxiety that emerges in *Hagar's Daughter*.

> *Scott v. Sandford* asks a specific question:

Can a negro, whose ancestors were imported into this country, and sold as slaves, become a member of the political community formed and brought into existence by the Constitution of the United States, and as such become entitled to all the rights, and privileges, and immunities guaranteed by that instrument to citizens?

> The verdict is unequivocal on this point:

A free negro of African race, whose ancestors were brought to this country and sold as slaves, is not a "citizen" within the meaning of the Constitution of the United States.... When the Constitution was adopted, they were not regarded in any of the States as members of the community which constituted the State, and were not numbered among its "people or citizens." Consequently, the special rights and immunities guaranteed to citizens do not apply to them. And not being "citizens" within the meaning of the Constitution; they are not entitled to sue in that character in a court of the United States, and the Circuit Court has not jurisdiction in such a suit.

The majority decision is quite lengthy and a striking example of strict construction, that the Court's judgment must be rendered within the confines of the "true meaning and intention" of the Constitution "when it was formed and adopted," and cannot be swayed by any subsequent changes in "public opinion or feeling in relation to the African race." The only issue here is original intent and, perhaps, how we determine that intent.

The Court's answer, in this instance, proves interesting in light of *Hagar's Daughter* and the ways issues pertaining to marriage, some not immediately germane to the central action of the novel, find their way into the discussion. Marriage laws in Maryland and Massachusetts provide clear evidence of intent. At issue is the degree to which the generic rights assigned to "all men" by the Declaration of Independence apply to African Americans descended from slaves or, more materially, the degree to which African American descendants of slaves form part of the "people" who, in the Preamble of the Constitution, undertake "to form a more perfect union, establish justice, insure domestic tranquility, provide for the common defense, promote the general welfare, and secure the blessings of liberty to ourselves and our posterity." That they were not included, that the African slaves and their descendants "had for more than a century before been regarded as being of an inferior order, and altogether unfit for association with the white race, either in social or political relations," can be ascertained from laws banning interracial marriage in Maryland and in Massachusetts passed in 1717 and 1705, respectively. The Maryland statute permits the enslavement of both parties entering into an interracial marriage:

that if any free negro or mulatto intermarry with any white woman, or if any white man shall intermarry with any negro or mulatto woman, such negro or mulatto shall become a slave during life, except for mulattos born of white women, who, for such intermarriage, shall only become servants for seven years.

The white partners will also suffer the same seven-year sentence to servitude.[1] In Massachusetts, the punishments extend to those who contract the marriage:

that none of her Majesty's English or Scottish subjects, nor of any other Christian nation, within this province, shall contract matrimony with any negro or mulatto; nor shall any persons, duly authorized to solemnize marriage, presume to join any such in marriage, on pain of forfeiting the sum of fifty pounds.

These laws provide clear evidence of how unfit as partners, how unwelcome in the families of white people negroes and mulattos were. Still in force at the time of the revolution, they offer "a faithful index to the state of feeling towards the class of persons of whom they speak," erecting "a perpetual and impassable barrier" between white master and enslaved African. Emancipation was powerless to reverse this condition, "this stigma, of the deepest degradation, [which] was fixed upon the whole race." In Massachusetts, the law was revised in 1786 and 1836, the ban extended to include Indians, the penalties increased, and any such marriages declared null and void, "degrad[ing] thus the unhappy issue of the marriage by fixing upon it the stain of bastardy."

The catalogue of similar statutes continues, including laws in Connecticut, New Hampshire, and Rhode Island, all, seemingly, havens of liberal sentiments. Connecticut, in spite of a 1774 law banning the further importation of slaves (largely, the court points out, because it was "injurious to the poor" and "inconvenient"), passed legislation in 1833 penalizing the creation of schools offering instruction to "persons of the African race not inhabitants of the State" without first securing the consent of civil authorities in the town where the school was to be located. In 1815, New Hampshire passed legislation limiting participation in the state militia to free white citizens, a law still in force in 1855. In 1822, Rhode Island forbid the marriage of "any white person with any negro, Indian, or mulatto," a law reenacted in the revised code of 1844. Given these and other restrictions, the Declaration of Independence's discussion of inalienable rights and the Constitution's purposes as stated in the Preamble could not possibly have extended to people of African descent, no one of whom "had ever migrated to the United States voluntarily." To extend such rights and protections to such people would be logically inconsistent, in general, and inconsistent, in particular, "with the caution displayed in providing for the admission of new members into this political family," the federal government having reserved the power of naturalization to itself.

Finally, as if to drive the last nail in the coffin, the decision notes laws in Washington, D.C., restricting African Americans' rights to assembly and residency:

> And even as late as 1820 ... in the charter of the city of Washington, the corporation is authorized "to restrain and prohibit the nightly and other disorderly meetings of slaves, free negroes, and mulattoes," thus associating them together in legislation.

The statute fixes different penalties for slaves and for free negroes and mulattoes, the latter two facing $20 fines per offense, or six months at hard labor if the person proved unable to pay the fine. The same charter also acknowledges municipal authority "to prescribe the terms and conditions upon which free negroes and mulattoes may reside in the city." Taken together, the limits on marriage, military service, education, First Amendment rights, and residency justify denying people of African descent the Declaration's general guarantees of life, liberty, and pursuit of happiness, or the Preamble's specific intentions to "insure domestic tranquility, provide for the common defense, promote the general welfare, and secure the blessings of liberty to ourselves and our posterity."

The decision and the body of evidence it cites also explain why Hopkins frames the novel in the ways she does. The representation in the law of the citizenry as a family unit along with prohibitions in Massachusetts law against the marriage of English, Scottish, or, indeed, any member of any Christian nation with people of African descent, for instance, all provide a foundation for the novel's considerations of marriage, both between slaves in the opening chapter and between whites and people of mixed race thereafter. People of African descent, necessarily the offspring of slaves, represented an altogether lower life form, an attitude that allowed slave owners to sell spouses separately but which even appears in the progressive Harvard-educated Cuthbert Sumner, who supports the rights of the emancipated slaves in general, contributing "large sums to Negro colleges" but "on the same principal," giving "liberally to the Society for the prevention of Cruelty to Animals": "Negroes were classed together in his mind as of the brute creation whose sufferings it was his duty to help alleviate" (265–66). Though his reasons may be somewhat different, he is just as horrified as Ellis Enson was, in his pre–Civil War capacity as Southern gentleman and slave owner, by the prospects of being joined in marriage to a woman of mixed race. Within the logic of the Dred Scott Decision, an unfit marriage partner is equally ill suited to be embraced by the political family unit created in the adoption of the Constitution. Some habits die hard.

The passage of the Thirteenth Amendment and the resolution of the Civil War did little to change these basic attitudes. Legally, rulings like *Plessy v. Ferguson* allow apartheid policies to continue unchecked while social and "scientific" policies sanctioned by eugenics, seemingly the more proximal cause of Sumner's fears with regard to "amalgamation," to "polluting" gene pools, will continue to render African Americans as unfit marriage partners for whites. With regard to the law, as Justice Harlan notes in his dissenting opinion, "the judgment rendered this day [i.e., *Plessy v. Ferguson*] will, in time, prove to be quite as pernicious as the decision made by this tribunal in the *Dred Scott Case*." Hopkins is writing under the shadow of that decision.

At issue in *Plessy* is the constitutionality of a Louisiana law requiring local train systems to provide separate though equal accommodations for white and "colored" passengers. Plessy, a man "of mixed descent, in the proportions of seven eighths Caucasian and one eighth African blood," in whom "the mixture of colored blood was not discernible," had taken a seat in a white carriage and was forcibly expelled and arrested when he refused to comply with the conductor's request to relocate to the car for colored passengers. Ironically, at least according to the Court's construction of the event, Plessy does not challenge the laws defining racial classification, but those assigning whites and blacks to different cars, not because the assignment was demeaning to black passengers, but because the assignment deprived him of the material advantages enjoyed by whites:

> It is claimed by the plaintiff in error [i.e., the party bringing the appeal, his contention that Judge Ferguson had ruled in error against Plessy's claims] that, in any mixed community, the reputation of belonging to the dominant race, in this instance the white race, is portrayed in the same sense that a right of action or inheritance is property.

His claim is that his assignment to the car for colored passengers denied him this advantage, his "property," an actionable claim, again somewhat ironically, under the Fourteenth Amendment.

As does the Dred Scott Decision, the decision in *Plessy* will cite marriage laws to support its position. Justice Brown's decision recognizes that the intent of the Fourteenth Amendment "was undoubtedly to enforce the absolute equality of the two races before the law," but that it was powerless "to enforce social, as distinguished from political, equality, or a commingling of the two races upon terms unsatisfactory to either." Segregation does not imply inferiority, as laws providing for separate schools in Massachusetts and the District of Columbia, among other places, have "been held to be a valid exercise of the legislative power," a point that Mr. Charles Sumner, an abolitionist, Massachusetts lawyer, newspaper editor, and senator Hopkins refers to in the opening chapter of *Hagar's Daughter* (6),[2] had disputed in *Roberts v. City of Boston* and which Justice Shaw had rejected. Laws restricting interracial marriage also provide precedence for the ruling in *Plessy*: "Laws forbidding the intermarriage of the two races may be said in a technical sense to interfere with the freedom of contract, and yet have been universally recognized as within the police power of the State. *State v. Gibson*, 36 Indiana 389."

In the case of *Plessy v. Ferguson*, since the railroad in question only offered local service and so was exempt from federal oversight of interstate commerce, the only question is whether the statute at the heart of the case is "reasonable," that "every exercise of police power must be reasonable, and extend only to such laws as are enacted in good faith for the promotion for the public good, and not for the annoyance or oppression of a particular class." Given prevailing attitudes and practices in Louisiana, the provision of separate rail cars for whites and blacks was deemed reasonable, no more unreasonable, for instance, "or more obnoxious to the Fourteenth Amendment than the acts of Congress requiring separate schools for colored children in the District of Columbia."

Brown adds two final points in closing, that (1) any sense of inferiority arising from enforced separation is a result of blacks' own sense of inferiority, that were the tables turned, with whites in the minority and facing similar laws, no white person would assume this sense of inferiority, and that (2) social prejudice cannot be overcome by legislation, by "an enforced commingling of the races":

> If the two races are to meet upon terms of social equity, it must be the result of natural affinities, a mutual appreciation of each other's merits, and a voluntary consent of individuals.... Legislation is powerless to eradicate racial instincts or to abolish distinctions based upon physical differences, and the attempt to do so can only result in accentuating the difficulties of the present situation.

We might specify, Brown writes, more exactly what percentage of blood defines being black, whether "any visible admixture" or "the preponderance" or "the preponderance of white blood must be in the proportion of three-fourths." Beyond such measures, we can only enforce equality before the law (e.g., jury service, voting rights), not social equality.

Set into the context of a murder mystery where much of the plot is being driven by racial attitudes as measured by the suitability of marriage partners, in this instance, women of mixed race who, like Plessy, appear white and who have otherwise acquired the "social" advantages of whiteness—education, wealth, property—and in a novel, at that, which alludes to biblical materials through its title character, words and phrases like *reasonable, good faith, natural affinity, mutual appreciation,* and *voluntary consent* all seem to resonate interestingly in sympathetic vibration to the striking of particular key notes in *Scott* and *Plessy*. These characters all have their reasons for what they do. Even Cuthbert Sumner's relief at escaping marriage to Aurelia, a woman of mixed race, may seem reasonable, given the social and (pseudo) scientific prejudices against such unions. Eugenics theory, echoed in Sumner's comments about maintaining the purity of the bloodline, will appeal to this standard of reason. By 1914, Harvard, Columbia, Cornell, and Brown, among others, will be offering courses on eugenics (Selden), and race mixing in marriage will be one of the particular targets, as Paul Lombardo points out: "By 1915, twenty-eight states made marriages between 'Negroes and white persons' invalid; six states included this prohibition in their constitutions." Madison Grant, an outspoken advocate of eugenics theory, argued in *The Passing of the Great Race* (1916), that racial mixing was "a social and racial crime" and would lead to "racial suicide" and the eventual disappearance of white civilization:

> The cross between a white man and an Indian is an Indian; the cross between a white man and a negro is a negro.... When it becomes thoroughly understood that the children of mixed marriages between contrasted races belong to the lower type, the importance of transmitting in unimpaired purity the blood inheritance of ages will be appreciated at its full value [qtd. in Lombardo].

Virginia's Racial Integrity Act, passed in 1924, is not struck down until 1967 when the Supreme Court rules that it and similar laws in fifteen other states violate the Fourteenth Amendment's equal protection clause. Cuthbert Sumner's concerns may be a touch anachronistic—Francis Galton first coins the term *Eugenics* in 1883, developing the idea from Darwin's work, the theory pushed forward by the rediscovery of Gregor Mendel's work in the early 1900s—just as Hopkins's concerns may be somewhat prophetic, but these ideas are all in circulation; their concerns are real, and they will seem eminently reasonable, at least in the abstract, to many people.

That, on the other hand, these ideas are not entirely reasonable seems to be Hopkins's point. In a form like the murder mystery which is driven by science and reason, by Holmesian observation and ratiocination, *Hagar's Daughter* seems somewhat contrary. *Hagar's Daughter* seems to represent something of a counter tradition. Chief Henson, for instance, professes himself willing to trust in women's intuition ("I have confidence in intuitive deductions," Henson comments to himself, when Jewel first visits him and expresses her suspicions sans evidence, that Benson is somehow responsible for recent events [190]); in another telling instance, Auntie Griffin, an old black woman who oversees the Enson estate, is accorded hoodoo powers, her second sight revealing things invisible to empirical observation and reason (228). Artistically, some higher authorial power emerges in the novel, managing the patterns of coincidence that, however contrary to the logic of realism that reigns in the conventional mystery, are discounted here. Reason has its limits, which is nowhere clearer than in the case of love. Ellis's love for Hagar and Sumner's for Jewel clearly grow from a "natural affinity," a sense of "mutual appreciation," their marriage vows a matter of "voluntary consent." Ellis's and Sumner's initial reactions upon discovering the mixed heritages of their respective wives, no matter how reasonable their misgivings seem, both succumb quickly to their stronger affections for these women, though, perhaps, not quickly enough in either case to avert the losses that result from their hesitation. If they had only trusted their instincts, or, as the allusions to Hagar's biblical namesake, emerging from the Abramic narrative, suggest, had they only had faith, things might have ended differently.

While the allusions to the biblical narrative open up another dimension in *Hagar's Daughter*, one that proves more epistemological than historical, at this level it seems clear that Hopkins is intent on confronting the historical forces embodied in documents like the *Scott* and *Plessy* decisions and in revising the historical narrative, in providing the foundation on which to erect a more perfect union, one which will accord the promises of the Preamble to whites and blacks alike. Given the roles that laws forbidding interracial marriage play in measuring the original intent of the Constitution or in providing support for the separate-but-equal policies of *Plessy*, the positive portrayal of interracial marriages in *Hagar's Daughter* and the real suffering that results when two otherwise noble, Christian gentlemen at first hesitate to honor their marriage vows is clearly subversive. Sumner's objections prove to be deeply hypocritical.

To this larger argument, Hopkins does add one more small piece. Marriage as a civil union, defined by the laws of man but sanctioned by a higher authority, provides the possibility of domestic tranquility in ways that both promote the general welfare and secure to our posterity the blessings of that union. The relationship is metonymic and covers almost all of the elements outlined in the Preamble to the Constitution, failing only to speak to the state's needs to provide for the common defense of its citizens. The character of Henry Smith, one of Chief Henson's operatives, supplies this one omission. Henry Smith is a disabled veteran of the Civil War, a black man, a member of the Massachusetts Fifty-fourth Regiment who lost a leg in the charge up Honey Hill. Soitos comments on Hopkins's inclusion of Smith as one indication of "her conscious use of affirmative black history, generally omitted, in this and other works" (68).[3] What is interesting is the way Smith tells the story of the siege of Fort Wagner and his role in it, one which includes his fleeing from the battle under heavy fire from the Confederates. He runs headlong into the rearguard, a black North Carolina regiment, "a provy guard," as Smith puts it, "stationed thar to return stragglers to their posts" (232). He can either return to battle or be shot for deserting his position; he is compelled under pain of death to stand his ground and fight. As heroic as the siege of

Fort Wagner proves, Smith does not romanticize the incident, laying no claim to having participated in some heroic action. He tells of being marched in parade formation directly into fire, of the mayhem that ensues in which he fights like a cornered animal, literally, using his teeth to tear out the throat of a Confederate soldier in the midst of hand-to-hand fighting, and of his fleeing the scene of battle only to be compelled to return. On one level, the description of such animalistic behavior is disconcerting. When he sees Colonel Shaw, the regiment's commander, taken by the Confederates,

> I fel' lak a she wil' cat, an' I jes' outfit a blin' mule. I tore an' I bit lak a dog. I got clinched wif a reb, an' dog my cats, fus' thing I know'd I was chawin' him in de throat an' I never lef' go 'tel he give a groan and I seed he was gone [232].

Thereafter, finding himself rapidly being surrounded, he runs for his life. On another level, his response is perfectly natural, instinctual, a clear example of a fight-or-flight response, and as such, perfectly human, not heroic. His claims are not extraordinary. Henry Smith is a human being, a man who participated in the defense of the union. He is and should be counted among the people of the United States, with all the rights and privileges and responsibilities citizenship entails.

Knowing, in a Biblical Sense

In *The Blue's Dectective*, Stephen F. Soitos argues that, from the beginning, African-American authors writing detective fiction reshaped the genre to reflect specific characteristics of African American life, a "sense of community and family life that doesn't exist in the mainstream detective tradition"(31), for instance, where detectives are almost always solitary, single, singular people, or in the ways they incorporate African American identities, traditions, and ways of knowing into their novels:

> African Americans were attempting from the very beginning to define a new approach to popular fiction that used detective conventions as a vehicle in which to express social critique of mainstream attitudes toward race, class, and gender. Detective writers such as Pauline Hopkins and J.E Bruce initiated the use of distinctive African American cultural tropes in four areas: alteration of detective personas, double-consciousness detection, black vernaculars, and hoodoo. Furthermore these writers signify on the conventions of detective fiction by the use of these tropes, establishing a tradition of black detection that extends over the twentieth century [52].

In Hopkins's case, Venus plays a central role in the solution of the case, thereby altering, or at least adapting the tradition. Sherlock Holmes, for instance, had employed the services of the "Baker Street irregulars" to gather information necessary to the solving of his cases. In *Hagar's Daughter*, Chief Henson is clearly an armchair detective, never really emerging from his office, who undertakes Jewel's request to investigate Elise Bradford's murder and Sumner's role in it as it represents "an uncommon riddle you have set me to solve" (190). He has also, it seems, noted an uncommon resemblance between Jewel and Hagar. In this instance, all of the information comes to him, first in Jewel's appearance and her "intuition" that Benson is somehow responsible for everything that has happened, and then in Venus Johnson's visit, whose connection to all the parties involved provides the necessary clues Henson needs to solve the crime. Venus has already determined who is immediately responsible for Jewel's disappearance and where he has taken her when she appeals to Henson for help. Henson needs to do little more than follow the leads supplied to him, to dispatch Smith and Venus, disguised as a young boy, to the Maryland plantation to confirm her suspicions and to rescue Jewel and Aunt Henny from their confinement there.

Soitos notes the role that hoodoo plays in *Hagar's Daughter*, in particular the curses and prophecies that form a background to the actions, most notably in the uncanny abilities of "witch women" like Auntie Griffin, reputed by whites and blacks alike to be in communication with evil spirits and to see into the future (228). Soitos credits Venus with similar mystical powers, something passed down from Aunt Henny, her grandmother, to Marthy, her mother, to her, arguing that Venus uses these mystical powers to intuit Jewel's and Aunt Henny's whereabouts, that hoodoo powers form the basis of her investigative skills (72–73). In this instance, his reading seems somewhat forced. Venus's suspicions arise from her intimate knowledge of Isaac, her father, and his character, joined with her own close observations of events in the Bowen household, including overheard conversations and private letters she has been privy to, augmented by her "innocent" questioning of Marthy and Oliver, her brother, about recent events. Isaac is a suspicious character, a known entity, whose sudden appearance with a large sum of money, the money needed to pay off the mortgage, indicates that he has been up to no good. Her hunches are the product of logical deduction, not mystical powers. As a descendent of the slaves serving the Enson-Sargeant estates and a maid in the Bowen household, she is ideally positioned to work out what, in general, is going on here.

The allusion to hoodoo powers and the curses and prophecies they support do, however, seem to suggest the existence of powers beyond rational comprehension, of forces at work in the world that are essentially mysterious, magical, and somehow accountable for events. In her fateful interview with Sumner, Elise Bradford alludes to these powers:

"I feel impelled to tell you what I am about to disclose, by an unseen power. Do you not believe in unseen forces influencing our acts?" she asked wistfully.

"I cannot deny that I have sometimes felt the same influence of supernatural powers that you speak of, and I do firmly trust that the world of shadows and mystery to which we are all bound may be one of infinite love, infinite calm and rest" [153].

In the case of *Hagar's Daughter*, the forces at work seem biblical, the allusion to Hagar providing the link.

Hagar, of course, plays a central role in the story of Abram/Abraham as the Egyptian slave girl given to Abram by his wife Sarai that he might beget a child, the heir this otherwise childless and aging couple lack (Gen. 16). Abram had complained to the Lord that, being childless, "my heir must be a slave born in my house" (Gen. 15: 3), and so it proved, at least in part to be, Hagar conceiving and giving birth to Ishmael. The Lord had told Abram that his progeny would be more numerous than the stars above (Gen. 15: 5), but that, aliens in an alien land, they would also be held as slaves for 400 years before being rewarded and their masters punished (Gen. 15: 13–14). Hagar's son seems to be implicated in that prophecy. Though we are later told, after Isaac is born, that Ishmael will also be father to "a great nation" (Gen. 21:13), his will be a difficult life. An angel appears to Hagar:

"You are with child and will bear a son.
You shall name him Ishmael,
Because the Lord has heard of your ill-treatment.
He shall be a man like the wild ass,
His hand against every man
And every man's hand against him;
And he shall live at odds with all his kinsmen" [Gen.16:11–12].

Ishmael, the footnotes tell us, means "God heard." He is evidence of the crimes committed against Hagar ("Because the Lord has heard …") and the answer to a prayer. As Abram's child, even though he is the son of a slave, he will participate in the blessings promised to his father.

The immediate point of the reference is clear enough: Hopkins's Hagar is a slave girl lent to a childless couple thereby providing them with an heir to their estate, just as Sarai lends her slave to Abram that he may father a child and heir to his. But the references seem to extend farther, for the larger narrative, the story of Abram being called out by the Lord, being promised that, in spite of being an alien in an alien land, his descendants will be uncountable, that they will hold dominion over all that Abram can see, seems prophetic, resonating through *Hagar's Daughter*. In the course of the biblical narrative, *Abram* is transformed into *Abraham*, from "exalted father" to "father of many nations," from the head of a family to the founding father of a great nation, a promised people taking possession of a promised land, an image of Manifest Destiny as Abram will take possession of all he can see, "north, east, south, west" (Gen. 13:14–15). While Ishmael is the son of a slave, he, too, will participate in that promise, a part of the larger prophecy.

Hopkins is not writing allegory, but much of the story seems to echo the biblical narrative in one way or another, extending at length through the story of Lot, Abram's nephew, and of Isaac and even of his sons, Jacob and Esau. Twice in the course of his travels, Abram will disguise himself as Sarai's brother, a ruse that Isaac and Rebecca will repeat, fearing that first Pharaoh and later Abimelech will not hesitate to kill her husband that they might claim Sarai for themselves. A brother, however, poses no obstacle; his favor might even be courted. In both instances, Pharaoh and Abimelech will be punished for taking a married woman from her husband, their kingdoms rendered infertile until Sarai is restored to Abram, revealed to be her husband, and reparations made. The frequent use of disguise, the dramatic revelations of identity, the honoring of the marriage contract, even the repetition, the same story told three times, all have a place in *Hagar's Daughter*.

Seemingly significant in the biblical narrative is the revelation that Abram/Abraham is, in fact, Sarai/Sarah's brother. In Gen. 20, Abimelech asks Abraham why he has misrepresented himself. Abraham responds:

> I said to myself, There can be no fear of God in this place, and they will kill me for the sake of my wife. She is in fact my sister, she is my father's daughter though not by the same mother; and she became my wife [Gen. 20: 11–13].

Though of "mixed blood," Abraham and Sarah share a father and a common inheritance. The theological and genealogical lines here become tangled, as they will when Lot's daughters, after fleeing the destruction of Sodom and Gomorrah, sleep with their father in order to beget heirs, or, in a variation, when Jacob disguises himself as his brother Esau so that he might steal Isaac's blessing. What does seem clear, somewhat ironically, is the sanctity of marriage, protected against the moral laxity of the Egyptians, of Abimelech, of Sodom, and the need to preserve the patrimony from being lost, even through incest. (Rebecca seems intent on stealing Isaac's blessing for Jacob because Esau has married a Hittite woman, an unfavorable match in Rebecca's eyes [Gen. 26: 34–35].) The point seems to be the need to save the patrimony from being seized by the morally degenerate, of preserving Abraham's legacy from those who would corrupt it. Framing *Hagar's Daughter* as she has done, moving from Chapter 1's portrayal of the founders of the Confederate States of America as the fallen angels in *Paradise Lost* to the final chapter's comment that "the idolatry of the Moloch of Slavery must be purged from the land and his [Sumner's] actual sinlessness was but a meet offering to appease the wrath of a righteous God" (283–84), these comments coming in both cases within the need to honor marriage vows, even among enslaved peoples, Hopkins is invoking the larger themes implicit in the stories of Abram/Abraham.

Working out the exact terms of the implied comparison, given the strangeness of the biblical materials and their fragmentary nature, however, is difficult. It becomes clear that the Enson-Sargeant estates need to be saved from falling into the hands of the morally degenerate and wholly unworthy younger brother, St. Clair, and that Ellis, marrying Hagar in his fortieth year (just as Isaac and Esau are both 40 when they marry), must honor this marriage contract, the mixed-race woman, a slave, worthy of his love and respect, however unconventional the marriage proves, just as the Lord's promise to Abram will extend to Hagar and her children. But the points of contact seem to shift, capable of multiple constructions. In this regard, Harold Bloom's commentary on Abram, offered in *The Book of J*, may help:

> Martin Buber, a great interpreter of the Bible, was not in the normative tradition, and read J's Abram as a seer, the first prophet of Israel: "With Abraham what matters is not his character as God finds it, so to speak, but what he does, and what he becomes." What Abram does is to respond immediately to Yahweh's call; what Abram becomes is Abraham, the father of the Jews, the Christians, and the Muslims, all of whom are the children of Abraham [197].

Ellis Enson seems, finally, to play this role. Troubled by the letter of the law, that according to Maryland statutes, his marriage to the mixed-race Hagar is null and void, he hesitates and nearly loses everything that has been given to him, the blessings he has received. By the end of the novel, he sees more deeply and acts without hesitation, accepting Hagar, Jewel, and even the illegitimate son of his fallen brother into his household, realizing the lessons that Buber and Bloom find in Abraham. Ellis sums up this lesson for Sumner, who has just discovered the truth of Hagar's origins and is struggling to come to terms with it:

> My dear boy, I know just where you are. I went all through the old arguments from your point of view twenty years ago. I wavered and wavered, but nature was stronger than prejudice. I have suffered the torments of hell since I lost my wife and child.
>
> He rose from his seat and strode down the room, then back again, pausing before the young man.
>
> "Sumner," he said, with impressive solemnity, "race prejudice is all right in theory, but when a man tries to practice it against the laws which govern human life and action, there's a weary journey ahead of him, and he's not got to die to realize the tortures of the damned. This idea of race separation is carried to an

extreme point and will, in time, kill itself. Amalgamation has taken place; it will continue, and no finite power can stop it" [270].

The conversation concludes:

"'A boy's will is the wind's will, And the thoughts of youth are long, long thoughts,'" he quoted softly. "You will learn one day that there is a higher law than that enacted by any earthly tribunal, and I believe that you will then find your nature nobler than you know."

"You make me feel uncanny, Enson, with your visionary ideas. Thank God, I have my wife; there I am safely anchored" [271].

The discovery that Jewel is Hagar's biological daughter almost immediately following this conversation will leave Sumner unmoored.

The biblical narrative, clearly there but often seen aslant from the corner of the eye, the story about prophecy and about Abram's coming to see and fulfill that vision, becoming Abraham in the process, represents an alternative way of knowing the world, a competing paradigm, one in which the mechanical representations of empirical science, the selective breeding protocols of eugenics, for instance, prove ineffective for explaining the higher principles governing human nature. This mysticism is hoodoo, or something like it, and it is Ellis/Chief Henson and his willingness to accept the evidence of intuition or the word of a black woman, the access to the uncanny, that establishes the viability of this alternative tradition. The Old Testament, this "wisdom literature," offers a typological structure that is working toward fulfillment in the present, a testament to the powers of prophecy, an older way of knowing that is native to the Auntie Griffins in the world and which Ellis Enson, in his own way, has come to appreciate and to participate in.

An Unconventional Construction

Hopkins, as Bloom might put it, is not in the normative tradition, and the story she tells, however dependent it is on the conventions of genre fiction, seems to be exploring the limits of conventionality, particularly in its depiction of what can only be considered, at least at the time, an unconventional marriage. So-called conventional wisdom would legislate, and had, in fact, already legislated, against the union of a white man and a mixed-race woman. In reading *Hagar's Daughter*, these kinds of prohibitions just seem wrong, foolish, unfounded. At least to the contemporary reader, Sumner's horror at learning of Aurelia's mixed blood, repeated with the discovery of Hagar's and then Jewel's heritage, seems exaggerated, beyond reason, exposing the limits of his own imagination and the inherent hypocrisy of his liberal support for

African American issues. It seems to be of a piece with the hypocrisy of our good Christian minister lecturing Walker on the inherent value in selling husbands and wives together, not separately, if a buyer can be found who will purchase both, or of a democratic country championing rights which are self-evident for some but evidently not for all people. The conventional constructions, the letter of the laws in each case, violate the spirit of the higher principles that should guide actions in instances like these.

On one level, our emotional response to the action, our feelings that the unions of Ellis and Hagar, of Sumner and Jewel are natural, normal, sensible, and that the objections leveled against them are unnatural seem an instance of the power of genre fiction, as Phyllis M. Betz notes, to "normalize" the abnormal by representing unconventional relationships within the formulaic conventions of the romance or mystery novel (8). According to the roles they play in the romance, the honorable Ellis could not help but fall in love with a woman like Hagar, the love destined by the formulas of romance to outlast the obstacles it faces. That the obstacle in this case is as obdurate as slavery and racial prejudice hardly matters. According to the narrative conventions, the love is real and the fears unfounded, and so, at least in part, is the case here.

But the formulas don't work quite the ways they should. Nothing is more conventional than the discovery of a token, a locket with a secret compartment, that will reveal Jewel's identity, transforming her from stepdaughter into Hagar's actual daughter lost long ago and long presumed to be dead. This discovery, as Hazel V. Carby points out in her introduction to the novel, creates new problems at the same time that it solves old ones:

> A number of magical resolutions conclude *Hagar's Daughter*. The most magical of all is the rediscovery of a lost child through a locket (such magical signs were common popular fictional narrative devices for returning an orphan to his or her parents). The secrets of the "little hair trunk" lead to the discovery of Hagar's daughter but not to the restoration of a moral order. Conventional popular fictional use of disguise and double identities indicates a disruption of the natural order of events in a society or community. The revelations and fictional resolutions of popular fiction signal the reestablishment of the disrupted moral and social order in the characters' lives. But the resolutions to *Hagar's Daughter* reveal the contradictions inherent in Hopkins's attempt to use popular and easily accessible narrative forms to question the morality of, rather than to restore faith in, the social formation. The capture and imprisonment of the villains do not return Hopkins's fictional society to happiness. Nor are the heroes and heroines secured in their social positions when threats to expose them cease. Blackness is the source of their vulnerability [xl–xli].

The anticipated resolution doesn't resolve many of the problems raised in the novel. The unmasking of St. Clair/Benson and Walker/Madison will allow a long-delayed justice to go forward. These two are demonic forces, fallen angels, proverbial snakes in the grass whose crimes, including in St. Clair's case, complicity in the Lincoln assassination, can now be known and punished. The process of discovery that unmasks Benson and Madison will also reveal Hagar's past, and, in a somewhat loosely linked chain of causation, Jewel's identity as Hagar's daughter. While these discoveries allow for the restoration of Ellis Enson's family, they simultaneously disrupt Sumner and Jewel's marriage, at least long enough for the two of them to be separated, thereby initiating the final tragedy, Jewel dying before she and Sumner can be reconciled. In this case, rather than revealing the character's identity and his or her fitness to enter into a marriage, as often happens in Shakespeare, that marriage reining in the forces that threaten to disrupt the social order, the token seems to reveal Jewel as unfit, an unsuitable partner for a white man.

The problem Carby identifies appears in the ways the conventions are perceived to work, that "conventional popular fictional use of disguise and double identities indicates a disruption of the *natural order* of events in a society or community" and the unmasking of those characters a step toward restoring the *natural order* of things. In this case, Ellis's love for Hagar and Sumner's for Jewel seem perfectly natural, well within the natural order of things; the problem is in the unconventional nature of these relationships, that they cannot be legally sanctioned, that they defy community standards. It is not the natural order but the community standards that are at fault, not Jewel's mixed blood but the social stigma attached to it that causes Sumner's hesitation, or, perhaps, it is Sumner's all too conventional New England philanthropy that is at fault. In either case, the fault is in the conventional construction. We need a more radical vision. The laws of man prove in this instance to be imperfect reflections of a divine order, "the world of shadows and mystery to which we are all bound," as Sumner puts it, one that Sumner hopes "may be one of infinite love, infinite calm and rest" (153). The inherent contradiction here is between the rule of law and the ends of justice, or in *Plessy*, the idea that legal equality can be enforced without achieving social equality. That the conventional construction doesn't quite work in the novel only underscores how inadequate the conventional attitudes recorded in law and public opinion prove to be: "the sin is the nation's" (283).

Hagar's Daughter proves to be a remarkably interesting and sophisticated, if not wholly successful, work. It is interesting in the ways it engages the historical moment and the ways it reflects on and challenges the received "wisdom," providing in its place an alternative vision, a different way of knowing and being in the world. The novel will question both the conventional wisdom and the wisdom in conventions. There are more things in heaven and on earth than are dreamt of in our philosophy, a point that Marthy stresses in conversation with Oliver:

> "Now, ma, you don't believe all them old signs about hoodooing and such stuff. There isn't a thing in it, it's nothing but superstition."
> "Don't talk to me 'bout yer suferstition; there is some things in this wurl that college edication won't 'splain, an' you can't argify an' condisput 'em, neither. I've had my trials, Oliver, but tryin' to bring you an' yer sister to a realisin' sense of the sin in the wurl is hard on me, an' it lays on my mind" [172].

Hopkins seems to have labored under the same anxieties that Marthy faces. On this level, the book is wholly successful. If it has its weaknesses, they are largely the weaknesses of the genre, the plot machinery rather creaky, the prose overly dependent on adjectives and adverbs, the whole thing preachy, didactic, at least in places. Hopkins is prone to authorial intrusion, telling, not showing.

The work is, as well, remarkable prescient, the issues it takes up, in some cases, still being debated a hundred years later. Justice Harlan's dissent in *Plessy*, that the doctrine of separate but equal would, in time, turn out to be "quite as pernicious" as the findings of the Dred Scott Case, proved prophetic, this unfortunate decision persisting for over half a century before being set aside in *Brown v. Board.* A half-century after *Brown*, we are still struggling with the inequitable distribution of educational and economic resources in our society. Debates over affirmative action still seem to rehearse arguments that appeared in *Plessy* and which Hopkins engages in her novel. The laws restricting interracial marriage would take even longer, until 1967, to be declared unconstitutional; the depiction of romantic relationships between whites and blacks would remain rare in popular culture, on television and in the movies, for at least the next forty years. And the tensions that arise in the novel, in the problems inherent in using forms like the romance or the murder mystery, forms more typically employed in conservative ways to reproduce rather than reform prevailing social structures, the problems inherent in using such popular forms to explore minority experiences, continue to be a concern. Hopkins, it seems, was right to be worried: "The thoughts of youth are long, long thoughts."

Original Sins

Read in isolation, especially more than a hundred years after its initial publication, *Hagar's Daughter* can seem puzzling, even problematic at a number of levels, as the foregoing discussion makes clear. The promises of emancipation and the realities of the post–Reconstruction period where legal rulings like *Plessy v. Ferguson* and (pseudo-) scientific eugenics theories combine to perpetuate the caste prejudices prevalent throughout slavery clearly establish the issues, all having to do with the wisdom and legality of interracial marriages—of social equality—that the plot centers on. Still, problems persist: the episodic form of the novel, perhaps, to some degree, the product of serialization, itself a somewhat odd choice following the more conventional publication of her first novel, *Contending Forces*, in book form; the novel's focus on its white characters, or characters who at least initially seem white, published in a magazine primarily aimed at an African American readership; the novel's romantic resolution, seemingly supportive of miscegenation, of the racially mixed union of the novel's central characters. This last point, while it might be seen simply as Hopkins's defiance of eugenics, proved to be a trend in Hopkins's work and the subject of discussion in the *Colored American Magazine* letters to the editor section. In her study of Hopkins's contributions to the *Colored American Magazine*, "'The Case Was Very Black Against' Her: Pauline Hopkins and the Politics of Racial Ambiguity at the *Colored American Magazine*," Sigrid Anderson Cordell notes at least one reader who found such resolutions disconcerting. Cornelia A. Condict, Cordell writes, complained that "the fiction [printed in the *Colored American Magazine*] favors miscegenation as a romantic ideal," that the journal's stories, as Condict writes,

> without exception ... have been of love between the colored and whites. Does that mean that your novelists can imagine no love beautiful and sublime within the range of the colored race, for each other? ... The stories of these tragic mixed loves will not commend themselves to your white readers and will not elevate the colored readers [qtd. in Cordell 59].

Cordell points to one possible explanation, that in addition to its primary African American audience, the magazine needed to appeal to a liberal white readership whose support, financial and otherwise, was necessary to its survival (52–53).

Condict's complaint, at least in Hopkins's case, is compounded if *Hagar's Daughter* is read in conjunction with "Talma Gordon," a short story Hopkins published in the *Colored American Magazine* in 1900. "Talma Gordon," which seems to represent Hopkins's first entry into the mystery genre, shares some central plot points with *Hagar's Daughter*, primarily a woman's discovery of her own mixed racial heritage and questions of her suitability as a marriage partner for a white man. Much as in Hagar's case, a childless couple adopt a mixed-race child and raise her as their own, the adoption, in this instance, concealed by a trip to Europe. That child, raised as white, is eventually married to Capt. Jonathan Gordon, a cotton manufacturer, former ship's captain, and descendant of an old New England Puritan family who traveled to this country on the *Mayflower*. After the birth of two daughters—Jeannette, who favors her father in appearance and complexion, and Talma, who favors her mother—Mrs. Gordon's mixed race is revealed in the birth of her third child, a boy with distinctive Africanized features. Neither mother nor child survive childbirth, allowing the secret to be concealed, though it does result in a private settlement from Mrs. Gordon's parents to appease Capt. Gordon's "righteous wrath" (18). Capt. Gordon remarries, has a second son, and thereafter amends his will, leaving his daughters only enough to provide for their maintenance, the bulk of the estate bequeathed to his son. Jeannette only learns of her own mixed racial heritage and that she has been largely dispossessed as a result of a conversation she overhears between her father and stepmother. Talma only learns of these details in a letter from her sister delivered to her after her sister's death. The story's cast of characters is entirely white, or at least appears to be, with the mixed racial heritage of the Gordon women concealed even from them.

These details are, of course, only slowly revealed in the course of the story, following the murder of Capt. Gordon, his second wife, and their infant son, all of whom have had their throats slashed. While suspicion falls on Talma, who had recently quarreled with her father over his refusal to permit her marriage to a young white man, she is found not guilty at trial, the circumstantial evidence insufficient to win a conviction. After a sojourn in Europe and the death of her sister, Talma returns, her health failing, to be cared for by the family's physician, Dr. William Thornton. Thornton, who relates the particulars of this story, solves the mystery of the Gordon murders when one of his patients confesses on his deathbed, the motives entirely unrelated to the family drama surrounding the revelations of Talma's mixed heritage. Talma's suitor, still hoping to marry her in spite of her father's earlier refusal, is horrified, however, to learn the truth of her heritage, just as Cuthbert Sumner is similarly horrified to learn of Hagar's and then Jewel's mixed blood. In this case, the rejection is almost comical. Talma's suitor exclaims, "God! Doctor, but this is too much. I could stand the stigma of murder, but add to that the pollution of Negro blood! No man is brave enough to face such a stigma" (19). In fact, the doctor proves to be brave enough, and in the last line of the story, he reveals the identity of his until now mysterious wife, Talma Gordon.

In her study of Hopkins's life and work, *Pauline E. Hopkins: A Literary Biography*, Hanna Wallinger identifies Hopkins's primary concerns in her four novels as "historiography, the discussion of the slave past and ancient Africa, and their legacy in the America of her time; the fate of the beautiful mixed-race woman; the heroism of her male characters, their manliness and civil courage; and ancient African glory and the future of race leadership" (9). "Talma Gordon" clearly anticipates at least two of these interests, Talma's fate as a beautiful mixed-race woman and Dr. Thornton's civil courage in marrying her, an act not only defying popular opinion but of civil disobedience given the prevailing prejudices and legal prohibitions against miscegenation. That miscegenation has a deeper meaning, connecting the story to these other concerns, will also prove to be the case. If nothing else, the story reinforces one of Hopkins's often repeated lines, that, as Enson tells Sumner in *Hagar's Daughter*, "amalgamation has taken place; it will continue, and no finite power can stop it" (270).

On one level, the story as told seems to be directed at the wisdom of American imperialism. The story is framed by an unidentified narrator, a member of The Canterbury Club of Boston, here convened at Dr. Thornton's Beacon Street residence for its regular monthly meeting. Thornton's home, the narrator notes, is "usually closed to society" (1), and his wife "entirely unknown to social life" (1); this meeting, consequently, is something of a special occasion. The evening's topic for discussion is "Expansion: Its Effect Upon the Future Development of the Anglo-Saxon Throughout the World" (1). The topic seems particularly appropriate to Hopkins, coming so early in her association with the *Colored American Magazine*, marking her return to public life after a decade of silence. After an early theatrical career, Hopkins had left the stage. Wallinger points to historical concerns as the reason:

> She [Hopkins] chose to weather the "Nationalist Nineties," as John Higham [author of *Strangers in the Land: Patterns of American Nativism, 1860–1925*] calls this decade, with work largely not artistic. Since the 1890s were characterized by national and international unrest, this was a wise choice. On the international plane, the Spanish-American War, the military occupation of Cuba, the annexation of Guam, the Philippines, Puerto Rico, Hawaii, and Wake Island demonstrate the imperialistic agenda of the time [44].

Coupled with domestic issues including labor unrest, immigration restriction, economic depression (1893–97), the *Plessy v. Ferguson* ruling, attempts to limit African American voting rights, and an estimated 100 lynchings a year between 1893 and 1904 (Wallinger 44), Hopkins seems to have found continuing her theatrical activities untenable. In this context, the subject for debate is clearly significant.

The debate, at least initially, elicits the expected responses. Herbert Clapp, "eminent jurist and politician" (1), notes the economic and political advantages to be gained by expansion, while Joseph Whitman, "theologian of worldwide fame," noted "the great opportunity which expansion would give to the religious enthusiast" (2). Hopkins's comment that "none could doubt the sincerity of this man, who looked once into the idealized face on which heaven had set the seal of consecration" (2) cannot be more ironic, as the action of the story proves. The idealism inherent in these lines of argument meets its real-life counterpart in Capt. Gordon, whose activities as pirate in the East Indies, including the murder of his first mate in order to protect the location of his concealed treasure, turns expansion into exploitation. That Gordon traces his heritage to Mayflower Puritans casts doubt retroactively over the noble intentions of even our founding fathers. The apple, we can imagine, doesn't fall very far from the tree.

This much seems obvious. What is somewhat less than obvious is Dr. Thornton's response to the question. Thornton sees expansion as leading inevitably to amalgamation, and that expansion cannot be pursued unless we are willing to accept that consequence. Thornton says, "Did you ever imagine in spite of our prejudices against amalgamation, some of our descendents, indeed many of them, will inevitably intermarry among those far-off tribes of dark-skinned peoples, if they become part of this great Union?" (2). Thornton believes that such intermarriages will occur among all classes, not just among the lower class, as another club member, a college president, suggests. Surprisingly, rather than opposing this outcome, Thornton professes himself "most emphatically" in favor of such unions,

> when they [the marriage partners] possess decent moral development and physical perfection, for then we develop a superior being in the progeny born of the intermarriage. But if we are not ready to receive and assimilate the new material which will be brought to mingle with our pure Anglo-Saxon stream, we should call a halt to our expansion policy [3].

Civil prohibitions against intermarriage will be powerless to stop "the God-implanted instinct that made Adam" (3) and that led Adam to accept Eve (4) and cling to her, Thornton's reasoning suggests, even in the face of certain punishment. Thornton concludes: "So it is with the sons of Adam ever since, through the law of heredity which makes us all one common family. And so it will be with us in our re-formation of this old Republic" (3). It is at this point in the story that Thornton takes over the narrative duties and proceeds, by way of example, to tell the story of the Gordon murders, the daughters' discovery of their mixed racial heritage, and, in the end, to introduce to the company his wife, the former Talma Gordon. The doctor speaks from experience.

The references to Adam, the operations of providence, an irresistible sexual attraction, and the common genetic heritage of all people, all descendants of Adam, establish a line of argument that emerges in Hopkins's fiction and nonfiction works alike, particularly in her 1905 self-published pamphlet

A Primer of Facts: Pertaining to the Early Greatness of the African Race and the Possibilities of Restoration by Its Descendants—with EPILOGUE Compiled and Arranged from the Works of the Best Known Ethnologists and Historians. Wallinger has reprinted this text as an appendix to *Pauline E. Hopkins: A Literary Biography*, noting that Hopkins draws on biblical, ethnological, and historical arguments then in wide circulation, ideas most immediately available to her in William Wells Brown, *The Rising Son* (1874); Martin R. Delany, *Principia of Ethnology: The Origin of Races and Color* (1879); Rufus L. Perry, *The Cushite; Or, The Descendants of Ham* (1893); and George Washington William, *History of the Negro Race in America, 1619–1880* (1883). Hopkins borrows liberally from these authors, the arguments based both in biblically inspired monogenesis, defined by Shawn Salvant in "Pauline Hopkins and the End of Incest" as "the single-origin theory of human genealogy" common in nineteenth-century ethnological debates (660), and in Ethiopianism, that "western civilization originated in mighty, ancient Ethiopian kingdoms," as John Nickel puts it (55). In short, Hopkins's argument in *A Primer of Facts*, echoing her sources, is that humankind traces its heritage to Adam, that Adam, as such, incorporated in himself all races, that in complexion, giving his composition, he would have been clay colored, reddish or yellow (Wallinger 293–4). Racial divisions thereafter emerge in Noah's three sons, each of whom proves distinct: Shem, Noah's color (i.e., clay colored like Adam); Ham, dark in complexion; Japheth, light skinned. Following the destruction of Babel, each son and family migrate, Shem east into Asia, Japheth north and west into Europe, and Ham south into Africa (Wallinger 293–95). Each population reproduces true to type owing to the "economy of the Creator," racial differences reinforced by climate, among other environmental factors (Wallinger 296–97). Civilization takes root in Ethiopia among the descendants of Ham and his son Cush, moving from Ethiopia to Egypt, all one kingdom in the beginning, from Egypt to Greece, from Greece to Rome. Western civilization is thus established in Africa and thereafter transmitted through the subsequent rise and decline of these kingdoms. That Ethiopia will rise in prominence is foretold in Psalms 68:31, a passage Hopkins frequently cites in her work: "Princes shall come out of Egypt; Ethiopia shall soon stretch forth her hands unto God."

Amalgamation, seen in this light, will restore humankind to a pre–Babel, pre-flood condition. Hopkins cited Acts 17:26 in support, "Of one blood I made all nations of man to dwell upon the whole face of the earth." Southern caste prejudice, the notions of social inequality reinforced by rulings like *Plessy v. Ferguson*, prove to be the immediate obstacle. Hopkins quotes a lengthy passage from Jeannette Robinson Murphy's *Southern Thoughts for*

Northern Thinkers in *A Primer* to baseline these attitudes. In one passage, Murphy describes the impossibility of whites and blacks meeting as equals:

> The whole trouble and difficulty lie in just one thing and nothing else. We are willing to give the Negro an all-around mental, moral, physical and spiritual education, but we insist upon the utter segregation and social isolation of the colored man. No proposed standing army can ever change the attitude of the white South upon this question. No qualifications or highest education of the Negro could ever make the true Southern man welcome that Negro into his family or hold out to him the tiniest tip of social recognition, for he believes that the mingling of a higher race with a lower one is an abomination unto the Lord. Around this pitiful point future wars and causes of war lie [Wallinger 308].

Hopkins's response several pages later is that white Southern gentlemen forced themselves on black women, first perpetrating the offense Murphy complains of (Hopkins: "Tears and heart-burnings are the portion of the Southern white woman, and like Sarah of old, she wreaks her vengeance on hapless Hagar") and that rather than polluting Anglo-Saxon bloodlines, amalgamation will improve genetic stock: "Anglo-Saxon blood is already hopelessly perverted, with that of other races, and in most cases to its great gain" (Wallinger 311).

In "Furnace Blasts," a two-part essay Hopkins published under her J. Shirley Shadrach pseudonym in the February and March 1903, editions of the *Colored American Magazine*, Hopkins had made much the same point. She had written that "the greatest objection to Negro enfranchisement is found in the menace of social equality which it is contended will inevitably lead to amalgamation" (qtd. Wallinger 66). To the question "Shall the Anglo-Saxon and the Afro-American mix?" she responds, "They have mixed" (qtd. in Wallinger 66). Nevertheless, given the prevailing caste prejudices that, in general, make it impossible for whites and blacks to enter into marriage as equal partners, "the time for amalgamation is not yet," though she adds that the "future American" will be a product of amalgamation (Wallinger 67).

Dr. Thornton's remarks—that we are "sons of Adam," that we compose "one common family," that in the future amalgamation will restore this condition—"And so it will be with us in our re-formation of this old Republic"—directly anticipate language and ideas that Hopkins will return to repeatedly in her novels and essays. This line of argument also provides a response to readers like Condict troubled by the positive portrayal of mixed-race marriages. And it also seems to qualify, to some extent, readings like that Sigrid Anderson Cordell advances in "'The Case Was Very Black Against' Her" that "what sets [Hopkins's] fiction and journalism apart from that of her female counterparts—both black and white—is her blunt depiction of brutality and violence and the explicit link that she draws between violence and social, political, and racial oppression" (52–53). In "Talma Gordon," Cordell contends that Hopkins's narrative technique will concentrate attention on the history of violence, especially sexual oppression, common under slavery and the ways it emerges in the present. She writes:

> Hopkins utilizes a story-within-a-story technique to recount the brutal murder of a white man who turned against his own daughters after learning that their mother was part black. By creating layers of frame-tales to be stripped away by the reader, the narrative structure explicitly reveals three aspects of social history: first, the historical reality of violence against black women in the United States; second, the extent to which white upper middle-class identity depends upon perpetuating and hiding that violence; and, third, that this situation creates enormous potential for rage on the part of the oppressed [Cordell 53].

Clearly, many of the elements Cordell describes are there: the abandonment of the mixed-race child who, in time, becomes the first Mrs. Gordon; Capt. Gordon's "righteous wrath" at learning of his first wife's racial heritage and his ability, as a result, to essentially blackmail her parents, winning a financial settlement for damages done; Talma's abandonment by her would-be fiancé when he learns of her mixed blood; even Jeannette's murderous intentions which are only prevented because her father had already been murdered, all possibly reinforced by the story's conflation of imperialism with piracy in Capt. Gordon's character which, by extension, seems to challenge traditional narratives of the Puritans and the purity of their motives in traveling to this continent. Cordell has a case. Even today, for instance, writers referring to Thomas Jefferson's children almost never include in the number the children he fathered with Sally Hemings in spite of DNA evidence demonstrating that he fathered at least one child and maybe as many as six children with Hemings in addition to his six white children.

And yet, in both "Talma Gordon" and *Hagar's Daughter*, the romantic resolutions, clearly in keeping with generic conventions, offer a more positive vision than Cordell describes. In both cases, the critical action occurs when a childless white couple adopts a mixed-race child and raises her as their own, welcoming that child into their family, a child loved and supported, offered all of the education and advantages available in upper middle-class white society, a child who is fully equal and worthy of their love. That the child may be the result of a past that permitted the sexual exploitation of black women is clearly the case. That this child also becomes the answer to a childless couple's desire for children and, by all appearance, the object of their love, is also the case. It is tempting to read the parents' inability to conceive a child, to perpetuate their bloodline, as symbolic of Anglo-Saxon sterility, a genetic dead end that amalgamation, as Hopkins sees it, will repair. The beautiful mixed-race woman is both a testament to an unfortunate past and the promise for the future. Talma and Hagar are the future.

Hopkins does not, as a result, so much repudiate eugenics theories as offer an alternative reading, one that links biblical and ethnographic conceptions of race current in the literature of her time to biology. It would, to some degree, be surprising if she did repudiate eugenics and the biologistic paradigms that governed early-twentieth-century scientific understanding; colorism, for instance, remains an issue in the African American community, never fully repudiated even in the face of the black-is-beautiful movement of the late 1960s, appearing as an issue even in Stephen L. Carter's *The Emperor of Ocean Park* (2002). "The thoughts of youth are long, long thoughts," as Longfellow suggests, the line Hopkins ends *Hagar's Daughter* with (284). What does seem to emerge in these early pieces, however, is a sense of prophecy being fulfilled or perhaps typology, of the Old Testament prefigurations finding completion in a "New Testament." The Old Testament stories and prophecy are there in the promise to Hagar and in Psalm 68. Jewel, at the end of *Hagar's Daughter*, in her note to Sumner following the revelation of her own mixed-race heritage, describes her own caste prejudice in Old Testament terms:

> I know your prejudice against amalgamation: I have believed with you. My sin, for it is a sin to hold one set of God's creatures so much inferior to the rest of creation simply because of the color of the skin, has found me out. Like Miriam of old, I have scorned the Ethiopian and the curse has fallen upon me, and I must dwell outside the tents of happiness forever. I know you pity my poor mother; she has been so unhappy. I am proud of my father; he is a noble man. I will write again tomorrow and perhaps see you; but, oh, pray not today! [281–82].

Miriam, Moses's sister, had been punished by God for speaking against Moses's wife, an Ethopian, a Cushite. Miriam's skin turns white, leprous—she is a thing unclean—and she is exiled from the camp, following Moses's intercession, for seven days (Numbers 12:1–16). Cuthbert Sumner's eventual response is also telling, couched in language from the Psalms and Song of Solomon: "Many waters cannot quench love, neither can the floods drown it. All Thy waves and Thy billows have gone over me, but the heart is not easily closed. Love is strong as death" (282). The first and last sentences derive from Song of Solomon 8, verses 7 and 6, respectively, while "all thy waves and Thy billows have gone over me" derives from Psalm 42:7, a Psalm of the soul in sorrow thirsting for God. Verse 8, however, provides hope: "Yet the Lord will command his lovingkindness in the daytime, and in the night his song shall be with me." Amalgamation has taken place and will take place and will, in time and under the proper conditions, work to the improvement of all humankind, as Dr. Thornton suggests. Jewel's hesitation in meeting Cuthbert—"oh, pray not today"—and the twenty-four hours it takes Cuthbert to realize that his love for Jewel supersedes his prejudices against amalgamation prove to be the problem, precipitating the final tragedy, one that could have been avoided had either of them acceded more swiftly to accept their love.

3

"A Mystery Tale of Dark Harlem"

Rounding Up the Usual Suspects

Biological Determinism

Early in *The Conjure-Man Dies* (1932), John Archer, a Harlem physician, is called across the street to the apartment of N'Gana Frimbo, a self-described "psychist," when one of his clients discovers Frimbo unconscious and bleeding from a head wound. Frimbo, or the man everyone believes to be N'Gana Frimbo, is already dead, having been suffocated after being stunned by a non-fatal blow to the side of his head. The police are duly summoned and, in the company of Perry Dart, one of ten African American members of the Manhattan police force to be promoted to detective, Archer and Dart survey Frimbo's apartment. The search initially yields a well-appointed if very masculine bedroom and a study, holding an extensive library, including a number of philosophical treatises on determinism, cause and effect, and the science of history. The room also holds Frimbo's framed Harvard diploma. Archer, who, like his creator, Rudolph Fisher, is a well-educated and clearly well-read doctor, finds the scene anomalous: "A native African, a Harvard graduate, a student of philosophy—and a sorcerer. There's something wrong with that picture" (27–28). As the survey continues, this mystery will deepen with the discovery of a fully-equipped laboratory including, among other things, what Archer believes to be a television receiver (this piece of information is not divulged until much later in the book) and several specimen jars holding human male "sex glands." This assemblage of materials doesn't seem to add up: Frimbo is a native African—he, in fact, turns out to be the king of Buwongo, "an independent territory to the northeast of Liberia, with a population of approximately a million people," the population organized into 48 tribes (215, 218)—who has been educated at Harvard, and who has subsequently established himself in Harlem as a "conjure man," or so Archer and Dart assume, a hoodoo priest of sorts, telling fortunes and casting spells, collecting two dollars a visit from gullible and superstitious Harlemites; Frimbo, in fact, does more business than the very reputable Archer does across the street. When considered in this light, things don't, indeed, add up.[1]

This scene contains at least one more mystery. Archer is intrigued by the contents of Frimbo's library, which do seem curious:

> The doctor was glancing along the rows of books. He noted such titles as Tankard's *Determinism and Fatalism, a Critical Contrast*, Bostwick's *The Concept of Inevitability*, Preem's *Cause and Effect*, Dessault's *The Science of History*, and Fairclough's *The Philosophical Basis of Destiny*. He took this last from its place, opened to a flyleaf, and read in script, "N'Gana Frimbo," and a date. Riffling the pages, he saw in the same script penciled marginal notes at frequent intervals. At the end of the chapter entitled "Unit Stimulus and Reaction," the penciled notation read: "Fairclough too has missed the great secret" [27].

In the course of Archer and Dart's investigations, the murder mystery will be solved. Their efforts will be assisted by a chance discovery by Bubber Brown, a former city street sweeper/garbage collector idled by the Depression[2]—he has recently set up as a private detective specializing in tracking the activities of spouses suspected of straying, an activity seemingly immune to economic fluctuations—and, ultimately by Frimbo himself, whose miraculous reappearance along with the simultaneous disappearance of the corpse midway through the initial investigation complicates the plot. In most ways, the plot remains relatively true to the formulas of the Golden Age puzzle mystery, with the obvious exception of the Harlem location and the African American cast, and, true to form, the solution of the murders proves perfectly prosaic, at least in terms of motive, a jealous husband eliminating his wife's lover. What is not revealed, however, is the "great secret" that Fairclough has missed and which dies with Frimbo, or, for that matter, the enigma that Frimbo himself represents. Frimbo's function in the book, his relationship with issues and matters of interest both at the time and in the study of African American detective fiction, proves ambiguous at best. While he speaks to the Harlem Renaissance's interest in reclaiming African roots and heritage, he also represents the hoodoo trope Soitos identifies as one of the ways African American writers have adapted the murder mystery to represent African American interests and worldview (4). On the other hand, Frimbo has chosen not to return to Africa and reclaim his position as king of Buwongo, and he would probably dispute being identified as hoodoo priest/conjure man. This is a label others have applied to him, not one he would necessarily accept.

As a murder mystery, much of the novel is relatively conventional in construction, as most critics point out, from the variations it plays on closed-room/country-house formulas to the ways that the Archer/Dart team recalls the collaborative efforts of earlier crime fiction, most notably Doyle's pairing of Holmes and Watson.[3] The Golden Age mystery has simply been relocated into Harlem, allowing Fisher to play a variation on a very recognizable theme, though in an urban setting that anticipates the ways American authors will transform crime fiction in the hard-boiled novel. It also, just as clearly, lays the groundwork for the police procedural, given the amount of attention devoted to the mechanics of investigation, from the posting of officers to secure the location to the collection and evaluation of physical evidence, especially fingerprints, to the interviewing of suspects to, finally, the use of forensic evidence—dental work and the analysis of blood samples—to determine the identity of the victim and to corroborate or challenge the testimony given by eyewitnesses. Crime scene investigation plays at least as large a role in the novel as do the Golden Age architecture and urban interests. The story represents something of a hybrid, just as the narrative engages a number of interests: forensic, anthropological, philosophical, medical, psychological, sociological, literary. The interwoven strands, supported both by Fisher's extended treatment of setting and characters in other novels and short stories and by patterns of allusions to philosophical and medical figures and to popular culture, ground the narrative, providing it with a high degree of realism and authority.

That the novel is also aware of itself as a conventional construction is also clear. The story includes four detectives, not just one, from the irrepressibly parodic Bubber Brown to the highly professional and competent Dart (who may, in fact, represent the DuBoisian "talented tenth" of those ten African American officers promoted to the rank of detective) to the "pedantic" Archer, as Adrienne Gosselin describes him ("World," 607; "Psychology"), a young physician possessing a wide range of interests, a man clearly proud of his knowledge, to Frimbo himself, whose methods and motives contrast with those of the other three investigators. The four competing constructions of events these detectives offer, phrased in four idioms, informed by four different bodies of experience, each one, as far as it goes, either offering a partial or an inaccurate account of events, if nothing else, highlight the heterogeneous character of the materials that have gone into the construction of the work. In fact, one of the book's recurring motifs is the attention it gives to language and storytelling: Archer and Dart provide simultaneous translations of Jenkins' testimony, accounting for his "limitations of vocabulary" (66); Frimbo retells Archer's story, inserting the "drama" into Archer's simple chronology of events (224–25); Archer "corrects" Dart's assessment of

Frimbo's mental state, that he's "a nut," supplying a more clinically accurate phrasing (290); and Bubber Brown embellishes his own part in the investigation (272), the result sounding like a pulp-fiction plot, perhaps, or a low-budget B-movie, not unlike those he attends to while away idle hours in the course of the book. In general, the book frequently comments on dialect and language use as indications of social class. How each investigator reconstructs the story of the crime is equally revealing of the assumptions he brings to the table and the ways these assumptions determine the character of the tale he tells.

Equally interesting is the intermixture of real and fictional elements in the allusions and anthropological details that provide a sense of authority to the text. Some, most obviously the references to Herbert Spencer and Freud, are grounded in history, while the altogether plausible list of authors and titles quoted above seems to be purely fictional. The Library of Congress catalogue, at least, contains no such references. References to "Janski [sic] and Moss" (200) as pioneers in identifying blood types are accurate, though their work is really secondary to that of Karl Landsteiner, a Viennese physician and researcher whose discovery of blood types in 1901 and whose further research into antigens, antibodies and immune reactions provides the foundation for understanding the agglutination tests Archer describes. Landsteiner received the 1930 Nobel Prize for Medicine for his work, something Fisher must have surely known.[4] Still, the reference to Jansky and Moss, and not to Landsteiner, may be significant. Landsteiner, Jansky, and Moss, working in Vienna (1901), Czechoslovakia (1907), and the United States (1910), respectively, each described a system for typing blood, all three still in use three decades later (Harding), though the alternate systems resulted in some confusion. Douglas B. Kendrick describes the issues:

> The way was opened to the solution of this special problem [i.e., agglutination and hemolysis from admixture of incompatible bloods] in 1900, when Landsteiner (11) published his epochal work on the identification of blood groups, based on his previous demonstration of the presence of isoagglutinating and isoagglutinable substances in the blood. Jansky in 1907 and Moss 3 years later, without knowledge of Jansky's studies, worked out the reciprocal agglutinating reactions of the four blood groups and classified them accordingly. The confusion that arose because of differences in nomenclature was eliminated after World War I, when the numbers previously used to designate blood groups were replaced by the letters A, B, AB, and O, each group thus being designated by the agglutinogens in Landsteiner's original scheme [4].

Archer explains these general principles to Dart in analyzing the blood samples he has taken from the corpse and from Frimbo, and in so doing identifies his own blood type as Type II, using the older system in the process of being replaced by Landsteiner's. The alternate systems used to describe the same phenomenon, the confusion of terms entailed by using alternate nomenclatures, and the replacement of one system by another in an attempt to standardize reference all seem telling in the context of the story, given the multiple detectives, the stories they tell, and the languages they employ.

The anthropological details of Frimbo's tribal roots will, like this somewhat puzzling reference to Jansky and Moss and not to Landsteiner, also prove somewhat anomalous. Rather than reflecting actual peoples and places and practices as they might have done, Frimbo's African experiences—the Buwongo territory, the Malindo fertility ritual and the "rites of the gonad"—all seem to have been invented. Each one, again, seems quite plausible, but no one of the three seems to have had an exact reference.[5] Of the three, the seemingly parodic "rites of the gonad" is the only one to correspond to contemporary practices and medical theories, curiously akin to theories like those championed by Eugen Steinach in circulation in the 1920s that led W.B. Yeats, for instance, to undergo a Steinach Procedure in 1934, a vasectomy-like operation which he credits with reviving his creative powers and which earned him the sobriquet of the "gland old man" in the Irish press. Sigmund Freud would also have a vasectomy "hoping that it might delay the return of his recurrent oral cancer" (Sengoopta) but without success. (The much-rumored implantation of monkey testicles seems to be apocryphal, at least in Yeats's case, though this procedure was advocated by Serge Voronoff, a French-Russian surgeon.) Truth can be stranger than fiction, in some cases.

Again, though it seems a minor point, Frimbo's interest in male gonads as a repository of ancestral heritage (269) is not too far off from those theories being advanced by Steinach and which were in active play both in the medical and popular literature at the time Fisher is practicing medicine and writing *The Conjure-Man Dies*. In "'Dr Steinach Coming to Make Old Young': Sex Glands, Vasectomy and the Quest for Rejuvenation in the Roaring Twenties," Chandak Sengoopta describes what now seems a rather strange interest in all things gonadal:

> In the 1920s, research on the endocrine glands—especially the sex glands—was widely expected to lead to revolutionary new ways of improving human life. The medical marketplace was crowded with glandular techniques to revitalize the aged. "Monkey glands" apart, the Austrian physiologist Eugen Steinach's simple vasectomy-like operation was perhaps the most popular of these. Steinach was one of the leading endocrine researchers of the early 20th century and the Steinach Operation was based on rigorous laboratory research. It was much more than a simple, scientific error, and its history shows us how early endocrine research was shaped by broader social and cultural forces [122].

Research beginning in the late nineteenth century with the injection of testicular extracts from dogs and guinea-pigs sparked something of a medical craze—the "so-called organotherapy with extracts of every conceivable tissue became a fin-de-siecle panacea for virtually every conceivable disorder" (Sengoopta 122)—and led to a significant body of research in the early decades of the twentieth century:

> By the end of the First World War, all this research had reached a critical mass. The ductless glands and their still mysterious secretions came to acquire an air of omnipotence in the 1920s. "We know definitely now," announced a popular medical work of the 1920s, "that the abnormal functioning of these ductless glands may change a saint into a satyr; a beauty into a hag; a giant into a pitiful travesty of a human being; a hero into a coward, and an optimist into a misanthrope" [Sengoopta 122].

Steinach's work was widely quoted in the medical and popular press—Sengoopta's title is taken from a 1922 *New York Times* article, for instance—and he was nominated for a Nobel Prize in Physiology six times between 1921 and 1938 (Sengoopta 123). And aside from Yeats and Freud and some number of wealthy millionaire men seeking rejuvenation, some women, including the novelist Gertrude Atherton, underwent a similar procedure involving the irradiation of the ovaries, another "therapeutic" use of x-ray technology not unlike that which Dr. Archer describes on the opening pages of "John Archer's Nose" to dissolve a "retained thymus."

Implicit in these treatments is the sense that biology, at some level, determines destiny. Steinach had, for instance, attempted to cure homosexual males by implanting them with testes extracted from a heterosexual male, an experiment that failed, but which Sengoopta writes "clearly demonstrates the narrow biologistic principles with which Steinach sought to intervene in the complex world of human sexuality" (123). And, in fact, the emphasis on rejuvenation develops a distinctly political purpose following the war, as Sengoopta writes:

> The revitalization of individuals was not merely a medical task but the key to reviving a tired civilization and redeeming humanity, especially after the First World War, which had robbed Central Europe of a large part of its young male population. In America, the German sympathizer George Viereck argued that the Steinach operation could help Germany recover speedily from its post-war economic destitution by making its older population more productive [24]. Gertrude Atherton called upon Germany to use the Steinach operation to create a new breed of superman-leaders that could restore the nation's lost glory [25]. After the Great War, "biology," says historian Paul Weindling, offered "creeds of national regeneration, combining the scientific with resonating categories of nature, life and the race" [26]. The Steinach Operation was but one illustration of that trend [126].

Frimbo's rite of the gonad seems to fit this model perfectly, a means of "reviving a tired civilization," African in this case, and of "redeeming humanity," that humanity that African Americans had been deprived of. It is a little hard to determine Fisher's tone of voice here, just how ironic his treatment of this material is, just as it is hard to determine Archer's response to Frimbo, whether he is truly impressed, as he seems to be, by the strength and character of Frimbo's mind, or whether, as he later tells Bubber Brown, he is convinced that "It [Frimbo's mind] has its share of rubbish" (255), a comment that seems to lack some commitment. In spite of the somewhat satirical treatment Steinach's research received in the popular press, and in spite of it having been proven wrong, Steinach's work represented serious and reputable science and clearly had its adherents.

All of which would clearly represent something of a problem, a source of anxiety for an African American physician/author, for any people whose biological characteristics had been credited as certifying their inferiority. Frimbo's philosophical interests in determinism, fatalism, cause and effect, the science of history, inevitability and individual destiny clearly reflect this concern, just as his and every other character's obsession with skin color, an incessant refrain that figures in every physical description, that appears in almost every interchange between Bubber Brown and Jinx Jenkins, for instance, equally attests to this concern. Brown's and Jenkins's insults frequently connect the color of their skin to their lack of intelligence, a theme sounded early in the investigation as the two await questioning:

"Trouble with you," said Bubber, "is you' ignorant. You' dumb. The inside o' yo' head is all black."
"Like the outside o' yourn."
"Is you, by any chance alludin' to me?"
"I ain't alludin' to that policeman over yonder."
"Lucky for you he is over yonder, else you wouldn' be alludin' at all."
"Now you getting' bad, ain't you? Jus' 'cause you know you got the advantage over me."
"What advantage?"
"How could I hit you when I can't even see you?"
"Well if I was ugly as you is, I wouldn't want nobody to see me."
"Don't worry, son. Nobody'll ever know how ugly you is. Yo' ugliness is shrouded in mystery."
"Well yo' dumbness ain't. It's right there for all the world to see. You ought to be back in Africa with the other dumb boogies."
"African boogies ain't dumb," explained Jinx. "They' jes' dark. You ain't been away from there long, is you?"
"My folks," returned Bubber crushingly, "left Africa ten generations ago."

"Yo' folks? Shuh. Ten generations ago, you-all wasn't folks. You-all hadn't qualified as apes" [32–33].

Evolution, intelligence, and skin color are all intermixed, inseparable, and seemingly obsessive, though, as the narrative points out, the insults here lack force:

> Thus as always, their exchange of compliments flowed toward the level of family history, among other Harlemites a dangerous explosive which a single word might strike into instantaneous violence. It was only because the hostility of these two was actually an elaborate masquerade, whereunder they concealed the most genuine affection for each other, that they could come so close to blows that were never offered [35].

The nature of these insults is typical, "as always," nothing unusual between these two or unusual in the verbal sparring that linguists and literary critics have described as typical in the speech of young African American males. That Fisher feels a need to do commentary suggests, at least in part, that he's addressing a white readership, one unaware of the conventions in play here. His black readership would recognize the routine.

Frimbo is equally concerned with such matters, but at a more philosophical level. To the native African, the Euro-American conception of race seems something of a mystery. In what has become the most famous interchange in the book, Frimbo corrects Archer, suggesting that the circumstances surrounding the death of his servant do not, by any means, constitute the mystery here, even though the case remains to be solved:

> "Mystery? That is no mystery. It is a problem in logic, and perfectly calculable. I have one or two short-cuts which I shall apply tomorrow night, of course, merely to save time. But genuine mystery is incalculable. It is all around us— we look upon it every day and do not wonder at it at all. We are fools, my friend. We grow excited over a ripple, but exhibit no curiosity over the depth of the stream. The profoundest mysteries are those things which we blandly accept without question. See. You are almost white. I am almost black. Find out why, and you will have solved a mystery."
>
> "You don't think the causes of a mere death a worthy problem?"
>
> "The causes of *a* death? No. The causes of death, yes. The causes of life and death and variation, yes. But what on earth does it really matter who killed Frimbo—except to Frimbo?"
>
> They stood a moment in silence. Presently Frimbo added in an almost bitter murmur:
>
> "The rest of the world would do better to concern itself with why Frimbo was black" [230].

The mysteries of life and death and variation, evolutionary concerns, are worthy of attention, as are the larger philosophical questions, especially the degree to which biology determines destiny, that such speculations give rise to. The solution of an individual crime, especially in the Golden Age mystery novel, is a problem in logic, a puzzle capable of solution, something that might divert the mind for a time relieving Holmes of his existential angst, perhaps, but not the final solution.

Frimbo and his seeming psychic abilities to see into things, to discern past events of which he has not been told or to foretell the immediate future, that is, to discern cause and effect in the life of another person, and his claim to be free, to exist outside of such causal forces himself, seem to be part of the mystery here. His clientele certainly believe that he is in possession of paranormal powers, which they associate with those of the hoodoo priest, the conjure-men of the title. He claims no such powers. Doty Hicks, for instance, accuses Frimbo of having cast a spell over his brother, the proprietor of Patmore's Pool Hall, a charge Frimbo dismisses as "superstitious nonsense": "I am no caster of spells," he tells Hicks. "I am a psychist—a kind of psychologist. I have done nothing to your brother. He simply has pulmonary tuberculosis—in the third stage" (114). Frimbo offers a naturalistic explanation/diagnosis, there being nothing mysterious in this situation. Hicks's enlisting of a self-proclaimed hoodoo priest whose "magic" proves to be little more than superstitious nonsense and completely ineffectual only serves to advance Frimbo's claim.

Frimbo claims extraordinary powers, that he alone is free from the deterministic effects of the past and that, as free, he can change the future, at the same time that he claims that he has no special abilities. This somewhat contradictory strain emerges, for instance, in his interview with Jinx Jenkins. As to his ability to discern Jenkins's name, age, and marital status, there is nothing mysterious here, only a "process of reason, based on observation" (68), something "that can be learned by anyone" (69). This line sounds very Holmesian, though Frimbo's explanation is a bit different:

> "There are those who claim the power to read men's lives in crystal spheres. That is utter nonsense. I claim the power to read men's lives in their faces. That is completely reasonable. Every experience, every thought, leaves its mark. Past and present are written there clearly. He who knows completely the past and the present can deduce the inevitable future, which past and present determine. My crystal sphere, therefore, is your face. By reading correctly what is there I know what is scheduled to follow, and so can predict and guard you against your future" [68].

On the other hand, he also claims possession of a secret handed down from "son to son through four hundred unbroken generations of Buwongo kings," a "dangerous secret" that "my fathers knew when the kings of the Nile still thought human flesh a delicacy":

The voice sank to a lower pitch still, inescapably impressive.
"Frimbo can change the future." He paused, then continued, "In the midst of a world of determined, inevitable events, of results rigidly fashioned by the past, Frimbo alone is free. Frimbo not only sees. Frimbo and Frimbo alone can step in at will and change the course of a life" [69].

To prove his point, Frimbo predicts that Jenkins will soon find his needs for food and shelter well fulfilled, but that he will be "more unhappy than you are now," and that he will rejoice only when this guarantee of food and shelter is lost. These predictions come true almost immediately when Jenkins is arrested and incarcerated, seemingly implicated in Frimbo's murder. Prison will certainly meet his immediate needs, though he will never be more unhappy.

Frimbo repeats and expands on these points later in the book in his conversation with Archer. Archer is amazed by the accuracy of Frimbo's description of the details of Archer's early life and the struggles he has endured to become a physician. Frimbo responds that his recasting of Archer's story represents no mystical power, nothing even telepathic, though Fimbo does suggest that telepathy is possible, "a simple matter of transforming energy," a human power similar to that used in radio and television broadcasting. In this instance, however, Frimbo's "powers," such as they are, are little different from Archer's diagnostic routines:

> "But this is much simpler than [telepathy]. Is it at all mystifying that you should walk into a sick room, make certain examinations, and say, 'This patient has so-and-so. He got it in such-and-such a way approximately so long ago; he has these-and-these changes in such-and-such organs; he will die in such-and-such a fashion in approximately so long'? No. I have merely practiced observation to a degree of great proficiency; that, together with complete faith in a certain philosophy enables me to do what seems mystifying. I can study a person's face and tell his past, present, and future" [226].

Much of the rest, Frimbo admits, like his ability to produce a person's name without being told, is a "trick of the trade," the result of his being able to observe his subjects surreptitiously. Archer accepts much of this explanation but still wonders about Frimbo's ability to predict the future. Frimbo's explanation, as above, is relatively direct and echoes the biologistic model he has already alluded to:

> "The future is as inevitably the outcome of the present as the present is of the past. That is the philosophy I mentioned."
> "Determinism?"
> "If you like. But a determinism so complete as to include everything—physical and mental. An applied determinism" [226].

Frimbo's clairvoyance is literally little more than an extension of Archer's diagnostic routines. Having observed certain symptoms and knowing a good deal about human physiology and the disease-causing mechanisms that have produced these observable results, Archer can see the eventual outcome, the teleology of the disease. Frimbo's only extraordinary claim is that he alone is free from this system of causes and effects (227).

The extraordinary claim is not, at least at one level, all that extraordinary. Frimbo is, in effect, reading social construction and playing the probabilities. In spite of their differences in experience, education, and social class, Archer and Jenkins are both black. For Archer to have succeeded in the ways he has done, he must have done so against the odds, with a great deal of sacrifice, both personal and on the part of parents. Jenkins, by contrast, has been "jinxed," the more typical results of limited educational and economic opportunity, which is more than apparent in his taciturn disposition and which promises, given his present company and penury, to result in incarceration in the not too distant future. Race in 1930s America, a (pseudo)biological factor, and past constructions of race still determine present and future possibilities. That this biological factor also determines the ways these characters think about themselves and others, given the rampant colorism within the community, is also clear. While Frimbo is not immune to such treatment, his personal history and the unique perspective it provides grant him a freedom the others do not have. Spider Webb, the numbers runner, is entrapped in the hegemonic systems that define life in Harlem; Frimbo has somehow managed to figure the racket out, consistently beating the odds. That he has beaten the odds is clear; how he has done so, the exact mechanism in this case, is left unexplained.

There is slightly more going on here, however, than may be immediately apparent. Frimbo, at least, would not fully own the foregoing description, just as he would not accept the conjure-man label from the book's title. This is how others see him, not how he sees himself, and, in fact, the source of Archer's anomaly. It is, in a sense, a matter of perspective. Frimbo's belief is rooted in the work of Herbert Spencer and his argument that evolutionary theories explain everything, that everything, at bottom, is biological, and that biology is organized through evolutionary principles.[6] Frimbo opens his discussion with Archer on just this point, the claim, according to Spencer's model, that "Psychology [is] considered as the physiology of the nervous system" (214), that is, as a matter of biology:

> Easily and quickly they began to talk with that quick intellectual recognition which characterizes similarly reflective minds. Dr. Archer's apprehensions faded away and shortly he and his host were eagerly embarked on discussions that at

once made them old friends: the hopelessness of applying physico-chemical methods to psychological problems; the nature of matter and mind and the possible relations between them; the current researches of physics, in which matter apparently vanished into energy, and Frimbo's own hypothesis that probably mind did likewise. Time sped. At the end of an hour Frimbo was saying:

"But as long as this mental energy remains mental, it cannot be demonstrated. It is like potential energy—to be appreciated it must be transformed into heat, light, motion—some form that can be grasped and measured. Still, by assuming its existence, just as we do that of potential energy, we harmonize psychology with mechanistic science."

"You astonish me," said the doctor. "I thought you were a mystic, not a mechanist."

"This," returned Frimbo, "is mysticism—an undemonstrable belief. Pure faith in anything is mysticism. Our very faith in reason is a kind of mysticism" [214].

Spencer had attempted to "harmonize" much of science by using evolution as a kind of unified field theory, a theory that Frimbo can only partially accept. The "simple" application of physico-chemical principles to psychology seems reductive. He proposes a somewhat more complicated model, one informed by Einsteinian principles of relativity. The mechanics of human psychology are more complicated than biology, by itself, can explain, just as Newtonian mechanics can only take us so far.

Such narrow biologistic theories prove to be no more adequate than Steinach's attempts to reduce the complexities of human sexuality to a function of the endocrine system. Frimbo's rite of the gonad thus proves a rather ironic means of saying as much. Working in his laboratory, Frimbo is both pursuing his passion and exercising his ancestral rites, the "rites of the gonad." Sexual relationships he pursues, he tells Archer, as "necessary to comfort," adding, rather notoriously, "like blowing one's nose" (268). However dismissive the simile proves, the point is clear, that sex is a purely biological function. His research he pursues "because I like it," or, more exactly, "because a part of it lifts me out of the common order of things," exercising that rite "which has been a secret of my family for many generations, whereby I am able to escape the set pattern of cause and effect," that is, more specifically, the rite of the gonad:

"Yes," Frimbo said, a distant look creeping into his deep-set eyes. "The germplasm, of which the gonad is the only existing sample, is the unbroken heritage of the past. It is protoplasm which has been continuously maintained throughout thousands of generations. It's the only vital matter which goes back in a continuous line to the remotest origins of the organism. It is therefore the only matter which brings into the present every influence which the past has imprinted upon life. It is the epitome of the past. He who can learn its use can be master of his past. And he who can master his past—that man is free" [269].

The biology is a little off here—it is the mitochondrial DNA (mtDNA), which is inherited from the mother, a matrilineal trait, not the father, not some testicular substance, that provides the unbroken biological link—but the point is clear: The sum total of our biological existence, our essential humanity, is located here. Frimbo's thousands of generations trumps Bubber's ten generations out of Africa; recent historical events and the causal forces they exert are of little importance when read against the immensity of human experience. Frimbo is, in effect, declaring himself free from the conventional constructions of race that African Americans labor under and claiming a far older right, the right to think for himself. Herbert Spencer seems to have gotten that part right, being as much a champion for individual rights as he was an advocate of evolutionary theory. It is, in the end, a matter of perspective, a question of "relative-ity," one might say.

Alternative Epistemologies: Reading the Evidence

The Conjure-Man Dies proves to be interesting at a number of levels, among them the degree to which it focuses on the mechanics of detection, on logic, on physical evidence, and given its four detectives, on the different ways that their experiences and assumptions color the investigation. For both Dart and Archer, who discuss investigative practices on several occasions in the novel and who both claim to follow the evidence, detection is an empirical science which is likened to medical diagnosis. Both, however, prove to be quite mistaken in their attempts to reconstruct the crime. Dart's knowledge of the Harlem underworld, especially of the gambling bosses Spider Webb works for, and Archer's psychoanalytic profile of Frimbo both lead to dead ends. Frimbo, for his own part, seems no more successful in his attempts to solve the crime. His scheme succeeds, in a sense, in revealing the perpetrator, but only insofar as it tempts the killer to complete the crime by killing Frimbo, his original and intended target. Beyond that, Frimbo seems to have underestimated the destructive force of sexual jealousy. The physical evidence which seems to tie Jinx Jenkins to the crime, itself probably enough to satisfy the burden of proof in most courts, also turns out to be unreliable. And Bubber Brown, who is consistently clueless as to what is going on, manages quite by chance to retrieve the one piece of evidence, a skull that Frimbo is attempting to incinerate in the building's coal-fired furnace, which provides Archer and Dart with the one piece of evidence that proves to be reliable. Following the disappearance of the corpse, they can't even prove that a crime has been committed, much less identify the victim. Brown's find reveals that Frimbo's servant, and not Frimbo himself as it first seemed, had indeed been murdered. Why he had been murdered and by whom remain a mystery to them until the final pages of the book.

Dart claims in his conversations with Archer that he is operating inductively, following the evidence to the conclusion, not fitting the facts to a foregone conclusion, a point that Archer reminds him of midway through the investigation:

> There was once a man—nice fellow, too, even though he was a policeman—who delivered some remarks on premature conclusions. His idea was to fit conclusions to facts, as I recall, not facts to conclusions. And he admitted—nay, insisted—that by such a system, it would only be necessary to accumulate enough facts and they'd sort of draw their own conclusions. You will observe that this fellow was a lineal descendant of Francis Bacon—despite their difference of complexion—in that he inherited the tendency to reason inductively rather than deductively. But such is the frailty of human-kind that even this fortunate chap occasionally fell into the error of letting his imagination, instead of his observation, draw the conclusions; whereupon he would suddenly look about in bewilderment and say that something didn't hitch up with something [206].

Two immediate problems appear in this formulation, one, that Dart's professional experiences have led him to formulate a number of hypotheses which color his observations, much as Archer's study of medicine and the prevailing paradigms have colored his, and two, that even the most basic observations, in this case, the assessment of fingerprint evidence, rest on certain assumptions. The instrument used to strike the initial victim, having been recovered, yields a readable fingerprint. Dart assembles the people present in the house when the murder occurred and proceeds to have them all printed, telling them, "You all know the meaning of finger prints"(142), as though their meaning was self-evident, unambiguous. The fingerprint on the club belongs to Jinx Jenkins, as does the handkerchief that Archer had removed from the victim's trachea. The physical evidence seems compelling, but it rests on one assumption, as Archer will point out:

> Simple statement of fact. The discovery of a finger print is not necessarily any better evidence of its owner's presence than the discovery of any other object belonging to him. Don't misunderstand me. I know that as a means of identification, its value is established. But as proof that the owner's fingers put it where it was found—that's another matter. That is a belief based on an assumption. And the fact that the assumption is usually correct does not make it any the less an assumption [278].

Archer proceeds to demonstrate that fingerprints can be transferred and that, in addition, the fingerprint in question is rather improbably placed on the club, not where it would naturally appear if the club had been used as a weapon.

In spite of his protest to the contrary, Dart is often guilty of attempting to fit the facts to a conclusion. He pronounces Frimbo a woman-hater based on his initial survey of Frimbo's bedroom and its lack of any evidence of feminine influence (25). Later in the book, having uncovered the policy war and Frimbo's role in it, Dart hypothesizes that Frimbo was killed to forestall any further losses and that Frimbo's servant was employed by the boss to carry out the hit. The servant is willing to do so because he "is already envious of his master's success—the way black servants are with black masters" (286–87). This principle might prove true in Dart's experience, but it is clearly a belief based on an assumption which, even if usually correct, is no less an assumption. The perception might prove generally true of African American men, given the tortured history of master-servant dynamics from slavery forward, but it is not true of the African Frimbo, whose kinship to the murdered servant, oriented within the mutual responsibilities of king to subjects and subjects to king that characterize Buwongo tribal society, describes an entirely different dynamic, one that Dart cannot even imagine. Archer's attempts to diagnose Frimbo as a paranoid personality and to suggest that Frimbo murdered his own servant as a result of this paranoia prove no more accurate. The hapless Bubber, again, turns out to have been right from the beginning, that "monkey business," "cheatin," is the cause, though he could never have explained how so in this instance.

Things are not always as they appear, and appearances, colored by prevailing notions, the unacknowledged assumptions brought to experience, prove to be deceiving. In the African American mystery, as Charles Heglar points out in his comparative study of Fisher's, Himes's, and Mosley's works, the role induction plays in the solution of the mystery becomes important thematically:

> A final point must be made about the implications of the three authors' shared emphasis on induction as a method for discovering the criminal or finding a solution. Although induction is the common method of detective fiction, African American writers use the method, in contrast to deduction, to make a telling point about the larger society. Since deduction begins with a theory and works to integrate particular details, it is most frequently presented in black detective novels as the method of institutional, but uninformed, authority; deduction in such a context supports the racist theory which assumes that blacks are criminals and blindly works toward designating some individual within the group as the perpetrator. On the other hand, the black agents of detection employ induction, which works from the accumulation of facts to an explanation; this method recognizes differences among members of the same race as

well as a broader range of possibilities in terms of motivation and action. Each author's pair of detectives works to unravel a mysterious murder, or stop a confidence scheme, or find a missing person by accumulating information without the blinders of imposed theory. It is the only way they can arrive at a universal or a poetic instance of justice [305].

But as Fisher demonstrates in *The Conjure-Man Dies*, even induction isn't immune to assumptions.

Detection, like medicine, may be an empirical "science," an organized body of knowledge build on experimental methods, but that does not mean it is free of assumptions, as Thomas Kuhn famously demonstrated in *The Structure of Scientific Revolutions*. Even the most empirical science is based on certain bodies of belief, organizational ideas that are not themselves empirically provable; these are foundational principles that simply must be accepted on faith. That the world makes sense, that nature operates according to a series of invariant natural laws, that those laws are discoverable and describable can only be assumed, never proven; as Kuhn argues, no fact emerges independent of theory. Simply put, we see with our brains, not our eyes; perception, a physiological response to stimuli, is always accompanied by an act of interpretation. Kuhn's work, appearing thirty years after *The Conjure-Man Dies*, clearly transformed the ways we understood science to operate, but much of what is most innovative in Kuhn's analysis is rooted in philosophical and psychological investigations emerging in the early decades of the twentieth century, in Josiah Royce's seminars at Harvard, for instance, which T.S. Eliot attended as a doctoral candidate in philosophy, the influences of which are traceable in his dissertation, *Knowledge and Experience in the Philosophy of F.H. Bradley*, in his poetry, and in his literary criticism, including the Charles Eliot Norton lectures, *The Use of Poetry and the Use of Criticism*, delivered at Harvard in 1932. These ideas emerge in Gestalt psychology which finds its way into Wittgenstein's work of the 1920s and 1930s, most specifically in *The Philosophical Investigations*. The positivism driving nineteenth century studies generally and suggested by the fictitious works of philosophy Archer finds on Frimbo's shelves, most specifically Dessault's *The Science of History*, were being challenged and replaced with a more sophisticated understanding of epistemology. Fisher's work seems to fit seamlessly into this discussion.

The alternate constructions of events each character offers, based on distinct bodies of experience and phrased in different languages, represent different paradigms/alternative epistemologies. Each is, in that sense, a "cultural construct," and each one, as a result, is a fiction, something made up. It is tempting to read Fisher's use of fictitious philosophical works and of Frimbo's imagined African heritage as a self-conscious acknowledgement of the fictive worlds we inhabit, a point seemingly reinforced in the text's Bakhtinian character. Or it could just be that the busy doctor hadn't the time or interest in doing the background research that would yield more authentic philosophical and anthropological sources. In either case, Bubber Brown seems the perfect representation of all these points. He is the most clearly conventional character, a perfectly stereotypical "stage Negro"; he is also the most ardent (and clumsy) of empiricists, as his investigations of domestic affairs demonstrate, letting himself into young ladies' rooms so that he can observe their activities for himself; and he is also the most colorful of storytellers, as his account of rescuing the skull from the furnace demonstrates:

> And he related, how, at great personal risk, which he ignored because of his friend's predicament, he had voluntarily entered the stronghold of mystery and death, ignored the undertaker's several corpses—four or five of them lying around like chickens on a counter—descended past a company of voodoo worshipers who would have killed him on sight for spying on their secrets, and so into the pit of horror, where the furnace was merely a blind for the crematory habits of the conjure-man [170–71].

Each character tells his story, and while each one is perhaps more plausible than Bubber's, the account each one offers is no less conventional in construction, which, in the end, seems to be the point of *The Conjure-Man Dies*.

Fisher is sometimes criticized for not fully engaging and opposing in his novel the prevailing prejudices then current in American thought. He seems, at least on the surface, to have imported the Golden Age puzzle piece directly into Harlem, having exchanged country house for brownstone, the British countryside for the Harlem blackscape. His Archer and Dart are genteel figures, especially when measured against Chester Himes's Coffin Ed Jones and Grave Digger Johnson, or against Easy Rawlins in Walter Mosley's books, all figures who arise from the streets, whether the tenements in Harlem or the world of Fifth Ward Houston. Archer and Dart are well-spoken, clearly educated, upwardly mobile people, rendering them somewhat problematic, perhaps, in the same ways that the patrician figures in Stephen L. Carter's books, set in the Gold Coast neighborhood of Washington, D.C., or in the Sugar Hill section of Harlem, initially seem somewhat problematic, defying the odds, if nothing else. When read somewhat more closely, however, Fisher, himself a physician, seems both to be engaging the "biologistic" paradigms rooted in endocrinology that rendered behavior a product of physiology, the "biology-is-destiny" constructions of naturalistic fiction, and, in his multiple investigators and attention to procedure and the philosophical underpinnings of detection, the constructions of genre. Though relatively conservative in certain regards, *The Conjure-Man Dies* proves to be remarkably successful in the end in the ways it challenges medical, generic, and social constructions, one model for how the mystery genre can be made to serve minority interests.

The Scent of the Crime

Archer and Dart do return in "John Archer's Nose," a long short story published in 1935, a work which, while relatively slight, seems to amplify some of the general tendencies and themes of the *The Conjure-Man Dies*. Like the novel, "John Archer's Nose" is a largely conventional puzzle mystery, something of a locked-room variant, centered on the murder of a young man in his bedroom in a fifth-floor walk up, only one way in, with several other family members present in the apartment at the time. While the initial investigation focuses on the family, the only ones seemingly with access to the bedroom, the solution turns out, as in *Conjure-Man*, to be relatively prosaic. The killer had entered and exited the bedroom through a window looking out into a narrow airshaft, the adjoining apartment vacant and unlocked, also with a window opening onto the airshaft, a short step away. Tenants in Harlem, the story explains, typically install their own locks on exterior doors when they rent apartments and then take those locks with them when they leave (218). This detail, along with an earlier description of the apartment's floor plan—"nothing unusual about the arrangement of rooms—several bedchambers off a central hallway, with the living room at the front end and a kitchen and a dining room at the back" (194)—provides a sense of scene, details of vernacular experience that residents of Harlem would have recognized and that provide commentary and interpretation for readers not native to the area.

In this case, the solution to the crime turns out to be literally right under their noses. Archer detects a particular odor in the murdered man's bedroom, a smell he also picks up in the apartment's living room and kitchen, though nowhere else in the residence. The smell, it turns out, is emanating from a charm, some fired hair wrapped in cloth, the deceased man's mother is wearing on a cord around her neck. The charm is a folk remedy she has made and is hoping will somehow ward off the tuberculosis her son was dying from—prior, that is, to being stabbed to death—and from which her husband died before him. The woman trades in such remedies, her services advertised in a local Harlem paper. The newspaper is, in fact, lying on the dining-room table open to that ad when Archer and Dart search the premises, though neither seems to notice that ad among the others, only remarking on the

Harlemites' propensity to believe in superstitious nonsense. Earlier that day, Archer had witnessed the death of an eighteen-month-old child whose parents had preferred to use just such a folk remedy rather than the x-ray treatment Archer had advocated and which would have quickly cured the problem. Superstition, Archer tells Dart, had killed the child (186). Though Archer doesn't immediately place the scent or connect the two deaths, he will eventually do so, finding that the murdered man's mother had sold the dead child's parents the fried-hair charm their son was wearing at the time of his death. The child's grief-stricken father, having lost his only son, is avenging that child's death by killing the old woman's children. While Dart focuses his investigation on the murdered man's family, Archer determines both the means of entry and the motive for the killing and with Dart's permission, dispatches two officers to bring the killer to the dead man's apartment where he readily admits to the murder. Much as happens on serial crime dramas like *CSI*, Dr. Archer discovers the link between these two, seemingly unrelated deaths after witnessing the first himself and then being called quite by coincidence to the scene of the second. He is, as luck would have it, ideally positioned to connect these two deaths.

For the most part, Fisher places the story securely within the conventions of detective fiction, as his language more than makes clear. Standing in the kitchen, having completed their initial inspection of the apartment, Archer and Dart review their findings. The narrative notes that the apartment possessed "no *apparent* entrance or exit other than its one outside door" (194, italics added) and then tracks the odd direction the conversation takes, that "*characteristically*, the doctor indulged in wordy and *somewhat irrelevant* reflection during the tour of inspection" (194, italics added), in this case his disquisition on smell, "[d]iscernible in higher dilutions than any other *material stimulus*." Dart notes the newspaper spread out on the table and remarks on the superstitious natures of the typical Harlemite, "your people," as he calls the residents of Harlem, linking the erudite and light-skinned doctor, clearly something of an anomaly in Harlem, at least in Dart's experience, to the general population. Archer concludes, tellingly, that "this crime has a specific smell ... which I think we should find *significant if we could place it*" (194, italics added). The whole passage proves wonderfully ironic: The *somewhat irrelevant* discussion of smell proves relevant; the reference to the detective and doctor's opening conversation about *your people* being, in the detective's estimation, 'the most superstitious idiots on the face of the earth" (185) also proves to be the case; the people in question all connect to the doctor, literally *his people*; everyone, the doctor included, act in characteristic ways; and the *significant if we could place it* turns out to be perfectly true.

And these lines are all delivered in the presence of the telling detail, the newspaper ad, a signpost pointing them toward the solution of the crime. All of the evidence, in one way or another, is under their noses, in front of their faces. Fisher deploys the generic conventions and the expected language at the same time that Archer, somewhat oddly, in his typically pedantic style, runs on about the inadequacies of language, at least with regard to odors, that "in a language of a quarter million words, we haven't a single specific direct denotation of a smell," that "we haven't even such general direct terms as apply to colors—red, green, and blue. We name what we see but don't name what we smell" (194).

As in other places, it is a little hard to know what to make of this material, of the degree to which Archer acts as Fisher's alter-ego, as readers often assume, the physician Fisher reflected in Doctor Archer's scientific approach to diagnosing illness, whether medical or social. Biographical sketches of Fisher, especially of his college and medical school career, however, suggest distinct and competing interests, the English major, champion orator, and eventual author of short stories and novelistic fiction clearly alive to the affective elements in language, while the chemistry major, medical student, and eventual roentgenologist might affect a more positivistic strain, a clinical language emphasizing denotation, signs and signification, observable and measurable effects. Archer is clearly something of a positivist, opposing the clarity of scientific and clinical observation to the darkness of superstition. When Archer surprisingly concedes to Dart's assessment of the people of Harlem being "the most superstitious idiots on the face of the earth," he cites his experience that morning in evidence. The conversation is worth quoting at some length:

> "I've had a cogent example today of what you complain of."
> "Superstition?"
> "Of a very dark hue."
> "State the case. Let's see if you can exonerate yourself."
> "I lost a kid."
> Dart reached for his glass. "Didn't know you had one."
> "A patient, you jackass."
> Dart grinned. "Didn't know you had a patient either."
> "That's not funny. Neither was this. Beautiful, plump little brown rascal—eighteen months old—perfectly developed, bright-eyed, alert—and it passes out in a convulsion, and I was standing there looking on—helpless."
> "If it was so perfect, what killed it?"
> "Superstition."
> "Humph. Anything for an alibi, hey?"
> "Superstition," repeated Archer in a tone which stilled his friend's banter. "That baby ought to be alive and well, now."
> "What's the gag line?"

"Status lymphaticus."

"Hell. And I was just getting serious."

"That's as serious as anything could be. The kid had a retained thymus."

"I'll bite. What's a retained thymus?"

"A big gland here in the chest. Usually disappears after birth. Sometimes doesn't. Untreated, it produces this status lymphaticus—convulsions—death."

"Why didn't you treat it?"

"I did what I could. Been seeing it for some time. Could have cleared it up overnight. What I couldn't treat was the superstition of the parents."

"Oh."

"Specially the father. The kid should have had x-ray treatments. Melt the thing away. These kids, literally choking to death in a fit, clear up and recover—zip—like that. Most spectacular thing in medicine. But the old man wouldn't hear of it. None of this new-fangled stuff for *his* only child" [186].

The musical hall routine ("I lost a child." "Didn't know you had one"), the "dark hue" of superstition practiced by Harlem's dark-skinned peoples, even the (unexpected) insensitivity of Dart's "What's the gag line?" turning out to be all too literally true, the child having choked to death, unable to breath, finally, because of his enlarged thymus, are all remarkably ironic, though perhaps no more ironic than Archer's diagnosis of *status lymphaticus* as a result of a retained thymus. Though widely diagnosed at the time and typically treated with x-rays, retained thymus and *status lymphaticus* turn out to be as mythical as the therapeutic effects of fried-hair charms. While the diagnosis and treatment of *status lymphaticus* were already controversial in the 1930s, it is again hard to tell what the physician Fisher's attitudes on this question were.

In "Status Lymphaticus: Sudden Death in Children from 'Visitation of God' to Cot Death," Ann Dally describes the history of *status lymphaticus*, its prevalence in the medical literature in the opening decades of the twentieth century, the developing controversy at this time, and its utter disappearance from the medical literature after 1965 (71). Dally reports that *status lymphaticus* was first described by A. Paltauf, a Viennese professor, in 1889 and "soon became prominent in the western world," being widely covered in the medical literature between 1890 and 1930 (71). She describes the historical circumstances that led to the diagnosis of this condition and its prevalence in medical practice, tracing its roots to earlier unexplained deaths of children, the cause of death listed as "visitation of God" on early death certificates; in the nineteenth century to the sudden deaths of children anesthetized by chloroform; and thereafter to other unexplained deaths of children, what we would today classify as sudden infant death syndrome or cot death. The diagnosis of *status lymphaticus* served an important legal function, allowing coroners in England, who were "specifically ordered [by the Coroners Act of 1887] to differentiate between natural and unnatural death" (Dally 73), to do just that. The unexplained deaths of children, which could no longer be attributed in the increasingly secular nineteenth century to divine intervention (Dally 70), bureaucratic requirements, and questions of legal liability all combined to support the diagnosis of *status lymphaticus*. Once called "the most important problem in medicine" (Dally 70), and still being cited as late as the 1950s by one hospital pathologist as the cause of "almost all difficult deaths" (Dally 71), "yet now," Dally writes, "as far as doctors are concerned, it does not exist and it never did exist" (71).

Archer's description of the thymus as "a big gland, here in the chest. Usually disappears after birth," is not, in fact, wholly accurate. As Dally describes it,

> the thymus is a lymphatic organ that lies close to the thyroid gland in the front of the neck. It straddles the windpipe and, like other lymphatic tissue, it is relatively large in small children and gradually diminishes in size [74].

It does not, in fact, disappear, only diminishing in size following the onset of puberty. While late-nineteenth-century medicine found the thymus to possess no immediately discernible function and so advocated its removal, "we now know that it is important in the developing immune system" (74). Removal, in fact, was facilitated by the discovery of x-rays and the fact that lymphatic tissue was particularly sensitive to x-ray exposure. X-rays were used as early as 1907 to shrink an "enlarged" thymus (Dally 78). Moreover, the use of x-rays to shrink thymic tissue was advocated as a prophylactic measure for all infants, in general, and specifically called for prior to the administration of anesthesia where an enlarged thymus was suspected, as pathologist William Boyd recommended in a 1932 article (Dally 78). What constituted a "normal" versus an "enlarged" thymus, however, was open to question as no reliable measurements existed, at least through the end of the nineteenth century (Dally 74). In a 1954 article on the thymus, Geoffrey Keynes comments, "It seems to be extraordinarily difficult to get at the truth concerning even the size of this enigmatic organ" (qtd. in Dally 79), noting that adult organs vary in weight from 2.7g to 32g. The attribution of death to thymic causes, Keynes concludes, constituted "no more than a confession of ignorance" (qtd. in Dally 79). Dally comments on the persistence of a diagnosis with no clinical evidence to support it, that "in spite of the evidence against it, it continued to suit people's beliefs, hopes, and fears" (79).

In spite of the prevalence of *status lymphaticus* in the medical literature through much of the first half of the twentieth century and the standard use of x-rays to shrink thymic tissue, many of the same questions Keynes notes in 1954 about the size of the thymus and its identification as a cause of unexplained deaths appeared in a 1931 report published by the Medical Research Council and the Pathological Society of Great Britain and Ireland (Dally 80–81). The report specifically noted variation in the size of the thymus and that no clear correlation existed between cases of sudden death and larger than normal thymuses. The report reinforces conclusions already published in an earlier report by M. Greenwood and H.M. Woods entitled "Status thymolymphaticus considered in the light of current work on the thymus," as Dally notes:

> In 1927 an extensive analysis of deaths from *status lymphaticus* announced as "a critical examination of a curious phase of modern medical teaching," said that diagnosing in life was "largely nonsense," and that if thymic weight is the criterion, status lymphaticus and its associated conditions were "mere verbalisms." Such a diagnosis has "no more value than affirmative evidence in cases of witchcraft" and "the diagnosis ought to be abandoned" [81].

The 1931 MRC report describes *status lymphaticus* as "a good example of medical mythology": "A nucleus of truth is buried beneath a pile of intellectual rubbish, conjecture, base observations and rash generalization" (qtd. in Dally 81). While these reports remained controversial and did not immediately eliminate the diagnosis or the prescribed course of treatment, the language, at the very least, reverberates interestingly, an ironic counterpoint to Archer's diagnosis, his positivistic attitudes and language, and the general action of "John Archer's Nose."

Without medical records from Fisher's practice, it's impossible to say to what degree he was, as a physician, aware of the controversy surrounding *status lymphaticus*, whether he subscribed to the conventional medical practices of the time or opposed a practice for which no compelling clinical proof existed. That John Archer is convinced of the dangers an enlarged thymus poses and of the need to irradiate it is clear. But as always, Fisher's detective fiction always seems to be peculiarly self-conscious of conventional construction. As a character in Fisher's stories, Archer is himself "a mere verbalism," whose claimed empirical observations are clearly colored by prevailing medical theories, theories which cannot be empirically verified. He sees, in effect, what he expects to see or has been taught to see by the orthodox medical practices of the time, itself a linguistic construct, a paradigm. As a character, he behaves "characteristically," in keeping with the conventions of the genre. That the conventional construction seems open to question is also the case.

Just as Archer's anomalous use of an obsolete Roman numeral nomenclature to identify blood type in *The Conjure-Man Dies* seems little more, perhaps, than a quirk of character, the references in "John Archer's Nose" to *status lymphaticus* as a result of an enlarged thymus seem, at first glance, of little critical significance, no more, perhaps, than one instance of modern medicine's triumph over the superstitious practices associated with hoodoo, witchcraft, and conjure men. On the other hand, Fisher's choices in both cases may serve deeper thematic purposes. As an example of contemporary "medical mythology," a product of "intellectual rubbish, conjecture, base observations and, rash generalization," *status lymphaticus* may parallel Frimbo's Rite of the Gonad and its seeming parody of late-nineteenth/early-twentieth-century theories of biological determinism, theories in which the endocrine glands, which include both the testes and the thymus, played a central role. Eugenics, similarly believed in as scientifically grounded, represents another instance of medical mythology, of intellectual rubbish, conjecture, base observation, and rash generalization. In that regard, Dart's insistence when addressing Archer on referring to the people of Harlem as "your people" seems equally significant: John Archer's science, in this case, is not different in kind, only in degree, from the folk remedies and witchcraft of the suspicious Harlemites. But with only two data points, we can only speculate on the thematic lines these stories define. In that regard, Fisher's untimely death has left us with at least several unsolved mysteries.

4

Plus ça change
Chester Himes's Harlem Domestic Series

Formula Fiction

Enjoyable as they are to read and in spite of the critical acclaim these books have received, Chester Himes's series of ten novels set in Harlem, running from the late 1950s through the 1960s, are not fully successful works. Described frequently as "surreal," the books often seem cartoonish in their outrageous casts of characters and depiction of violence, the stories sketched in broad strokes. They frequently depend on stock characters and conflicts and a prepackaged prose, all quite colorful, perhaps, but still formulaic, which also proves to be true of the two central characters, Coffin Ed Jones and Grave Digger Johnson, with their matched set of outsized 38-caliber revolvers, their impeccable marksmanship, and their penchant for violence. The typical resolution, at least in the early books, where love blossoms and is affirmed in the midst of chaos, is equally clichéd. The closing lines of *Run Man Run*, one of the least cartoonish of the bunch and the only one of the novels in which the two detectives do not appear, is a case in point. Jimmy is lying in a hospital bed, recovering from multiple gunshot wounds; he has just survived a racist white detective's campaign of violence. Jimmy tries to justify to his girlfriend, Linda, a nightclub singer, why he purchased a gun and confronted Detective Walker. He had hoped to force Walker into the open to prove that Walker was, indeed, responsible for the murders of Jimmy's coworkers at a Manhattan cafeteria and to prove that Walker had been tracking Jimmy in an attempt to eliminate him as the final witness to the original crime. Jimmy's efforts were probably unnecessary, though he couldn't have known as much, in that the detective's brother-in-law, investigating the original crime, had already built a compelling case against Walker. Jimmy defends his actions:

It was only then that he took her look for disapproval. "What's a man gonna do?" he questioned hotly. "I couldn't keep running all my mother-raping life."

"Shush!" She leaned over and sealed his mouth with her lips. They tasted hot, wet and breathless. "You just scared the living shit out of me," she confessed, quickly adding, "But I love you for it."

His eyes, which were all that could show it, lit with hope. "Then we're still engaged?"

She looked at him indignantly. "You fool, you think I'm going to lose you now? All I been through!" [*RMR* 192].

Jimmy has come to New York to study law at Columbia rather than attempt to integrate the law school in his home state of North Carolina; he wants to save his mother and sister from the embarrassment of so public a spectacle. His use of the all-purpose expletive "mother-raping" to describe his current life marks something of a shift for him, a polite, well-educated and well-spoken young man who has, on occasion, voiced his concerns over Linda's tendency to talk shit. Otherwise, the dialogue is strictly b-movie in nature, as is the resolution. In fact, these books, with their short running times and penchant for action—the car chase in *For Love of Imabelle*, the run-away tire in *All Shot Up*, for instance—are cinematic in nature, further reinforcing the cartoonish nature of their characters and conflicts.

The results can seem problematic. On one level, the Harlem series represents a remarkable achievement, the first commercially viable series, at least in France, to feature an African American detective and to be set in an African American environment. These pieces work, in general, as Stephen F. Soitos suggests in *The Blues Detective*, especially with regard to their substitution of African American figures and "blackscape" for the more conventional white figures and settings of the traditional hard-boiled novel; in their exploration of the black vernacular experience, of the material elements of African American culture; and in their use of "double-consciousness" detection, as Grave Digger and Coffin Ed remain liminal figures in these books, minority black detectives in a majority white system, the "man" on the streets of Harlem. Being black law-enforcement figures marks them as doubly suspicious, as suspicious on the streets where they grew up as in the department where they are employed. These elements will clearly drive the plots and provide ample opportunity for thematic development, primarily their exploration of the prevailing racist attitudes institutionalized within the larger culture and the ways these histories have resulted in Harlem.

By contrast, the books do not seem to explore the hoodoo elements/alternative epistemologies prevailing in black culture as clearly as they might. Aside from a manifestly misplaced spiritualism that seems common throughout, Himes gives little attention to this fourth element Soitos identifies as central to the tradition. The ministers, fortune-tellers, and folk healers, when they appear, all prove to be fraudulent, con artists of one kind or another, always working a scam. Himes leaves the mystery of faith largely unexplored, why so many people are seemingly so willing to place their faith in false prophets. Jackson's belief in his minister's healing powers seems as misplaced in *For Love of Imabelle* as his belief in the counterfeiter's ability to raise the denomination of ten-dollar bills to one hundreds.

At that level, the books tend to be primarily naturalistic, "realistic" in a conventional sense. Coming to Himes's Harlem after reading Rudolph Fisher's *The Conjure-Man Dies*, one is struck by how wholly corrupt Harlem has become, how predatory the relationships prove, how little one can trust anyone. Fisher's genteel young physician and his detective friend, Archer and Dart, bemoan the corrupt nature of Harlem, and Fisher, in his other works, does explore the ways that naive country people, newly arrived from the South, fall prey to Harlem con men, but little of this world is observable in *The Conjure-Man Dies*. Our one contact with the underlife of Harlem is Bubber Brown, whose irrepressible comedy-hall character ameliorates any of the obvious evil that will emerge in Himes's work.

As Himes portrays Harlem in *For Love of Imabelle*, Harlem is truly malevolent. In short order, Jackson, a Harlemite educated in a southern Negro college and now employed as a janitor and driver for H. Exodus Clay's funeral home, is betrayed by his live-in girlfriend, conned by counterfeiters, and bilked by a fraudulent U.S. marshal; he is beyond desperate when his attempts to bribe the marshal and repair his misfortunes so that he can reclaim Imabelle all fail. He loses money he has "borrowed" from his employer's safe, first in the daily numbers racket and thereafter at an all-night craps game. Only Goldy, Jackson's twin brother, a heroin addict who supports himself through the charitable contributions he receives disguised as a Sister of Mercy, seems in a position to help. Everyone in the book, with the notable exception of Jackson, is working an angle. Love, law, and religion all become the occasions for furthering the fraudulent schemes of Himes's Harlemites, whereas for Jackson, Imabelle is all that truly matters.

Little changes in the course of the book. With the notable exceptions of Jackson, a hopeless "square," and the detectives Coffin Ed Jones and Grave Digger Johnson, the rest of the assembled cast is motivated solely by self interest, manifested in an insatiable greed. The picture is nothing if not Darwinian. Himes describes Harlem half way through the book:

> Looking eastward from the towers of Riverside Church, perched among the university buildings on the high banks of the Hudson River, in a valley far below, waves of grey rooftops distort the perspective like the surface of a sea. Below

the surface, in the murky waters of the fetid tenements, a city of black people who are convulsed in desperate living, like the voracious churning of millions of hungry cannibal fish. Blind mouths eating their own guts. Stick in a hand and draw back a nub.

That is Harlem [*FLI* 93].

The only rule is the rule of force, which is what Coffin Ed and Grave Digger represent:

> Grave Digger and Coffin Ed weren't crooked detectives, but they were tough. They had to be tough to work in Harlem. Colored folks didn't respect colored cops. But they respected big shiny pistols and sudden death. It was said in Harlem that Coffin Ed's pistol would kill a rock and that Grave Digger's would bury it.
>
> They took their tribute, like all real cops, from the established underworld catering to the essential needs of the people—gamekeepers, madams, streetwalkers, numbers writers, numbers bankers. But they were rough on purse snatchers, muggers, burglars, con men, and all strangers working any racket. And they didn't like rough stuff from anybody else but themselves. "Keep it cool," they warned. "Don't make graves" [*FLI* 49–50].

In this instance, justice, such as it is, is strictly retributive. When Coffin Ed is blinded by one of the con men who throws acid in his face, Grave Digger tracks the man down and shoots him through the eyes, once with his own pistol and once with Coffin Ed's, an Old Testament eye-for-an-eye justice. In the end, Jackson seems to survive the ordeal, carried through it by his blind love and faith in Imabelle, and Imabelle, the recipient of that grace, also seems to escape any responsibility for her actions.

H. Exodus Clay, the undertaker and Jackson's employer, bails both of them out. In spite of his losses, he has been more than amply repaid by the wealth of dead bodies this business has left behind. In the ten books that make up Himes's Harlem series, Jackson will be mentioned twice in later books, once when he is unavailable to drive the hearse because he and his "wife" Imabelle are at church (*Big Gold Dream* 13), and in a later book, when it is reported that the burial of so many bodies has paid dividends, finally allowing Jackson to marry Imabelle (*Cotton Comes to Harlem* 157). Jackson is hopelessly square but protected somehow by his faith in God and his love for Imabelle, regardless of how unworthy either the church or the woman he believes in prove to be; he is perhaps the only recurring character in the series who seems to escape unscathed and uncorrupted by his adventures in Harlem—that, at least, is the unwritten implication—and the one mystery left unsolved in these books. Everything else will submit, in the end, to rational explanation.

A Prevailing Pessimism: The Presence of the Past

The Conjure-Man Dies, in general, seems an optimistic work, much like the Golden Age mysteries it emulates. Doctor Archer, Detective Dart, and the Harvard-educated Frimbo bring a gentility, a professionalism, and a possibility of advancement, even in spite of the economic downturns of the depression, all buoyed by the artistic and anthropological interests of the Harlem Renaissance. They bemoan the corrupt state of 1930s Harlem, but the satiric edge of the book, making sport of naturalism's theories of deterministic biology and the eugenic principles they support, suggests an idealism, a means of reimagining the current state of affairs. Writing in the late 1950s, early '60s, Himes might have had reason for optimism, given the Supreme Court's ruling in *Brown v. Board*, declaring the beginning of the end to government-sanctioned apartheid policies and the stirring of the Civil Rights Movement that arose in its wake. Himes's response, however, is anything but optimistic. On one level, his anxieties seem to mirror Pauline Hopkins's concerns. Writing in the opening years of the twentieth century, Hopkins is seeing the promises of emancipation going unrealized as new reasons and official rulings appear offering new sanctions for old ways. Much the same thing happened following *Brown*. Some recent commentators have noted the blunted impact of the Brown ruling, that the Supreme Court's call for integration to occur "with all deliberate speed" evidently meant "very slowly" (Sullivan 48). The more things change, the more they stay the same. It is also possible to argue that Himes's incarceration as a young man, his lack of recognition as a writer, his leaving the United States for France all contributed to the darkness of these books. The overt racism of the past, however, if anything, seems destined to continue in covert ways, a cold war replacing the open hostilities between races. Just as Jimmy will find it necessary to purchase a gun and openly confront Walker in his attempt to "force him into the open" in *Run Man Run*, Himes will similarly force issues in *Plan B*, the armed rebellion Tomsson Black secretly foments revealing how little things have changed.

The early books in the series can, at times, suggest a possibility of change. *The Real Cool Killers*, for instance, provides a clear instance in its formulaic ending of one such moment. In fact, the first four books, *For Love of Imabelle, The Real Cool Killers, The Crazy Kill*, and *Run Man Run*, all trace a similar trajectory, with the central figures in each emerging from the mayhem and madness these books describe to find love. Individual and personal acts of devotion seem to provide the only possible defense against the prevailing disorder and corruption of Harlem; at the very least, they represent some possibility of finding a degree of personal satisfaction and fulfillment within these straightened circumstances.

The plots in these books are nothing if not convoluted, and the stakes seem to rise book by book, the violence and disorder proving more difficult in each case to contain. In *The Real Cool Killers*, Coffin Ed's daughter will be at the center of the action, focusing attention on the family drama. In this case, a white man, sitting in a Harlem bar, is accosted by one of the patrons; he flees into the street, where a second patron of the bar pursues him, pistol in hand, and in short order, the white man, a "big Greek," is dead, a bullet in his brain. The spectacle attracts a crowd, including a group of young men dressed in Arab costume, the members of a black teenage gang that calls themselves the Real Cool Moslems. Coffin Ed and Grave Digger arrive almost immediately, quick enough to arrest the bar patron, pistol still in hand, standing over the body, but mayhem soon breaks out when one of the Moslems, in response to the detectives' questioning, attempts to douse Coffin Ed with a bottle of cheap perfume. Fearing another acid attack, Coffin Ed opens fire, killing the gang member and wounding a bystander before Grave Digger can subdue him. In the scuffle, the gang members scatter, taking the accused killer with them.

The novel proceeds at this point as the police seal off the area and conduct an apartment-to-apartment search while Grave Digger follows up on the available leads, starting at the bar where the whole business began. The investigation will ultimately reveal that the dead white man, a well-to-do salesman for a soft drink company, was paying teenage black girls $100 a session to allow him to flog them with a whip he keeps in the trunk of his car, sadistic acts that he then documents photographically. His initial assailant proves to be the father of two of his victims. His killer—neither the pistol-toting bar patron whose gun, it turns out, is a starter's pistol capable only of firing blanks, nor the leader of the black gang, who takes responsibility for the killing but whose home-made zip gun proves not to match the caliber of the bullet extracted from the man's head—turns out to be another of the white man's young victims, Sissie, who kills him to prevent him from beating her best friend. The friend in question is Coffin Ed's daughter. The official investigation is allowed to end before Sissie's role in the murder is uncovered, given the degenerate nature of the white man and the confession of the gang leader, who has been killed in the course of the investigation and whose confession has been publicly announced in the newspaper accounts of this sensational killing. Only Grave Digger knows the truth, and he isn't talking. As far as he's concerned, justice has been done; the killer in this case is unlikely to ever kill again.

The action in the novel, much as in *For Love of Imabelle*, is nearly continuous, unfolding simultaneously in several locations around the city as the (white) beat cops conduct their manhunt at the scene of the crime and as Grave Digger moves from bar to brothel to supper club and back to the bar, piecing together the story of the white man's perversion and the people, all of them black, who have assisted him in satisfying his desires. His investigation is strictly inductive, assuming nothing, not even what seems obvious to everyone else, that the man with the smoking gun must be responsible for the murder. The investigation will raise a number of questions, among them the seeming willingness of black people to allow white men to use black women to satisfy their sexual appetites, even those that prove to be distinctly perverted, and the Harlemites' excitement at the spectacle of a white man being pursued and shot by a black man on the streets of Harlem. The general response turns on several points: (1) the degree of misery and lack of economic opportunity pervasive in Harlem; (2) the fact historically that black women have been subservient to white men's desires, something that black men acquiesce in and may, in fact, take some peculiar satisfaction from, their women being, if nothing else, a source of income, their sexual services something that can be sold; and (3) the rare satisfaction that black people experience in seeing the tables turned, of a white man being pursued and shot down in the streets by black people. While the pervasive misery in Harlem and the satisfaction of seeing a white man killed by blacks both go unchallenged, there is some debate over the willingness of black men to sell their women to white men. The point, at least, provokes some discussion.

Law and justice prove to be two clearly different things in this case. Sissie is subject to legal action, guilty of first-degree murder, though her crime would almost surely be reduced to a lesser charge, manslaughter, perhaps, at trial. She is too sympathetic a figure, the victim too deserving of his fate to make a first-degree murder charge feasible. Tellingly, her role in the murder, the possibility that a young black woman might be responsible for the crime, never seems to occur to anyone but Grave Digger. The powers-that-be recognize that the physical evidence exonerates the dead gang leader, but they are willing to allow the fiction to go unchallenged. Reopening the case would require them to divulge the white man's crimes, the sadistic sexual pleasure that he derived from whipping young black women. Reopening the case would also require them to own the shoddiness of their own investigations, especially their readiness to accept the dead gang leader's guilt on face value in advance of the physical evidence. Their reading of the crime plays on racial profiles and stereotypes, a deductive move that proves to be wrong. Accepting the official account covers up a multitude of sins, provides closure, and suggests that some kind of justice has been served, even if the letter of the law has not been. A convenient fiction is allowed to cover an inconvenient truth, answering the needs of the dominant ideology. Grave Digger is complicit in this action, as guilty as the rest.

On the other hand, Sissie's selfless action is rewarded in the end. Sissy is an orphan, a gang leader's girlfriend, a young woman who has been sold by her boyfriend to a white man so that he might satisfy his sadistic pleasures; she is, in short, a young woman used brutally and used to the brutality of the world. As inured to violence as she is, however, she will not allow her friend, a young woman from an intact family living in a better part of the city, Jamaica, Queens (a new world, situated, it should be noted, on Utopia Parkway), to prostitute herself to satisfy this white man's perversion. Eve, short for Evelyn Johnson, known as Sugartit to the gang, has a chance to escape the past, and Sissie acts to protect that future. The novel ends with the revelation that Sissie fired the fatal shot and immediately thereafter with her visiting the blank-shooting assailant, Sonny, who is serving time in prison for disorderly conduct. She announces her desire to marry and settle down, pregnant, in fact, by her now dead boyfriend. Sonny, in spite of her pregnancy, proposes to her, willing to take her and the baby, promising to rebuild his shoeshine business when he is released from jail. Sissie is honest with Sonny, and Sonny is magnanimous in accepting her as she is:

> "I've done a lot of bad things."
> "Like what?"
> "I'd be ashamed to tell you everything I've done."
> "Listen, to show you I ain't scared of nothing you might have done, I want you to be my girl."
> "I don't want to play around any more."
> "Who's talking about playing around. I'm talking about for keeps."
> "I don't mind. But there's something I've got to tell you first. It's about me and Sheik."
> "What about you and Sheik?"
> "I'm going to have a baby by the time you get out of jail."
> "Well, that makes it different," he said. "We'd better get married right away. I'll talk to the man and ask him to see if he can't arrange it" [*RCK* 159].

Against the backdrop of hopelessness that seems pervasive in Harlem, some promise for the future appears, however trite the b-movie dialogue proves to be.

This kind of interchange and the satisfaction it brings clearly represent one of the "guilty pleasures" reading pulp fiction produces. The scene feels tacked on, certainly unexpected, and the dialogue couldn't be more banal, a b-movie cliché. Still, Sissie's heroic selflessness will meet its just reward in

Sonny's magnanimous offer of marriage, his willingness to accept her and the baby redeeming her from her unfortunate past, making an "honest" woman of her in the end. Comedy replaces tragedy, and we are happy to see some kind of order restored to these disordered lives, probably the only kind of order possible under these circumstances. The response parallels Grave Digger's willingness to accept the official account of the killing, allowing Sissie's actions to go unpunished. This is the best we can expect in a bad situation.

This willingness to accept this resolution, even to take some satisfaction in it, however, is the problem in this instance. It seems, in general, an example of the problems that Maureen T. Reddy notes in *Traces, Codes, and Clues: Reading Race in Crime Fiction*, primarily in that this resolution allows the racist assumptions/dominant ideology embedded in these books to go unquestioned. Hard-boiled fiction is, as Reddy points out, essentially racist:

> The primary pleasure of hard-boiled fiction lies in the reader's vicarious experience of prevailing, along with the hero, over mean characters from mean streets; the detective is the story, the sine qua non of the genre. Readers who consciously object to racism, sexism, and heterosexism may attempt to wriggle out of acknowledging the degree to which their beliefs are at odds with the ideology of that fiction by claiming that instances of racism and the like are understandable, given the period of the fiction's writing, and while deplorable, inessential. This argument cannot stand, however, because the ideology and the fiction are inseparable. The casual racism of some hard-boiled novels can be breathtaking [35].

Reddy goes on to cite Laura Mulvey's claims about classic Hollywood cinema, that viewers can only participate in and derive pleasure from these films by accepting their sexist perspectives, by "inhabit[ing] the male gaze" and "accept[ing] the woman's role as to-be-looked at" (37), arguing that the pleasures derived from reading hard-boiled fiction require similar commitments on the part of the reader:

> I make a similar claim about hard-boiled fiction, because refusing to stand with the detective, refusing the ritual of white/male/heterosexual bonding that hard-boiled fiction enacts, leaves one no place to stand at all as a reader of the fiction. It is not possible to read the fiction "innocently": either one engages in the bonding ritual, whether consciously or not, or one critiques it, refuses it, places oneself (or is placed) outside it. White/male/heterosexual bonding is not incidental to the reading of hard-boiled fiction but absolutely constitutive of its pleasures [38].

The question is whether the African American or Native American or lesbian writer of detective fiction, working in the tradition of the hard-boiled novel, can transform rather than simply transmit the prevailing forces in the genre.

In the resolution of *The Real Cool Killers*, Himes seems to have capitulated to these pressures, not to have transformed them. His shifting of the action to Harlem and his introduction of African American detectives foregrounds the racial questions and the racist assumptions implicit in the genre, but the valorization of individual action, often violent, in place of any higher civic or corporate responsibility or justice allows prevailing attitudes to go unchallenged. The response is pragmatic, not ideal, and that's the problem, as the novel ultimately plays inside the limited possibilities for achieving justice and the limited means available for its achievement. It accepts the collateral damage that accompanies these actions; it does not re-imagine the generic conventions of the hard-boiled mystery and the world they describe. In this instance, the past weighs too heavily on the present for any meaningful change to occur.

Insofar as *The Real Cool* Killers is the second book in the series, Grave Digger and Coffin Ed have a history. Coffin Ed bears the literal scars of his adventures in *For Love of Imabelle*, the result of having had acid flung in his face. He consequently reacts instinctively, blindly, when one of the Real Cool Moslems flings cheap perfume at him, killing the otherwise unarmed teenager and taking down a woman in the crowd. That young man, as it turns out, in spite of the company that he keeps, doesn't seem to be a bad kid; he lives with his elderly great grandmother, keeps pigeons, and happens to be the boyfriend of Coffin Ed's daughter. He is, at most, guilty by association, a young man who didn't deserve to die. Coffin Ed's response is understandable, accepted ultimately as the cost of doing business in Harlem, but not, in the end, acceptable. His is a natural response, a tough guy attempting to maintain order though the only means recognized on the street, or so the argument goes. It is an argument that has its limits.

Failing to bring Sissie to justice has other problems. The official explanation preserves appearances, allowing the public to believe that this white man, slumming in Harlem, has become the unfortunate victim of gang violence. It's an old story and one that is typically racist in construction. The real story, however, were it known, would require us to confront the racist realities still prevalent in society. The big Greek's whip is a not-too-subtle reference to that of the slave driver, a testament to how little has changed in the almost hundred years since emancipation. The elderly great grandmother, in fact, admits to the white policeman who interviews her during the apartment-to-apartment search for the Moslems that she was probably born before emancipation. She can't fully remember, and no accurate records exist, but it is quite possible that she was born into slavery, a relic of a past the results of which we are still living with. Honest black women will still find themselves functioning as "kitchen slaves" in the homes of well-to-do white people. The schools are still segregated in *Run Man Run*, bringing Jimmy north to attend law school. In *Cotton Comes to Harlem*, Colonel Calhoun mounts his "Back to the Southland" campaign, offering to pay $1,000 to any black man willing to return to the South and pick cotton, money he has stolen from a local back-to-African movement. Grave Digger and Coffin Ed will succeed in forcing the Colonel to return the money, but they will not be able to bring him to justice for killing a black man. Though the Colonel is indicted in New York, "the state of Alabama refused to extradite [Colonel Calhoun and his nephew] on the grounds that killing a Negro did not constitute murder under Alabama law" (*CCH* 157). *Plan B*, finally, will show just how little has changed since slavery. Himes's optimistic endings in these early novels will provide for some personal satisfaction but will leave the underlying structures unchallenged, both in terms of the larger historical narrative and with regard to the conventional structures of the hard-boiled novel.

Biological Determinism Revisited

The often surreal/graphic novel/cinematic nature of these books does not contradict the naturalistic elements in the genre, the more Darwinian aspects of these books. Grave Digger and Coffin Ed, harbingers of death in the predatory environment of Harlem, a world red in tooth and claw, represent a force of nature. Their attempts to maintain order through force of arms will be limited in the course of these books by the larger and more powerful systems of self-interest invested in the political structures of the city, the police department that protects those interests, and the racist attitudes that have historically furthered the economic interests of the dominant white culture. *Blind Man with a Pistol* will clearly show the two detectives succumbing to these superior powers. But the operations of chance, of random events, one of the key driving forces in evolution, also appear in these books, further complicating the picture and, in one instance, limiting the detectives' methods and effectiveness.

Biology, in one way or another, seems especially key in *Run Man Run*, a story centered on the fight-or-flight response supposedly rooted deeply in the central cortex of the brain. Walker is drunk, a serious alcoholic on a days' long binge, suffering from periodic lapses of memory. The alcohol has lowered his inhibitions, allowing his violent, racist tendencies free rein. This combination of factors places him in the Schmidt and Schindler luncheonette, holding a gun on Fat Sam, accusing him of somehow being complicit in the theft of his car. In fact, Walker has simply forgotten where he parked, the missing car a result of his alcohol-induced memory lapse. The thought occurs to Fat Sam "that white folks could believe anything, no matter how foolish or impossible, where a Negro was concerned" (*RMR* 13). Walker's behavior is particularly irrational and becomes even more so as the interview proceeds:

> Fat Sam had never seen a white man go insane like this. He had never realized that the thought of Negroes could send a white man out of his head. He wouldn't have believed it. He thought it was all put on. And now this sight of violence unleashed because of race terrified him as though he had come face to face with the devil, whom he'd never believed in either [*RMR* 16].

Still, Walker is as surprised as Fat Sam is when the gun he is holding discharges:

> Three sounds followed one behind another like a cold motor coughing.
> Fat Sam's eyes widened slowly in ultimate surprise. "You shot me," he said in an incredulous voice....
> The detective looked down in shock at the gun in his hand. A thin wisp of smoke curled from the muzzle and the smell of cordite grew strong in the small cold room.
> "Jesus Christ!" he exclaimed in a horrified whisper [*RMR* 16].

The action is accidental, probably the ultimate irony here. The gun Walker is holding is an unlicensed revolver fitted with a silencer, a gun he had retrieved from a crime scene, not his service revolver. The hair trigger was a surprise, even to him. Having shot Fat Sam, Walker feels that he has no other option but to finish the deed, killing Sam and the two other members of the night staff who can place him at the scene. His failure to kill Jimmy outright initiates the action of the book.

Given Walker's alcohol-induced rage and his (literally) unbridled racism, along with his employment as a police officer and his access to firearms, he is (literally) an accident waiting to happen. The killing is a random, senseless act, which is to say a mechanical operation, not something intended. The plot evolves out of this random act. Biology is destiny, or so this opening action seems to suggest.

The turning point in Grave Digger and Coffin Ed's career also seems the result of a random action, an accident. As the series progresses, official tolerance wanes for their brutal methods, no matter how effective. In *The Heat's On*, Grave Digger and Coffin Ed retrieve evidence from Jake, a drug-dealing dwarf, by hitting him in the stomach, forcing him to vomit up the inventory he has just swallowed (and is choking on) in order to escape detection. Jake loses consciousness, possibly a reaction to the drugs he has swallowed. He had been taken before the drug packets could be fully digested but also before he had had an opportunity to take anything to neutralize the effect of the drugs and the potential overdose they represent. Grave Digger and Coffin Ed had effectively pumped his stomach before the drugs could take effect. The problem occurs, however, when Jake dies from internal bleeding, the result of a ruptured spleen. The two detectives are held responsible for his death.

While their actions may have resulted in Jake's death, another more plausible source of this injury exists. Pinky, an albino giant, is attempting to flee from the scene and the beating he is in the process of receiving from a group of irate firemen who have discovered that Pinky is responsible for the false alarm they have just responded to. Pinky breaks away:

> The giant got to his hands and knees and pushed to his feet, shaking off firemen like a dog shedding water. He put his head down and started to run, plowing through a rain of blows.
> "The son of a bitch ain't human," a fireman complained.
> He got across the sidewalk and stepped onto the grass. His foot sunk into the belly of the unconscious dwarf. Globules of vomit spewed from Jake's mouth. No one noticed.
> He vaulted over the hood of a fire engine and got a lead on his pursuers [*HO* 13].

Jake's ruptured spleen is more likely a result of being trampled by the fleeing giant than of being hit in the stomach by Grave Digger.

The accidental, random nature of these events, the dangers implicit in hair triggers and lumbering giants, represent chance elements in an indifferent universe, "naturalistic" details out of which these stories evolve. They suggest a biological element in the series that, however unnoticed, drives the action in places. Biology seems, in one way or another, to represent destiny and in ways that reinforce rather than refute racist assumptions and prejudices. Himes's fictional universe transmits rather than transmutes hard-boiled conventions and the ideological implications inscribed in them.

Plan B

All of these problems will multiply in the final novels in the series, in *Plan B*, a novel that Himes all but completed and then abandoned, and *Blind Man with a Pistol*, which he published in 1969. *Plan B* seems to have been the earlier of the two novels, a book Himes was at work on in 1967, which seems to have been substantially complete in 1969, and which, incorporating the deaths of his two detectives, marked the intended end of the series. Himes published several excerpts from the novel as independent short stories in 1967 and 1972, the novel itself finally published in France in 1983, just prior to

Himes's death in 1984. Michel Fabre had discovered the nearly complete typescript of the novel along with a "synopsis" of the book's final ten pages, a summary "written out in expanded draft form with elaborate dialogues" (*Plan B* xiii), which he appended to the typescript and which then formed the basis of the French translation. The first American edition, incorporating some further revisions discovered after the French publication, appeared in 1993 in an edition edited by Robert E. Skinner. As Skinner and Fabre point out in their introduction to the American edition, *Plan B* clearly posed problems for Himes, who expressed misgivings both about the book itself and its commercial prospects, a book probably unpublishable in the United States at the time. It is a book, in general, that proves to be problematic on a number of levels, from the seeming reversal of roles played by the two detectives and the less-than-convincing explanation Grave Digger Jones advances for killing an unarmed drug addict early in the book, and the subordinate role the two detectives play in the book. That the book consists of a rambling multigenerational narrative which involves the frank depiction of sometimes perverse, white sexual behavior and the eruption of a race war in the United States render it additionally problematic. The fact that Grave Digger and his partner find themselves divided on the merits of this war precipitates their deaths, Coffin Ed at the hands of Grave Digger Jones, Grave Digger at the hands of Tomsson Black, the man responsible for the armed uprising. Himes set *Plan B* aside, allowing *Blind Man with a Pistol* to take its place as the final installment of the Harlem Domestic Series. The general question has always been why.

The larger part of the narrative focuses on the history of Tomsson Black, his radicalization and subsequent rise as the chief executive officer of a black corporate enterprise, Citterlings, Inc. The public purpose of the company is to provide economic self-sufficiency to a large number of indigent African Americans, an effort funded by a million-dollar grant made to it by a white foundation; its more immediate purpose, however, is to provide Black with the resources for acquiring and distributing military-style assault rifles to black men, chosen seemingly at random, to create a black military force capable of carrying out an extended guerrilla war against white society. The focus of the corporate enterprise is the development of a mammoth hog farm on 5000 acres of reclaimed Alabama swamp land, a project which will house, employ, and support 100,000 currently unemployed African Americans living in urban slums. The novel will trace this effort back to the initial settling of this land by slave-owning whites prior to the Civil War who prove totally inept at raising anything from this land other than large numbers of mentally deficient and sexually precocious children. These sections of the novel seem to exist primarily to establish the sexual proclivities of ante-bellum whites in backwoods Alabama and the existence of this abandoned and all but impenetrable parcel of land where run-away slaves and, later, black fugitives from justice find temporary refuge. The story moves from Alabama to Memphis to the University City suburbs of St. Louis before returning to Alabama, where Tomsson Black will find himself serving a prison term for the beating and rape of an affluent white woman aboard her husband's yacht while cruising in the Gulf. The two detectives appear only at the beginning of the book, when they respond to a homicide in Harlem, a drug addict having just killed his prostitute companion—the two have argued over an assault rifle the addict had just received and which he wanted to turn over to authorities—and at the end, when the two detectives are finally called in to investigate the source of these weapons. In the initial scenes, Grave Digger crushes the skull of the unarmed and strung-out drug addict with the butt of his pistol and is suspended. In the closing scene, he and his partner confront Black.

The story is clearly uneven, from its rambling multigenerational narrative set in the deep South, to its cartoonish depiction of well-hung black men being lusted after by randy white women unsatisfied by their under-endowed and sometimes homosexual husbands, to the story-stopping interview of Black by Harry H. Hopkins, former Dean of Harvard Law and current director of the Hull Foundation, the charitable organization that will fund Chitterlings, Inc.'s proposal. The two detectives, introduced at the beginning, disappear from the narrative until the end, serving only as a framing device. Throughout, the crude depictions of white sexuality, having all the subtlety of an R. Crumb *Zap Comix*, and the less than subtle depiction of race "relations," in every sense of the word, would probably have rendered the novel unpublishable at the time, as Himes feared. The racial and sexual stereotypes (e.g., white women lusting after well-endowed black men) along with Grave Digger's seemingly unmotivated killing of the addict, an action his partner attempts to cover up by concocting a story of a drug-crazed, knife-wielding suspect and which their white superiors are perfectly willing to overlook ("One more dead nigger meant very little to Captain Brice, and it saved the state the cost of convicting him for the murder of the woman" [*PB* 43]) both seem particularly problematic. Captain Brice would have dismissed the incident if Coffin Ed hadn't insisted on the addict's violent behavior, behavior at odds with heroin's narcotic effects. The stereotype, in this case, is out of keeping with actual behavior, and Brice has no option but to suspend Grave Digger pending a full and official inquiry into the incident.

The Harlem Domestic Series has never been noted for its subtlety, and the characteristically surreal nature of the series proves Kafkaesque in this case, *Plan B* more parable, Himes's version of *Amerika*, than mystery novel. It does, however, seem to reflect contemporary events, the race war and the incidents that precipitate it suggested by the 1965 Watts riots, and the sniper incidents modeled on the 1966 University of Texas Tower shootings. And the exaggerated response, the use of heavy artillery to destroy the Harlem tenement sheltering the lone gunman, with all the collateral damage that action entails, both recalls the military response in Watts and anticipates the 1985 bombing of the Philadelphia townhouse headquarters of MOVE, resulting in the deaths of eleven people, including five children, and the destruction of 61 homes.

In some ways at least, the incidents of *Plan B* are rooted in reality. Race riots had broken out in Harlem and then spread to several other Eastern cities and Chicago in the summer of 1964, each incident lasting several days, the precipitating incident the shooting of a black teenager by a white policeman in New York. These incidents, however, paled by comparison to the summer 1965 riots in Watts, set off by the arrest of a young black motorist for driving under the influence. His erratic behavior had been reported by a black citizen, and he did fail a field-sobriety test before being arrested and his car impounded, which seems to have been the immediate issue. Both his brother and then his mother had offered to drive the car home, only a few blocks distant from the site of the arrest. The riots that broke out lasted six days and resulted in 34 fatalities, 1032 people injured, nearly 4000 people arrested, and an estimated $40,000,000 in property damage (Governor's Commission). The report of the Governor's Commission, chaired by John A. McCone, assigned to investigate the event was significantly titled "Violence in the City: An End or a Beginning?"

When Captain McBride asks Coffin Ed what he would do, referring to the standoff between police and a sniper armed with a powerful assault rifle, Coffin Ed glibly responds, "I'd give them better housing.... Better schools, higher wages—" (*PB* 60). The gunman had just taken out two white policemen cruising the neighborhood in their patrol car. The policemen were substituting for the suspended Grave Digger and injured Coffin Ed. The McCone report, reviewing the 1964 riots, notes that, in spite of some circumstances unique to each site, "the fundamental causes were largely the same":

- Not enough jobs to go around, and within this scarcity not enough by a wide margin of a character which the untrained Negro could fill.
- Not enough schooling designed to meet the special needs of the disadvantaged Negro child, whose environment from infancy onward places him under a serious handicap.

- A resentment, even hatred, of the police, as the symbol of authority [Governor's Commission].

Where poor housing conditions clearly contributed in other cities to the unrest, in Watts, where housing standards far exceeded those in other black urban settings, black resentment seems to have been fueled by the passage of Proposition 14, a repeal of the Rumford Fair Housing Act. The police force was overwhelmingly white—four percent of the LAPD and six percent of the Sheriff's Department were African American, with even lower percentages of Mexican American officers (Governor's Commission). The schools in the four most disadvantaged Los Angeles districts were uniformly poor, with two-thirds of the students dropping out before receiving a degree. Fifth graders scored in the 18–20th percentile on vocabulary and the 19–24th percentile on reading comprehension; eighth grade scores declined, 13–16th percentile, vocabulary, 15–20th percentile, comprehension (Governor's Commission). While eleventh grade scores improved, largely because so many of the poorer students had already dropped out, the Commission report, in general, points out that students scoring in these ranges would be incapable of reading and understanding their textbooks, reading and understanding a daily newspaper, or of using reading for "ordinary purposes" in daily life. The illiterate and unemployed drug addict living in squalid conditions, the man who receives the assault rifle and who is brutally murdered by Grave Digger, seems representative of this underclass of under-educated, unemployable, ill-used people.

The McCone Report provides a snapshot of the despair that fueled the 1965 Watts riots; the 1964 riots in Harlem and Rochester, New York, in Jersey City, Paterson, and Elizabeth, New Jersey, in Chicago, Illinois, and Philadelphia, Pennsylvania; and that Himes describes at the center of life in Harlem. Thomas Pynchon describes how little conditions have improved in Watts a year after the riots. After a May 7th traffic stop of a young black driver by white policemen results in the "accidental" death of the black man, Pynchon writes that the incident

> brought it all into sharp focus, brought back long-standing pain, reminded everyone of how very often the cop does approach you with his revolver ready, so that nothing he does with it can then really be accidental, of how, especially at night, everything can suddenly reduce to a matter of reflexes: your life trembling in the crook of a cop's finger because it is dark, and Watts, and the history of this place and these times makes it impossible for the cop to come on any different, or for you to hate him any less. Both of you are caught in something neither of you wants, and yet night after night, with casualties or without, these traditional scenes continue to be played out all over the South central part of this city.

The 40th Armored Division of the California National Guard had been called in to quell the 1965 riots. Pynchon comments on Mayor Yorty's belief "in the virtues of Overwhelming Force as a solution to racial differences," similar in nature to the use of a tank to take out the sniper in *Plan B* or, twenty years after Watts and the year following Himes's death, the dropping of percussion bombs on a Philadelphia townhouse to end the MOVE standoff. In some regards, Himes's fiction is not as strange as it might seem, at least in some regards.

Pynchon's piece, along with the official report of the Governor's Commission, provides an interesting analogue to Himes's story, and it is interesting, as well, in its examination of psychology, "A Journey into the Mind of Watts." Watts is "besieged" by the white world that surrounds it, especially insofar as that world and its values are represented in the mass media:

> Watts lies impacted in the heart of this white fantasy. It is, by contrast, a pocket of bitter reality. The only illusion Watts ever allowed itself was to believe in the white version of what a Negro is supposed to be. But with the Muslim and civil-rights movement that went too.

Himes addresses the failure of this particular illusion, though in a slightly different way. Himes comments somewhat cryptically:

> While Americans suffer guilt over black segregation and restriction, in other white societies the assumption of black equality is summarily dismissed. This is why other white majorities treat their black minorities with greater consideration and politeness. They do not fear that blacks will ever attain equality or that they will even request it.
>
> Strangely enough, American blacks don't know this, and probably most whites don't either [*PB* 144].

Capitalist economics, driven by competition, may be the problem. If white Americans didn't view American minorities as sources of competition, or if those same minorities did not believe themselves equally entitled to compete for the economic advantages white Americans felt to be part of their birthright, then conflict wouldn't result.

The problem is that African Americans, lacking any sense of native heritage or value, have bought into the particular illusions empowering white Americans. In his interviews with Hopkins, Tomsson Black argues just this point: "In most instances, we can do no more than imitate.... We have so little tradition outside the structure of our national society, we have very few basic innovations to offer," with, perhaps, the single exception of jazz (*PB* 164). He continues in the following paragraph:

> We have taken our languages from the whites, our knowledge and education from the whites, our morals and religions from the whites, our definitions of

justice, ambition, achievement, clothing, shelter; in fact every aspect of our lives but reproduction, which is common to all life. We do not have any remembered tradition [*PB* 164].

Even the reclaiming of black standards of beauty, the idea that black is beautiful, is driven by white attitudes toward beauty and its association with power. When Hopkins interjects that black people "are beautiful too," Black responds:

> Of course, sir.... That is what I've been saying. "Too" is the operative word. We are human, too; we are intelligent, too; we are worthy, too; but we are not white, too, and that is the problem. We are everything but white in a white-dominated, white-oriented society. The one thing which we lack is white skin. So we must imitate the dominant group, as has every minority group in the history of the world. Unlike most minority groups, however, when we achieve our imitation even to perfection, we can not move over into the majority group and become assimilated because of the barrier of our skin [*PB* 165].

Tomsson Black had already demonstrated the extent of his capacity for self-conscious imitation, with his impeccable pin-striped suit, the black man "the more elegant of the two" compared to the tweedy Hopkins (*PB* 157), and in the overtly racist hiring policies at Chitterlings, Inc., where only those with the blackest skin were hired; high yellow and mixed-race African Americans need not apply (*PB* 148). He has perfectly imitated white attitudes and corporate structures. Hopkins concludes their interviews by asking if Black would allow himself to be psychoanalyzed to see to what extent his "subconscious attitudes" correspond with his stated positions (*PB* 171). The examination, however, is never completed, Hopkins dying a week later, significantly, of a heart attack.

Imitation seems to be the problem at several levels. For Black, the problem is emulating the white attitudes and values he seeks to displace. Having built a model corporate enterprise in Chitterlings, Inc., he seeks in his arming of black men to develop the military aspect of the military-industrial complex. The plan is to build a counter-force of armed black men capable, if needed, of carrying out a guerrilla-style attack on white society, to win by force what they have been unable to accomplish through legal channels. He doesn't, however, believe it will ultimately be necessary to deploy that force, that white America will concede to the threat, recognizing that genocide is their only viable option in this case, an option that they will find morally repugnant (*PB* 201). The success of the plan, however, depends on the development of an armed, disciplined, collective action, of the recipients of his rifles following the instructions accompanying them, that they learn their weapons and then wait for instruction. The desire to take individual vengeance, however, proves to be the fatal flaw in the design, one which Black realizes too late:

"I was a fool not to have anticipated it," he confessed. "Why should black men act any different from white men in a similar situation? Did black men value their lives any more than white men? Did black men value freedom any less? What was the difference between a black man and a white man whose antecedents had lived under the same society and with the same values and beliefs for three and a half centuries? Did the black man have hereditary slave compulsions passed down from one generation to another?" [*PB* 200].

Black believed risking genocide to be a "calculated risk" worth taking given that all formal channels of action had failed (*PB* 201). His plan was compromised, however, by an even more fundamental miscalculation, that armed black men would be capable of resisting their individual impulses and of acting collectively. The competitive impulses, the images of individual action, the impulses to take retribution no matter how suicidal the action might be were all too deeply ingrained in the national character to be denied.

That this story is framed by the falling out of the two partners seems appropriate. As members of the police force, they have always been associated with the prevailing power structures and not, clearly, immune to its effects. Their penchant for violence and retributive forms of street justice mark them ultimately as part of the problem. Coffin Ed's attempts to manufacture a plausible story that will clear his partner for murdering an unarmed, strung-out junkie is clearly no different from the attempt by white policemen in Watts to explain the "accidental" shooting of a black man at a traffic stop, the incident that Pynchon reports in "A Journey into the Mind of Watts." The two partners have always acted in concert before, one supporting the other in whatever way necessary. In this case the partnership fails. Grave Digger is uncharacteristically incensed by the junkie's murder of his prostitute girlfriend, failing to take from Coffin Ed the same advice he has offered Coffin Ed on other occasions. And he refuses Coffin Ed's offers of assistance, his willingness to testify that the murder was motivated by self-defense. Grave Digger insists that he acted alone:

"No, partner, I'm not going to let you stick your neck out for me. This was my own private feeling, my own private action. I don't ask you to feel like me, man, and I'm not going to let you share the blame. I did it. I killed this black mother myself, I busted his skull alone, and I'd do it again. I did it because that woman looked something like my ma looked as I remember her, a poor black woman wanting freedom. And I'd kill any black mother on earth low enough to waste her for that. But I'm not going to let you share this feeling, man, because this is for my mama" [*PB* 20].

While the stated reason, that the "woman looked something like my ma looked as I remember her," seems generally unconvincing, the emphasis on individual feeling, on personal memory, on individual action, however mysterious the underlying motivations, is clear.

The final scene, Grave Digger's shooting of Coffin Ed only to be shot in turn by Tomsson Black, is perfectly logical, the only action possible. The two partners disagree on the merits of Black's Plan B. Digger is willing to accept the risks, the need to do whatever it takes to achieve equal rights for African Americans, even if it ends in genocide, the annihilation of black Americans. Death proves preferable to prevailing attitudes. Coffin Ed, by contrast, sees the action as self destructive, any victory achieved at so great an expense as ultimately hollow. With no possibility of rapprochement, the only option is to kill or be killed. Digger kills Ed to prevent him from killing Black; Black kills Digger because he knows too much, because he is in a position to expose Black's responsibility for distributing guns and fomenting armed rebellion. It is a risk that Black is unwilling to take.

It also seems to be the only option for a series of murder mysteries conceived along conventional lines. Himes has not succeeded in disrupting generic formulas, only in relocating them, in reproducing, not reconstructing historical conditions. This point seems clear in the book. We have neither a viable past to reclaim nor a viable means of reconceptualizing and reconstructing society, only, as Black claims, the possibilities of reproduction, "which is common to all life." Himes's use of the form imitates to perfection the forms and formulas of the genre. We can't go back but have no means of moving forward. Blacks and whites can't live together, but they can't live apart. The two options available, to either comply or die, prove to be the same in reality, not distinctly different. It's not, in the end, surprising that Himes found this book impossible to finish. In unpublished notes from his autobiography which Skinner and Fabre quote in their preface to *Plan B*, Himes credits Phil Lomax with contributing the story of a blind man with a pistol which formed the resolution of the last novel in the Harlem Domestic Series that Himes would complete and publish:

> It [the incident of the blind man and his pistol] made a perfect ending for the story because I had launched on to a different kind of story where I could accuse everyone of inhumanity.
> Phil Lomax told me a story of the Blind Man with his pistol which was my story of all people: confusion, misunderstanding, confrontation with death at the hands of legality.... That was the story of all black people, but I never wrote it. I lost myself in trying to write a successful story about black people: *Plan B*. [*PB* xi].

The comment, again, proves to be cryptic, the *that* and *it* seeming both to refer to the completed *Blind Man with a Pistol* and a "story of all Black people" he had "not written," an ambition never realized because he had been sidetracked by the writing of *Plan B*. What is clear is that Himes found *Plan B* to be a problem, a project he had lost himself in in trying to write.

A Sense of an Ending, in Which Nothing Is Concluded

The abandoning of *Plan B* left *Blind Man with a Pistol* as the final installment of the Harlem Domestic Series. It is, in many regards, the most "literary" of the novels in the series because it is the least conventional offering in the group. It is a crime novel in which multiple crimes are committed but in which no single crime is solved, no one brought to justice. Grave Digger and Coffin Ed are present throughout, doing what they can to clear these crimes, but their efforts prove futile, even counterproductive on occasion. It is also the most unconventional of the novels structurally, more a series of not fully linked short stories, the chapters divided by occasional "interludes" printed in italics. And the chronology of events is confusing. Any sense of coherent, linear narrative has vanished. Officially, the two detectives have been assigned the task of investigating the possible source or sources of the recurring riots in Harlem. In this instance, there seems to be no mystery, the problems of unemployment, inadequate education, poor living conditions, black resentment all clearly in evidence. The *Interlude* that follows Chapter 15 pinpoints Lincoln as the cause:

> "I take it you've discovered who started the riot," Anderson said.
> "We knew who he was all along," Grave Digger said.
> "It's just nothing we can do to him," Coffin Ed echoed.
> "Why not, for God's sake?"
> "He's dead," Coffin Ed said.
> "Who?"
> "Lincoln," Grave Digger said.
> "He hadn't ought to have freed us if he didn't want to make provisions to feed us," Coffin Ed said. "Anyone could have told him that."
> "All right, all right, lots of us have wondered what he might have thought of the consequences," Anderson admitted. "But it's too late to charge him now."
> "Couldn't have convicted him anyway," Grave Digger said.
> "All he'd have to do would be to plead good intentions," Coffin Ed elaborated.
> "Never was a white man convicted as long as he plead good intentions."
> "All right, all right, who's the culprit this night, here, in Harlem? Who's inciting these people to this senseless anarchy?"
> "Skin," Grave Digger said [BMP 135].

The answers to some questions seem self-evident.

4. Plus ça change

What is never very clear are the connections between the multiple plot lines that emerge in the book. *Blind Man with a Pistol* includes no fewer than seven separate incidents, only a few of which seem connected. The book opens on two white patrolmen entering a squalid, dilapidated house—their interest has been piqued by the appearance of a sign in one of the front windows reading "Fertile womens, lovin God, inquire within" (*BMP* 8)—to discover an old black man, Reverend Sam, who claims to be a Mormon minister; his eleven wives, who, dressed as nuns, support the household by soliciting charitable donations on the streets; an estimated 50 children, the combined offspring of Sam and his wives, the children all naked and about to eat lunch, a swill that they eat from troughs without benefit of utensils; and Bubber, an older son, the preparer of the swill, whose distinguishing characteristics include his large size, harelip, and mental deficiency. An investigation of the premise will discover the shallow graves of three women buried in the basement. While a large black man with a harelip will appear later in the narrative, he is better dressed and possesses a far higher IQ than Bubber seems to own. Aside from this one tenuous connection, Reverend Sam and family are never heard from again, with but one very minor exception, in the novel.[1]

The final incident, a blind man armed with a pistol shooting up a subway car, is equally disconnected from the story. He appears in the next to last chapter, a blind man who refuses to accept the fact that he is blind and who wants to conceal his blindness from everyone else; he is also a gambler who loses consistently at craps. Taking the subway home after yet another misadventure at the craps table, he takes exception both to the belligerence of a disgruntled black gardener and to being described as "an old man" by a black woman who seeks to defend him from the gardener's verbal tirade. He opens fire just as the train is approaching the 125th Street Station, the passengers fleeing in panic from the gunman. Outside the station, Grave Digger and Coffin Ed are shooting rats as they scamper away from a building being demolished, part of an urban redevelopment program. The immediate effect of such redevelopment is to displace the former residents of the building and to erect in its place a building that none of the former businesses or tenants will be able to afford, abetting, not disarming existing anger. The four white patrolmen watching Grave Digger and Coffin Ed shoot rats prove typically racist, sorry only that the two detectives aren't shooting "nigger" rats (*BMP* 189). The panic-stricken people emerging from the subway, shouting about a shooting, draw the white policemen. The blind man emerges from the subway, fires his final bullet, killing one of the white officers purely by chance, before being shot and killed by the other three. The rumor mill immediately transforms the event into another senseless killing of a black man by racist white cops, and a riot ensues. The absurdity of the situation is not lost on Grave Digger and Coffin Ed, who are completely powerless to prevent the riot.

Blind Man with a Pistol presents a puzzle, the pieces of which don't ultimately go together to form a coherent picture. Two murders occur early in the novel, one a homosexual white producer cruising the black gay bars, the other Doctor Mubuta, who has been engaged by an aging black racketeer, Mister Sam, to restore his potency so that he can marry his young white fiancé. Mister Sam is already married, and his current wife, along with his son and his white wife, the old man's lawyer (supposedly having an affair with the current wife), the old man's chauffer, the teenage fiancé and another young woman called "Sugartit," never otherwise identified, are all present. A young black man wearing a red fez, ostensibly a Black Muslim, is implicated in both killings, but who he is, how he connects, why a Black Muslim, a group opposed to homosexuality, even appears at a gay bar, are all questions that are never answered. And, curiously, the narrative description of Mubuta's killing doesn't square with the seemingly honest, eye-witness account Anny, Old Sam's daughter-in-law, gives to Grave Digger and Coffin Ed.

A number of possible leads, allusions, references appear, though none of them seemingly productive. Mubuta's magic elixir, composed of animal sex organs, recalls Frimbo's rite of the gonad in Fisher's *The Conjure-Man Dies*, as does the off-hand use of the name *Bubber* in both books. For Mubuta, the rejuvenating potion, gotten from African medicine men, is his proposed answer to the "Negro Problem": It will allow black men, simply put, to outlive white men (*BMP* 39). While it's impossible to tell if anyone is buying into this scheme, it develops a veneer of plausibility, at least at that moment: "Within the frame of reference—light, heat and Harlem—at some time during the recitation they had all passed the line of rational rejection. It wasn't hard. It wasn't any harder to believe in rejuvenation than to believe equality was coming" (*BMP* 43). Beyond this, other slant references to Himes's earlier books—the Sisters of Mercy scam in *For Love of Imabelle*; the reference to a young woman named Sugartit, the street name Coffin Ed's daughter is known by in *The Real Cool Killers*—also appear, but never in ways that prove terribly informative, any more than the odd coincidence in the novel of two large black men with harelips, or the fact that the two elderly men in this book, both seeking young wives, are both named *Sam*. The one actual lead—that a young man wearing a red fez was seen leaving a gay bar in the company of a white man; that a man matching this description is seen running down the street, holding a pair of grey trousers, just prior to the white man's appearance, pants-less, his throat slashed; that immediately after this, a man wearing a red fez intercepts Doctor Mubuta as he tries to escape the brawl that has broken out at the rejuvenation and stabs him to death—never goes anywhere.

The only possible thematic link that appears in the book is the reference to the "Negro Problem" and the riots and the political activities that surround it. Three different groups, each with its own solution, will march on Harlem, all three parades converging on the same intersection at the same time, resulting in a riot. These three groups include an integrated collection of young people supporting interracial brotherhood, inspired by the Christian Gospel's call to love all men, the plan of an earnest if not very bright young black man, recently out of the armed services, and his white Swedish companion; a Black Power contingent, organized by a mysterious Doctor Moore, clearly a fraud, whose Black Power rallies and the donations they generate are just one of his money-making enterprises; and a group, under the direction of "General" Ham, a black preacher with a harelip from The Temple of the Black Jesus. Ham rejects the white Jesus and his message of peace and love as a scam, his church's aim to force the black Jesus down the throats of the white man until he chokes. Having ordered his followers to organize their demonstration, Ham disappears in a lavender-colored Cadillac with gold trim in the company of a buxom white woman showing a great deal of cleavage. All three parades converge:

> It was all really funny, in a grotesque way. The lynched Black Jesus who looked like a runaway slave. The slick-looking young man with his foreign white woman, riding in a car built for war service, preaching brotherhood. And last, but not least, these big Black Power people, looking strong and dangerous as religious fanatics, making black thunder and preaching Black Power [*BMP* 101].

When the inevitable riot breaks out, Grave Digger and Coffin Ed find themselves in the middle of it and emerge badly beaten for their efforts. They have been forbidden by the high command to use their guns.

It is obvious that things in Harlem are changing and have changed and yet haven't changed at all. The landscape is clearly late 1960s with its earnest young people preaching love, the Black Power and Black Muslim movements providing a counterforce to white power and religion, the appearance of mixed-race couples and of openly gay men and women seemingly everywhere. Grave Digger and Coffin Ed have been ordered to holster their weapons and denied their usual heavy-handed methods of interrogation. When they beat the information they are looking for out of an uncooperative source, that source immediately disappears behind corporate lawyers alleging police brutality and civil rights violations, something that would have never happened in the early books. The landscape has changed, and yet, in many ways, things haven't changed at all, the violence and poverty, the pimping and prostitution, the predatory scams, the false prophets preying on people who will believe anything, the number runners/daily lotteries run by organized crime, who augment their activities with the sales of illegal drugs, as often now hallucinogens as heroin, all still the same. If anything, things have gotten worse, not better.

Blind Man with a Pistol is Chester Himes's *Waste Land*. The nightmarish vision is clearly akin to Eliot's, the disconnected pieces of this discontinuous narrative "fragments I have shored against my ruins" (*WL* 431), with Himes playing the same cards, a kind of structuralist poetics where characters all blend one into the other. In *The Waste Land*, as the note to line 218 makes clear, all of the characters in the poem coalesce in the blind seer, Tiresias:

> Tiresias, although a mere spectator and not indeed a "character" is yet the most important personage in the poem, uniting all the rest. Just as the one-eyed merchant, seller of currants, melts into the Phoenician Sailor, and the latter is not wholly distinct from Ferdinand Prince of Naples, so all the women are one woman, and the two sexes meet in Tiresias. What Tiresias *sees*, in fact, is the substance of the poem.

In this case, the "blind seer," like Tiresias, "an old man with wrinkled dugs" (*WL* 228), carries a pistol, and his aimless shooting in the end, all the product of a misunderstanding, becomes an image in one way or another of all the characters in the book. Harlem has always been "rats' alley Where the dead men lost their bones" (*WL* 115–16). At the book's end, Grave Digger and Coffin Ed are reduced to rat catchers, shooting rats as they scurry out of the ruins of Harlem, much as the Fisher King sits fishing at the end of *The Waste Land*, waiting for the rains that will revive the broken land.

In what seems a throw-away line, Captain Anderson advises Grave Digger not to play Theseus:

> "Woe is us," Grave Digger said. "Every time we brush a citizen gently with the tip of our knuckles, there's shysters on the sidelines to cry brutality, like a Greek chorus."
> Anderson bowed his head to hide a smile. "You shouldn't play Theseus."
> Grave Digger nodded in agreement, but Coffin Ed's thoughts were on other matters [*BMP* 109].

As with so much else in this book, the reference to Theseus is obscure. As a young man journeying to Athens, Theseus had defeated a series of notorious robbers, establishing his credentials. Thereafter, he had most famously freed a group of noble Athenian youths offered in tribute to Minos by negotiating the labyrinth and killing the Minotaur. Anderson's warning may suggest that Grave Digger will be unequal to the task of entering into the labyrinth of Harlem's underworld, defeating the monsters residing there, and then returning. Alternately, he could be thinking of *A Midsummer Night's Dream* and Theseus's ability to bring order out of a disordered night. Or the allusion might be to Chaucer, where Theseus, in *The Knight's Tale*, attempts to contain the destructive passions of the two kinsmen Palomon and Arcite and their fight over the fair Emily by declaring a tournament. His efforts to settle the dispute without loss of life, however, are frustrated by the intervention of an irascible Uranus. Coming at the beginning of *The Canterbury Tales*, the tale is set in a pre-Christian world overseen by the operations of Dame Fortune where the only certainty is that those who rise will fall. Even a hero of Theseus's stature will be unequal to the challenges of creating order in so disordered a world. The two detectives, no matter how heroic their efforts, will be overmatched here.

The ending of the book is ambiguous. The two detectives are left standing, their lives spared, which is not the case in *Plan B*. But they also no longer have a viable role to play in this world. Times have changed, as Digger remarks to Ed in the closing pages of the book:

> Hell, Ed, you got to realize that times have changed since we were sprites. These youngsters were born just after we'd got through fighting a war to wipe out racism and make the world safe for the four freedoms. And you and me were born just after our pappies had got through fighting a war to make the world safe for democracy. But the difference is that by the time we'd fought in a jim-crow army to whip the Nazis and had come home to our native racism, we didn't believe any of that shit. We knew better. We had grown up in the Depression and fought under hypocrites against hypocrites and we'd learned by then that whitey is a liar. Maybe our parents were just like our children and believed their lies but we learned the only difference between the homegrown racist and the foreign racist was who had the nigger. Our side won so our white rulers were able to keep their niggers so they could yap to their heart's content about how they were going to give us equality as soon as we were ready [*BMP* 170].

While African Americans of their generation never believed these lies, the younger generation does, and "that's how we get riots," Grave Digger concludes.

Though it is something of a cliché, it is tempting to cite Yeats's lines from "The Second Coming," that "things fall apart" loosing "mere anarchy" on the world (3), or Eliot's lines from "Journey of the Magi," the sense of being "no longer at ease here, in the old dispensation" (41), much as Chinua Achebe did in titling his first two novels. But implicit in Yeats is the sense that things once added up and in Eliot that we have somehow seen the light, neither of which seems appropriate. Arnold, perhaps, seems more appropriate if no less of a cliché, that at the end of *Blind Man with a Pistol*, we are left "wandering between two worlds, one dead, The other powerless to be born" ("Stanzas from the Grande Chartreuse," 85–86). In that sense, *Blind Man with a Pistol* and *Plan B* both end on the same note. We can't go back, but we have no means of moving forward.

5

Entr'Acte
A Postmodernist Interlude

Prologue

Ishmael Reed's foray into detective fiction in his 1972 *Mumbo Jumbo*, his third novel, is remarkable in several ways. It is remarkable for the critical attention it has garnered, featured prominently, among other places, as one of Henry Louis Gates, Jr.'s, paradigmatic texts in *The Signifying Monkey: A Theory of African-American Literary Criticism*. First published in 1988, *The Signifying Monkey* is still, after more than a quarter century, the foundation text for African American literary criticism. *Mumbo Jumbo*, as a self-conscious postmodernist take on detective fiction, is clearly Signifyin(g) on generic constructions and the traditions of black letters. Even before its appearance in Gates's work, however, *Mumbo Jumbo*'s explication had occasioned an almost Joycean effort by exegetes intent on unraveling the allegories and allusions swirling through the text. At this point, those broad outlines are clearly enough established, the Harlem Renaissance setting of the novel linking to the Black Arts Movement of the '60s, the Atonist Path an expression of Western, imperialist, monotheistic Judeo-Christian, capitalist, soul-destroying repression seeking to eradicate the African, life-affirming, polytheistic exuberance that is Jes Grew. So much is obvious, or at least becomes so, by the end of the book, in the long scene of revelation where PaPa LaBas recounts the history of the struggle between the forces of Set and followers of Osiris, the Knights' Templar involvement in the action, and the responsibility of Hinkle Von Vampton and Hubert "Safecracker" Gould, founding members of the Knights Templar, for the recent murder of Abdul Sufi Hamid. Then again, much of the work is not exactly subtle; the subplot involving the *Mu'tafikah* (a group whose name derives from the Koran but which sounds suspiciously like "motherfucker") and their attempt to repatriate native works of art being held at the Center of Art Detention, now under the direction of

Biff Musclewhite, former chief of police, is a case in point. The regular substitution of *k* for *c* in words like *Amerika* and *Mumbo Jumbo Kathedral*, reaching as far back, perhaps, as Kafka's *Amerika*, was popular among '60s counterculture radicals critical of the fascist state, of the United States' imperialist activities in Southeast Asia, of the military-industrial complex that is America. Much of Reed's portrait of power structures and conspiracies is painted in broad brushstrokes, indeed.

Mumbo Jumbo is also remarkable, however, for the way it not only recapitulates and Signifies on both hardboiled conventions and earlier works of African American detective fiction, Rudolph Fisher and Chester Himes most specifically, but how it also anticipates in basic ways the historical perspective of Walter Mosley's Easy Rawlins series and the conspiracy theories, lost texts and alternate constructions of history that drive Stephen L. Carter's early novels. *Mumbo Jumbo*, published in 1972, is a historical novel, the primary action set in the 1920s, though with references to an earlier outbreak of Jes Grew in 1890s New Orleans; the book also includes an epilogue set sometime in the 1960s. Just as will be the case with the Easy Rawlins series, the periods chosen are important both in themselves and in their relationship to the present moment, the time of composition, each marking a period of promise and of acute anxiety, with *Plessy v. Ferguson* legalizing apartheid policies in the mid–1890s; with Woodrow Wilson's Jim Crow policies, with Ku Klux Klan recruiting activities throughout much of the country, including the Northeast, with lynchings across the South (as *Mumbo Jumbo* periodically reminds its readers), and with eugenics firmly established in textbooks, at state fair Fitter Families contests and in legislation all hallmarks of the 1920s. In the case of the 1960s, the Civil Rights Movement follows the failure of the *Brown v. Board* decision to spur school integration. Time is a particularly fluid business in *Mumbo Jumbo*, as disruptions in the narrative and as frequent anachronisms both in the narrative itself and in the non-narrative materials in the text—the photographs, quotations, citations—all attest. *Mumbo Jumbo* shares the surrealism and cinematic qualities of Himes's novels, while winking at Fisher in an off-hand reference to Frimbo's Funeral Home" (*MJ* 75) above which Woodrow Wilson Jefferson initially rents a room. At the same time its sense of Western culture as conspiracy, of postmodern paranoia, of texts, that if recovered and decoded, threaten to expose the whole affair, set the scene for Carter's *Emperor of Ocean Park*, *New England White*, and *Palace Council*.

As a work that Signifies on earlier texts and traditions, Gates argues that reference in *Mumbo Jumbo* is always doubled, a point which proves to be particularly true of its use of historical settings. Gates writes:

In *Mumbo Jumbo*, form and content, theme and structure, all are ordered upon this figure of the double; doubling is Reed's "figure in the carpet." The form the narration takes in *Mumbo Jumbo* replicates the tension of the two stories which grounds the form of the detective novel, defined by Tzvetan Todorov as "the missing story of the crime, and the presented story of the investigation, the role [sic: real?] justification of which is to make us discover the first story" [Gates 227].

While Reed's double might better be read as multivalent, supporting multiple references, or even perhaps as duplicity, a double agent whose very use of the conspiracy-theory form only serves to reify forces the novel clearly seeks on the surface to disrupt, a point that Andrew Strombeck, for instance, argues with regard to the sexist nature of Reed's work,[1] the reference to Todorov is telling. While somewhat reductive, perhaps, "the missing story of the crime," the already enacted insult in detective fiction by African American authors, invariably tracks to the historical repression of African peoples by Europeans and Euro-Americans, to the violence and brutality of the slave trade, to the institutionalized racism that runs through the history of the United States.

What is also remarkable is that given the still relatively active critical industry *Mumbo Jumbo* supports, PaPa LaBas's return in *The Last Days of Louisiana Red* has attracted relatively little notice. The *Modern Language Association's International Bibliography*, for instance, only catalogues a small handful of papers devoted to the book. *Louisiana Red* places PaPa LaBas in 1960s Berkeley and expands on some of the themes central to *Mumbo Jumbo*, but in a somewhat more conventional novelistic form than Reed employed in *Mumbo Jumbo*. Lacking the formal innovations of the earlier novel, *Louisiana Red* has generated little critical interest, which seems at least a little curious, given the attention *Mumbo Jumbo* has received. Reed's masculinist revision of the Antigone story may be part of the problem here.

Counterpoint

Reading *Mumbo Jumbo* has always posed something of a problem, particularly with regard to figuring out the relationship between the various textual elements of which the book is composed. Texts and their interpretation clearly stand at the center of the mystery as Gates argues in the chapter he devotes to *Mumbo Jumbo* in *The Signifying Monkey*. Reed's PaPa LaBas descends from the Esu-Elegbara line of tricksters that, as Gates points out, emerges as "Papa Legba (prounced La-Bas) in the pantheon of the loa of Vaudou of Haiti, and Papa LaBas in the loa of Hoodoo in the United States" (5).

5. Entr'Acte

Legba is "the divine reader, whose interpretations of the Book of Fate determines our understanding of the text" (Gates 24). According to Fon mythology, Legba "possesses all of the writing of each day" (Herskovits, qtd. in Gates 27) and is sent by Mawu, the author of man, "to bring each individual his Fa [fate], for it is necessary that a man should know the writing which Mawu has used to create him" (qtd. in Gates 27). Legba is the intermediary who must be worshipped if a man is to know "the writing that is his destiny," for "every man has a god whom he must worship, but that without his Fa he can never know his god" (qtd. in Gates 27–28). Coming to know the language from which we have been created, the god revealed therein, and the fate we face is the action of the book. As Gates puts it,

> Reed's third novel, *Mumbo Jumbo*, is a novel about writing itself—not only in the figurative sense of the postmodern, self-reflexive text but also in a literal sense: "So Jes Grew is seeking its words. Its text. For what good is a liturgy without a text?" *Mumbo Jumbo* is both a book about texts and a book of texts, a complex narrative composed of subtexts, pretexts, posttexts, and narratives-within-narratives. It is both a definition of Afro-American culture and its deflation. "The Big Lie concerning Afro-American culture," *Mumbo Jumbo*'s dust jacket states, "is that it lacks a tradition." The "Big Truth" of the novel, on the other hand, is that this very tradition is as rife with hardened convention and presuppositions as is the rest of Western tradition [220].

This dual movement in the text seems to emerge in the opening pages, a prologue to the novel that precedes the title page. In the space of five pages, the text moves from (1) a third-person narrative, the scene briefly sketched in the first paragraph and the action then handled largely through dialogue, detailing an outbreak of Jes Grew in New Orleans, to (2) a passage, printed in italics, describing the Wallflower Order's inability to curtail the Jes Grew outbreak of the 1890s which, failing to find its text, died out, to (3) an unidentified photograph of men, circa 1920s, dressed in white shirts, dark vests, plaid pants, hats (a jazz band uniform?), the group predominantly though not exclusively black, with Louis Armstrong and an unidentified white man, his back to the camera, visible at the left, to (4) a quote from Louis Armstrong describing the origin of "the second line," those people who spontaneously join the procession of mourners at New Orleans jazz funerals, to (5) an etymology of *Mumbo Jumbo* attributed to *The American Heritage Dictionary of the English Language* (*MJ* 3–7). The opening narrative is marked by several stylistic peculiarities, primarily the absence of quotation marks and tags distinguishing quoted speech from description, the general tendency to omit commas dividing items in a list, and the use of number forms where word forms would typically be used, e.g., "1 man approached the Mayor who is walking from bed to bed" (*MJ* 4). In "Literary Free Jazz? *Mumbo Jumbo* and

Paradise: Language and Meaning," Karen Omry describes these five sections as discrete narrative modes, functioning in ways that are analogous to modal music where "each part relates to the other, but [where] there is no overarching defining relation between the parts; as each moment passes, this relationship changes" (133). These pieces, which on first reading make up a seemingly random assemblage, will begin to cohere as the story progresses. The spontaneous outbreak of Jes Grew, manifest in the spirit of jazz and the Jazz Age but threatening, so some people would have it, "civilization as we know it" (*MJ* 4), connects the opening narrative with Armstrong, both photograph and quote, while the Wallflower Order emerges as the guardians of white Western civilization, "civilization as we know it," figures of repression who, incapable of dancing themselves, seek to prevent everyone else from joining the dance. What may initially seem to be nonsense, "mumbo jumbo," turns out to make sense, defining a field of forces in which these various pieces are suspended.

At this level, the intermixture of incompatible materials and narrative modes and the stylistic peculiarities of the text read as self-reflexive, postmodernist strategies allowing us to look at and not simply through the language. Omry suggests, even further, that the intentionally uncaptioned photograph provides an alternate way of knowing, mute testimony that "add[s] the literally unspeakable dimension of narration into [Reed's] story, a story of African American history that is both literally and figuratively unspeakable" (133). But, as Gates suggests, such elements seem to do more than function as postmodernist devices meant to call attention to the ways language both structures perception and ways of knowing, the conventional wisdom where the conventions of representation often prove less than wise.

The opening narrative reads like classic pulp fiction, or B-movie script, perhaps, though with something of a difference. A case in point is the description of Zuzu, the Mayor's female companion, "sprawled upon his knees" (*MJ* 3), as the story opens:

> A True Sport, the Mayor of New Orleans, spiffy in his patent-leather brown and white shoes, his plaid suit, the Rudolph Valentino parted-down-the-middle hair style, sits in his office. Sprawled upon his knees is Zuzu, local doo-wack-a-doo and voo-do-dee-odo fizgig. A slatternly floozy, her green, sequined dress quivers.
> Work has kept Your Honor late.
> The Mayor passes the flask of bootlegged gin to Zuzu. She takes a sip and continues to spread sprawl and behave skittishly. Loose. She is inhaling from a Chesterfield cigarette in a shameless brazen fashion.
> The telephone rings.
> The Mayor removes his hand and picks up the receiver; he recognizes the voice of his poker partner on the phone.

Harry, you'd better get down here quick. What was once dormant is now a Creeping Thing.

The Mayor stands up and Zuzu lands on the floor. Her posture reveals a small flask in her garter belt as well as some healthily endowed gams [*MJ* 3].

Slatternly floozy, healthily endowed gams, inhaling cigarette smoke in *a shameless brazen fashion* all emanate from hardboiled traditions of description, both the terms themselves and their sexist attitudes, with *fizzgig,* "a frivolous, giddy, restless woman or girl" (from ME *gigge,* girl; see GIGGLE) ("fizgig"), joining the fun. The scatted *doo-wack-a-doo* and *voo-do-dee-odo* provide a jazz-age vibe clearly suggestive, if somewhat short on specifics. *Doo wacka doo* is the title of a Will Donaldson song recorded in 1924 by the Paul Whiteman Orchestra, the title an onomatopoeic representation, so the lyrics tell us, of the cornet's waa-waa sound that drives women wild ("Doo wacka doo"). The *voo-do-dee-odo*" is less direct, similar, in general, to Betty Boop's "boop-oop-a-doop," though with a New Orleans twist. The entire passage is redolent of the 1920s and 1930s, compounded of equal parts of ragtime and hardboiled pulp-fiction. That "Doo wacka doo" was recorded by the Paul *Whiteman* Orchestra seems at least mildly ironic.

These are the most obvious effects. Other stylistic effects—the suppression of conventional punctuation in places, the peculiarities of syntax, the tendency to run near synonyms and/or nouns in apposition together into phrases, and the use of number forms instead of word forms—may not be so obvious. In the passage quoted above, Zuzu "continues to spread sprawl and behave skittishly"; she inhales cigarette smoke in a "shameless brazen" fashion. *Spread* and *sprawl* in the first case and *shameless* and *brazen* in the second say much the same thing. In discussing the Jes Grew outbreak, the doctor describes the disease's curious etiology:

> You see, it's not 1 of those germs that break bleed suck gnaw or devour. It's nothing we can bring into focus or categorize; once we call it 1 thing it forms into something else. No man. This is a *psychic epidemic* not a lesser germ like typhoid yellow fever or syphilis. We can handle those. This belongs under some ancient Demonic Theory of Disease [*MJ* 4–5; emphasis in the original].

The succession of verbs—"break bleed suck gnaw or devour"—or possible analogues—"typhoid yellow fever or syphilis"—run together. In this case, the substitution of *1* for *one* suggests one possible reading. The unconventional usage draws attention to the conventionality of the construction, disrupting readers' expectations, at least on one level. On another, the use of number rather than word forms suggests a level of statistical rigor, of accountability, of an exactness of denotation missing in words. And, as the novel progresses, we will also learn that *1* is a symbol of the Atonist Path (*MJ* 65), of their monotheistic, totalizing, repressive attempts to impose their unified will, their sense of civilization, on those who would follow Osiris. Language here is part of the problem, a means by which discipline is enforced, an expression of the Atonist agenda. Removing commas between items in a list turns multiple entities into a singular quantity, just as the removal of quotation marks distinguishing one speaker from another and those speakers from the narrative voice allows them to collapse together. The attraction is gravitational, a black hole exerting a powerful force that seeks to reduce all matter to a mathematical singularity. Hence the problem that Jes Grew confronts: "*So Jes Grew is seeking its words. Its text. For what good is a liturgy without a text? In the 1890s the text was not available and Jes Grew was out there all alone. Perhaps the 1920s will also be a false alarm and Jes Grew will evaporate as quickly as it appeared again broken-hearted and double-crossed (++)*" (*MJ* 6). The liturgy provides a form or public ritual, or perhaps a formula (its own math?), but one that lacks a language capable of expressing its belief system. The parenthetical double crosses, in general, seem to underscore the problem of symbolic expression, of the need to find a new language, a new means of conceptualizing experience, not an incremental addition to an existing language but a paradigm shift that will reconstruct reality in a revolutionary way.

These stylistic effects at this stage of the book are still not uniformly deployed. The Mayor questions the doctor, asking him for the results of his preliminary examinations of the victims and the ways the disease manifested itself in them:

> What *did* he see?
> He said he saw Nkulu Kulu of the Zulu, a locomotive with a red green and black python in its face, Johnny Canoeing up the tracks.
> Well Clem, how about his feelings? How did he feel?
> He said he felt like the gut heart and lungs of Africa's interior. He said he felt like the Kongo: "Land of the Panther." He said he felt like "deserting the master," as the Kongo is "prone to do." He said he felt like he could dance on a dime.
> Well, his hearing, Clem. His hearing.
> He said he was hearing shank bones, jew's harps, bagpipes, flutes, conch horns, drums, banjos, kazoos.
> Go on go on and then what did he say?
> He started to speak in tongues... [*MJ* 5; emphasis in the original].

Quotation marks appear in the doctor's recitation of the patient's visions, and commas likewise still appear in the list of auditory hallucinations, of the different instruments he hears. The manifestations are all "ethnic" expressions, folk forms. Even some of the more obscure allusions seem to parse. *Nkulu Kulu*, for instance, seems very close to *Nkulunkulu*, "great one" or "supreme being" ("Nkulunkulu"); "Johnny Canoing" seems to be the doctor's phonemic transcription of *Junkanoo*, a form of carnival with music, dancing and parades in the Bahamas and other Caribbean and Central American countries, a celebration dating back to slavery and possibly related to the Yoruba Egungun festivals; in fact, "John Canoe," the name given the male dancers in the festival, seems to be a corruption, via folk etymology, from *Junkanoo* ("Junkanoo"). Language, in general, seems unreliable and under Atonist control, though the usage is not fully consistent as natural language forms always admit variations. It is clear that the dominant dialect does not serve the interests and cannot express the mysteries of Jes Grew, as the patient's speaking in tongues suggests.

This section of the text, the narrative opening followed by the brief italicized description of the Wallflower Order's attempts to curtail Jes Grew, then gives way to the uncaptioned photograph described above, a visual image, a nonlinguistic means of signification, one that cannot be reduced to or co-opted by the dominant Atonist dialect. It simply is, a form of mute testimony, at least on one level, though serving rhetorical functions just as clearly on another level, the vantage point, framing, act of selection and arrangement of elements in the photograph arguing significance. Jazz, an idiomatic African American expression, and the suggestion of racial mixing that jazz fostered do, in this case, portend the beginning of the end of the segregated societies in the United States.

The intermixture of elements in the narrative seems more to underscore the problems than portend a solution to the larger issues of representation in the book. Omry, for instance, who argues that the intermixture of narrative forms in the novel is analogous to modal forms in music, sees something of a solution:

> The purpose of the modal narration is not to posit each mode in competition against the other. Rather, by including all forms of reality and of textuality, Reed stresses the impossibility of single meanings and invokes, instead, an acceptance of plurality with multiple interpretations co-existing simultaneously, or shifting, each one relevant for a different reader at a different time [134].

In fact, the photograph does seem, in some basic ways, to be in "competition" with the verbal text, to stand in mute witness to the text. The problem appears in the inability of parody to enact the paradigm shift we need, the parody playing inside of the pre-existing conceptual structures, not reimaging those structures. This is the problem that Strombeck, for instance, points to in "The Conspiracy of Masculinity in Ishmael Reed," that there is an inherent link, for instance, between the conspiracy-theory form and masculine desire: "The form itself reflects and reinforces masculine desire, a desire consistent with the historical origins of the secret-society conspiracy theory" (303). Citing Jameson's *The Political Unconscious*, Strombeck sees the attempt at appropriation to be the problem, "that [the appropriated] form cannot fully escape the moment of its production, because form maintains remnants of the struggles that raged around the moment"; hence, "The secret-society conspiracy theory, with origins in a white male sphere, maintains the structure that enabled it to function successfully as a white male form" (303). He compares the action here to Black Freemasonry, where the fact of freemasonry determines the possible forms of behavior, "no matter who is using it": "It is less *appropriated* for minority use then *inhabited* by minority subjects" (Strombeck 304; emphasis original to the text). As a result, Jes Grew will continue to look for its text, to search for words appropriate to its forms.

Time Signature

One of the immediate problems in following the action in the text is the intermixture of several different plot lines, all seeming to be happening simultaneously when, in fact, the events are at times being reported out of chronological order. This happens first in Chapter 9, where two otherwise unidentified men, a Wall Street broker and his friend, are killed when Beer Baron Schlitz's men hurl a bomb at Buddy Jackson and his date as they approach a bank at the corner of Broad and Market to deposit the previous night's cabaret receipts. Jackson, we have already learned in Chapter 7, has just wrested the Harlem protection trade away from Schlitz. The broker and friend are discussing a New York *Sun* article entitled "VooDoo General Surrounds Marines at Port-au-Prince" when they are killed (*MJ* 22–23). Twenty pages later, Schlitz, having dinner with Biff Musclewhite at the Plantation House where Charlotte, a French translator employed during the day at Mumbo Jumbo Kathedral, is appearing on stage, reports the attempted assassination of Jackson only to then be assassinated himself by two men posing as waiters in the restaurant (*MJ* 42–44). At this point, the narrative shifts back to PaPa LaBas, who had been introduced in the previous chapter, having attended the Chitterling Switch benefit with Earline, another young employee of Mumbo Jumbo Kathedral, where he engages in an extended conversation with Black Herman and Abdul Hamid. Now, one chapter later, he is answering a summons for allegedly allowing his dog "to soil the altar at St. Patrick's Cathedral" (*MJ* 46). We have no reason to believe that the Chitterling Switch benefit and the Plantation House dinner, reported in consecutive chapters, are not happening simultaneously, and that LaBas's court appearance does not then immediately follow the next morning. Nevertheless, LaBas emerges from court into the

5. Entr'Acte 113

commotion caused by Schlitz's bomb-throwing assault on Jackson (*MJ* 48). He returns to Mumbo Jumbo Kathedaral, where Charlotte tenders her resignation, having been offered the starring role in *Charlotte's Pick* at the Plantation House (*MJ* 51). In the following chapter, we follow Earline home from work, where she picks up a copy of the New York *Sun*, featuring an article about VooDoo generals and marines (*MJ* 53). The assault on Jackson (Chapter 9) actually occurs off-stage while LaBas is in court, and the Plantation House dinner, reported prior to that court appearance, doesn't occur until after Chapter 13, when Earline returns to her apartment at the end of the day. While the order of events can be worked out, the natural order of events cannot easily be accomplished by rearranging chapters, given the ways these materials are otherwise woven together.

A second instance of achronicity occurs in the early stages of the Hinckle Von Vampton narrative Hinkle Von Vampton is introduced in Chapter 14, immediately following the scene in Earline's apartment. His landlady observes him "1 night" dressed "like 1 of them knight fellers ... kissing some ugly nigger doll" (*MJ* 55). Amused by the spectacle, she invites her Mah-Jongg club to come witness these rituals (*MJ* 56). We are told both that Hinkle's apartment has been ransacked and that his work writing headlines at the New York *Sun* has begun to slip; his slip at work, the ransacking of his apartment, and the Mah-Jongg club's visit all occur in the same day. Chapters 15 and 16 then reveal that Von Vampton had written the VooDoo Generals headline and placed it in the newspaper while the managing editor was otherwise engaged in meetings. Summarily fired from his post, Von Vampton emerges from the building to find the newsboys hawking copies of the paper. "That night" he attends a lecture at the Knights Templar building and then returns to his apartment, where his landlady observes him praying to "the little black doll with the black curly hair" (*MJ* 61). The following morning he is kidnapped by agents of the Wallflower Order. The events of Chapters 15 and 16 again refer to material first reported in Chapter 9 and which precede the events recounted in Chapter 13, assuming, that is, that the New York *Sun* is a daily paper.

In general, time seems a somewhat fluid business in *Mumbo Jumbo*, with its intermixture of elements, often anachronistic, such as the chart showing the tonnage of bombs dropped in World War II, the Korean Conflict, and the war in Vietnam (*MJ* 163) that appears without warning in the midst of the long revelation scene at the Irvington-on-Hudson estate where LaBas relates the Osiris-Set conflict and the ways it has shaped history, or the references to the materials from which the Wallflower Order's headquarters has been built—"polyurethane, Polystyrene, Lucite, Plexiglas, acrylate, Mylar, Teflon, phenolic, polycarbonate" (*MJ* 62)[2]—and the use of television, "a new invention" (*MJ* 63) to monitor Jes Grew activity throughout the country. And, of course, Hinkle Von Vampton and Herbert "Safecracker" Gould, founding members of the Knights Templar, are centuries old.

The question here is clearly one of effect, of why events are given out of order, the different time lines out of sync, or why, in a story set in 1920, anachronistic elements like those described above intrude. That Von Vampton and "Safecracker" Gould are centuries old seems less out of keeping with the cartoonish, postmodern character of the book, somehow easy enough to accept, their presence an indicator of the history of oppression at the center of Western civilization, than the use of Lucite, Teflon, and Mylar in the construction of the Wallflower Order's headquarters or the insertion of statistics of bombs dropped in World War II, the Korean War, and the war in Indochina into LaBas's lecture on the history of the world. Moreover, the movement backward and forward in time, what might be construed as flashforwards and flashbacks had they been appropriately announced as such, disrupt the linear narrative, fracturing, as do these other anachronisms, the space-time continuum.

Time in detective fiction typically plays out in several ways, most typically showing how present circumstances are a result of past actions, demonstrating the on-going presence of the past in the lives of the characters. This movement is both a product of the dual narratives Todorov identifies in detective fiction, the untold story of the crime committed in the past setting the narrative of the present investigation, the story being told, in motion, and of the ways history, the construction of an alternate history, or the search for a usable history functions in detective fiction written by ethnic minority authors. *Mumbo Jumbo*'s Osiris-Set, Knights Templar-Jes Grew histories, in the ways they exaggerate such elements, seem to Signify on the tradition, just as the long speech LaBas delivers at the Irvington-on-Hudson estate parodies the scenes in Golden Age mysteries where Miss Marple or Hercule Poirot bring everyone together in the parlor to reveal the guilty party. The inclusion of period specific references—James Weldon Johnson and his active protest against the United States' invasion of Haiti, for instance, one of many episodes generally glossed over in American history—fulfills that general function.

The fragmentation of the narrative and the collapsing of future into present events, however, seem to move beyond these more conventional concerns. Approximately half-way through "Forms of Time and of the Chronotope in the Novel," Bakhtin inserts a discussion of "the problem of historical inversion and the folkloric chronotope," which suggests a possible approach to reading the temporal disruptions in *Mumbo Jumbo*. Having discussed the representation of adventure time in the Greek novel and the variations in the adventure novel of everyday life, Bakhtin writes that, "We have already seen that in any temporal representation some minimum sense of time's fullness is inevitable (and literature's primary mode of representation *is* temporal)" (146; emphasis original to the text). The present moment of the story must always inhere at least in minimal ways in past and future, creating a sense of the fullness of time:

> Where there is no passage of time there is also no *moment* of time, in the full and most essential meaning of the word. If taken outside its relationship to past and future, the present loses its integrity, breaks down into isolated phenomena and objects, making of them a mere abstract conglomeration [Bakhtin 146; emphasis original to the text].

While the long final scenes attempt to draw everything into temporal relationship, the intermixture of materials, often anachronistic in nature, through much of the book seems to fragment the text, producing in places a "mere abstract conglomeration" of isolated phenomena and objects.

In the ancient novel, Bakhtin notes, the "uncovering of social contradictions" led to "feeble first efforts at *new* forms for expressing time's fullness" (146–47; emphasis original to the text). While these early attempts were too weak to have much impact on the course of novelistic fiction, they did develop one distinctive feature, "historical inversion":

> This distinctive feature manifests itself predominantly in what might be called a *historical inversion*. The essence of this inversion is found in the fact that mythological and artistic thinking locates such categories as purpose, ideal, justice, perfection, the harmonious condition of man and society and the like in the *past*. Myths about paradise, a Golden Age, a heroic age, an ancient truth, as well as later concepts of a "state of nature," of natural and innate rights and so on, are all expressions of this historical inversion. To put it in somewhat simplified terms, we might say that a thing that could and in fact must only be realized exclusively in the *future* is here portrayed as something out of the *past*, a thing that is in no sense part of the past's reality, but a thing that is in its essence a purpose, an obligation [147; emphasis in the original].

Such seems to be the case with *Mumbo Jumbo*, a new form driven by the increasing recognition of social contradictions that leads to an act of historical inversion, positing a "thing that is in its essence a purpose, an obligation," all of those things Jes Grew symbolizes and which can only be realized in the future, here portrayed as something of the mythic past, the story of Osiris.

This historical dynamic seems potentially problematic. Bakhtin writes that the more the present and past are "enriched," the more "ephemeral" the future becomes

> deprived of that materiality and density, that real-life weightiness that is essential to the "is" and "was." The future is not homogeneous with the present and the

past, and no matter how much time it occupies it is denied a basic concreteness, it is somehow empty and fragmented—since everything affirmative, ideal, obligatory, desired has been shifted, via the inversion, into the past (or partly in the present) [147].

The effect, however, has a paradoxical effect, as "en route," Bakhtin continues, "it [the future] has become weightier, more authentic and persuasive. In order to endow any ideal with authenticity, one need only conceive of its once having existed in its 'natural state' in some Golden Age, or perhaps existing in the present but somewhere at the other end of the world ..." (148).

The present of the novel, 1920 New York, Jes Grew approaching, is bracketed by the 1890s Jes Grew outbreak in New Orleans and PaPa LaBas's annual lecture, set sometime in the 1960s, with which the book ends, past, present, and future—the fullness of time—all present. The Harlem Renaissance setting, in addition, doubles the Black Arts Movement, the present moment of composition reflected in the past. In effect, what is present in the novel and past in terms of composition has been "enriched," even to the point of investing 1920s New York with materials and technology still years in the future, all of these things seemingly in the grip of powerful gravitational forces, as are the otherwise disparate and often anachronistic elements of which the book is made. Again, the suggestion is of a black hole at the center of this universe, the pun seemingly intended, around which everything is centered, within which are mixed disparate materials all in the process of being amalgamated into a singularity, and from which nothing escapes, not even light. The reciprocal action Bakhtin describes fails here. The future, rendered increasingly ephemeral by the enrichment of the past, remains ephemeral, nebulous, an abstract possibility at best, no more persuasive than LaBas's annual lecture proves to be. Jes Grew will never find its text.

An Alternate History

One of the historical elements running through *Mumbo Jumbo* is the United States' occupation of Haiti from 1915 through 1934 and James Weldon Johnson's active campaign against it. Some details of American actions during the occupation are still not easy to come by. Searching for information on the Internet, for instance, yields somewhat contradictory results. A State Department website published by the Office of the Historian, for instance, records the failure of the Wilson Administration's efforts to force a new constitution through the Haitian legislature, one that would allow for foreign ownership of land. The website tells us that "the legislature was extremely reluctant to change the long-standing law and rejected the new constitution" ("U.S. Invasion and Occupation of Haiti, 1915–34"). By contrast, *About.com*'s Latin American History site, a reference site popular among undergraduates, reports that these efforts were successful: "A new Constitution, prepared in the United States, was pushed through a reluctant Congress: according to a debated report, the author of the document was none other than a young Assistant Secretary of the Navy named Franklin Delano Roosevelt" (Minster). The author, Christopher Minster, cites Hubert Herring's 1962 *A History of Latin America from the Beginnings to the Present* as the general source of his information. The history of U.S. occupation of Haiti is neither well known nor, at least according to accounts on popular websites, consistently represented.

With regard to the adoption of a new constitution, James Weldon Johnson provides some clarity. In the first of a series of articles published in *The Nation* in August and September 1920, Johnson reports that the Haitian assembly refused to approve the new constitution, at least in part because it would allow aliens to own property in Haiti. Johnson writes that "Haiti had long considered the denial of this right to aliens as her main bulwark against overwhelming economic exploitation; and it must be admitted that she had better reasons than the several states of the United States that have similar provisions" ("Self-determining Haiti: I. The American Occupation"). Thereafter, the legislature was dissolved and the proposed constitution approved by a plebiscite in "a flagrantly unconstitutional method" (Johnson, "Self-determining Haiti: I"). In this case, neither the State Department nor *About.com*'s Minster provides a fully accurate portrayal of events. Johnson concludes, "All of this has been done in the name of the Government of the United States, however, without any act of Congress and without any knowledge of the American people" ("Self-determining Haiti: I").

Press accounts of the American occupation of Haiti, as *Mumbo Jumbo* suggests, were strictly controlled. Haitian newspapers were forbidden from publishing anything critical of the occupation, while in the United States, "nothing that might reflect upon the Occupation administration in Haiti is allowed to reach the newspapers of the United States" (Johnson, "Self-determining Haiti: I"). In Part II of the series, "What the United States Has Accomplished," Johnson details both the very few improvements the occupation has fostered and the brutality of the U.S. Marines in policing the country, including the "slaughter of three thousand and practically unarmed Haitians," the enslaving of Haitian men under an obsolete *corvee* that obligated local men to contribute to the upkeep of public roads, the rape of Haitian women, the general contempt of the (white) marines for the (black) Haitians. One officer told Johnson, "The trouble with this whole business is that some of these people with a little money and education think they are as good as we are." Johnson responds: "and this is the keynote of the attitude of every American to every Haitian. Americans have carried American hatred to Haiti. They have planted the feeling of caste and color prejudice where it never before existed" ("Self-determining Haiti: II").

Johnson was in Haiti to investigate conditions there on behalf of the NAACP, of which he was then secretary. While Reed does not include Johnson's articles in the partial bibliography of sources appended to the end of the novel, the articles Johnson published in *The Nation* provide a context for elements in the novel. The intervention in and economic exploitation of Haiti under Woodrow Wilson and after, little recognized at the time, so it seems, because of close control of the press, lend a plausibility to the Wallflower Order's Haitian activities. That the interventionist activities and actions in Haiti then reflect American activities in Southeast Asia, another instance of the doubling Gates notes as central to the text, is also clearly the case.

Karmel

The Last Days of Louisiana Red, Reed's follow-up to *Mumbo Jumbo*, features a scene in which the two Yellings brothers, Street and Wolf, shoot each other, or, to be more exact, a scene in which their sisters, Minnie and Sister, listening to the radio, hear a report of their brothers' deaths. After a first announcement of a gun battle at Berkeley Marina where "*two men apparently in a case of mistaken identity mortally wounded each other*" (*LDLR* 107; italics original to the text), a second report follows with more detail:

> Radio: *More details are coming in on the shoot-out which took place at the Berkeley Marina today. In what was apparently a case of mistaken identity in which each man got the wrong one, two brothers, the popular Street* (the sisters gasp) *Yellings, leader of the Moochers, and Wolf, his brother, Vice President of Solid Gumbo Works, shot it out, leaving each other dead.* (Sister screams, throwing a hand over her mouth) *The scene of the double murder is shrouded in heavy fog. Eyewitnesses claim that when the blaze of gunfire ceased, the two men could be seen in the death embrace* [*LDLR* 107–108; italics original to the text].

In the following chapter, PaPa LaBas's housekeeper comments on how nice the funeral was, as reported by "one of the sisters at the Pick 'n Pack" (*LDLR* 110), a funeral LaBas had provided. He responds:

> "I did what I had to do. I told Wolf to get rid of that pistol. He wouldn't listen. When he drew the pistol, that made the Argivians nervous. They ran, leaving Street behind. He was forced by his stupid machismo to stay there and pull his.

A real old west scenario. I once saw a photo of Shattuck Avenue made in the 1850s. It looked like a set in *Shane*" [*LDLR* 110].

The housekeeper comments on how bad the fog was that morning.

This passage seems significant in several ways: the prevailing fog, the seemingly anomalous detail, probably wrong, that the shooting involved a case of mistaken identity, and the fact that the actions being related, the brothers' gun battle and their subsequent funeral, are neither one directly described, the first coming by way of a radio news bulletin, the latter related second-hand from a convenience store conversation, a matter of hearsay. The action of the book, as becomes immediately apparent, is modeled on Sophocles's *Antigone*, with some significant revisions. Wolf and Street, caught in a power struggle, confront and kill each other, just as their archetypes, Eteocles and Polynices, do in the play. That LaBas, playing the part of Creon, arranges for the brothers' burial, is clearly a departure. He had done what he could do to prevent this armed confrontation from happening in the first place, and failing, now fulfills his responsibility to the family. LaBas had been dispatched following the death of Ed Yellings, the boys' father, to look into the operations of the Solid Gumbo Works and to root out the corporate spies, the conspiracy afoot that had led to Ed Yellings's murder. LeBas also clearly suspects that Street's move to take control of the Solid Gumbo Works is a product of that conspiracy, that he is being used as a tool to disrupt operations at the Works. Had LeBas been able to work out the mystery of Ed Yellings's death, none of this need have happened. In this case, the violence takes place off stage, as Marian E. Musgrave has pointed out, in accordance with the dictates of Greek drama (65).

That the events are not directly witnessed but reported by intermediaries, "mediated" by radio broadcast and public perception in the marketplace, suggests more than an allusion to dramatic principles. Reed is clearly considering the ways popular-culture constructs mediate experience. The shoot out is "a wild west scenario," something pictured in historic photographs and then reconstructed in classic Westerns, *Shane*, for example, as LaBas's comment points out. On another level, the action is viewed through the lens of Greek mythology, archetypal in character, the brothers' deaths preordained, a matter of fate. The short chapter following the announcement of the brothers' deaths and including the conversation between LaBas and his housekeeper cited above, in fact, opens with LaBas, dressed in his "work" clothes, the witch doctor's black blouse and black pants, a "jet equilateral cross"—the Watson cross—on a chain around his neck, reading a copy of *Fate* magazine by candlelight (*LDLR* 109). *Fate*, we are told, "was pretty good at predicting the future," having foretold Kennedy's assassination a month before it happened. *Fate*, however, is only "pretty good" at predicting the future, and while the brothers play out their assigned roles in the *Antigone*-inspired drama at the center of the action, LaBas's Creon is clearly out of character, at least when compared to Sophocles's version of the myth. In the fog of perception, several outlines emerge, structures drawn from the mass media that mediate and seem to make sense of experience.

At this level, the "mistaken identity" line seems like a puzzled crime reporter's attempt to make sense of one brother killing another where no clear motive appears. The whole thing seems to be a tragic accident, not unlike Oedipus's encounter with his biological father, another case of mistaken identity which proves, in fact, to be no accident in the end. But this sense of mistaken identity at another level speaks to more than a mistaken perception, raising questions of identity and perception *per se*. Street, most clearly, is a character out of early 1970s Blaxploitation films, *Super Fly*, perhaps, as his first appearance in the novel suggests. Having escaped from the United States, he is the guest of a corrupt African ruler, living in luxury, overseeing a twenty-four-hour-a-day orgy. Maxwell Kasavubu, dressed in safari outfit, appears, just as Street dismisses his followers to the projection room to screen a film about a "Black superhero named 'Dong' ... who has it out with the mob and stays up all night playing cards" (*LDLR* 77). In the following chapter, Street is described as "wrapping his superfly cape about his shoulders and making loud noises with his funkadelic boots" as he descends the steps from his throne (*LDLR* 79). He imagines himself speaking to crowds in Golden Gate Park, on stage, dressed "in his great maxi coat made of condor feathers and his hat," the liberator of his peoples: "Why, maybe he could save his peoples. That's it. He would be the Moses of his peoples" (*LDLR* 80–81). The image is Atonist, the condor an endangered species on the brink of extinction, the image of Moses leading an enslaved people out of Egypt fully exploded in *Mumbo Jumbo*; Street is in the sway of a Western death-dealing mythology. The image of Street as the hero in a Blaxploitation film is completed in the martial arts match between Street and Minnie's bodyguard, Reichsfuhrer, a lesbian feminazi dressed in a Wonder Woman costume and expert in "Karate Kung Fu Thai Boxing Tai Chi Chaun Akido Tae Kwon Do Judo Jiu Jitsu Samurai Sword and Kick Boxing" (*LDLR* 93). He, of course, not only counters her attack but penetrates her defenses, in every sense:

> He then slaps her against the cheek and lifts her up and then gently rests her on him in a fashion that his Dong shoots up all in her hot wet orifice and like a sneaky SAM missile starts probing for them secret dark places. She starts convulsing and trembling like a 3-point Richter-scale earthquake, her passion stemming from a deep fault in her soul [*LDLR* 94].

5. Entr'Acte 121

Insofar as Street buys into this mythology, the image of the Black action hero, of the hypersexualized Black man and of women appreciative of his attention, whether they admit it or not, he can only respond as he does when confronted by Wolf.

The whole scene is cartoonish, clichéd, and deeply distasteful, just as many found Blaxploitation films troubling, not so much empowering as their proponents argued, but as reinforcing stereotypes, another pop culture form built on exploitation. LaBas will be equally dismayed by his encounter with Blue Coal and the orgy he presides over when LaBas crosses over into the spirit world at the end of the book to petition for the return of Minnie's soul. LaBas is all about the Business, about serving the Loas, and finds the disorder, the "lack of adequate bookkeeping," and Blue Coal's crisis management approach regrettable; LaBas is composing a report to the Board of Directors expressing his concerns as he returns East from Berkeley (LDLR 176). Oddly, in some ways, LaBas has been turned into the image of the "bourgeois Black," as Musgrave points out in "Ishmael Reed's Black Oedipus Cycle" (64–65). The "bourgeois Black," "those who had somehow managed to get a tenuous foothold in the society and had therefore a vested interest in the status quo," were considered in some circles "to be the real enemies of black progress" (Musgrave 65).[3] Employed as a lecturer at the Ted Cunningham Institute, a Booker T. Washington-like institution, and offended by Blue Coal's person and his operation of the Business, LaBas proves to be somewhat stodgy. Musgrave notes the irony, that "we are both surprised and delighted by Reed's conception of a bourgeois witch doctor" (65). That Wolf and his father Ed before him are equally bourgeois, all about business, is also the case. They are as typecast as Street is. Defined by these roles, they identify with the roles they have been assigned to play and act according to type. The duel does grow out of a case of mistaken identity, though not, perhaps, as we might first imagine.

Reed's investigations of the stereotypical images of African Americans in the media extends to the appearances of Amos, Andy, and Kingfish in the story, Andy and Kingfish seemingly determined by the characters and roles they played in *Amos and Andy*, much like Rosencrantz and Guildenstern in Stoppard's *Rosencrantz and Guildenstern Are Dead* are determined by the limited roles they played in *Hamlet*. Amos, by contrast, is not. As a limousine driver for the Solid Gumbo Works, he has escaped the hand-to-mouth existence, the life on the streets into which Andy and Kingfish are seemingly trapped, a case of arrested development. They remain the down-on-their-luck, malaprop-spouting, scheming comic stereotypes of radio and television. They have become Moochers, the liberationist/anti-capitalist sect that Minnie heads up, which in their case, mostly gives them a license to steal. When Kingfish offers to buy the next pitcher of beer, Andy expresses surprise:

> *Brown*: Why, Fish, you told me you didn't have no money. Where'd you get the money?
> (Kingfish beckons Brown to lean over; he whispers)
> *Kingfish*: I collectivized d tip on the next table the people left for the bartender. How's you like that for Mooching? Pretty clever, don't you think? [*LDLR* 47].

Kingfish even offers to pick up some food: "I seez they handin out some delectable supplications too. You want some weenies, Bro Brown?" (*LDLR* 47). Some things never change. This chapter is written in the form of a screenplay. Reed both composes whole chapters in screenplay form, as in this case, or incorporates elements of the screenplay, parenthetical stage directions, for instance, into the narrative in other places. Like *Mumbo Jumbo*, *Louisiana Red* is a mixed media affair. In "Two Crowns of Thoth: A Study of Ishmael Reed's *The Last Days of Louisiana Red*," Lorenzo Thomas sees this intermixture of contemporary and historical narrative forms as significant, that "the technique shows that Reed is quite as aware of the past as he is of the present ... and his idea of the past is continuous and unbounded" (8; ellipses original to the text).

It is significant, then, that Kingfish and Andy, both broke and on the street, seeing how successful the robed Hare Krishna supplicants are in coaxing donations from passers-by, decide to enter the "Karmel" business. The two had fallen out at the end of the earlier scene, arguing over whether Street should replace Minnie as the leader of the Moochers. Encountering each other on the street, they make up, "forgive and forget" (*LDLR* 113). Kingfish responds:

> *Kingfish*: That's right, Brown, I'll forgive and I'll forget. (Andy scratches his head) You know, I been thinking, Brown, the future is ours and all, but I'm still broke. The landlady put me out today. Aw, what I gonna do? Holy Mackerel there.
> *Andy*: Yeah, Fish, I'm in the same boat that you am. Pretty soon it'll be winter and I'm really uptight for money.
> (A youth in saffron-colored robes and a shaved head walks by. Fish studies the man as he solicits them. They refuse. He smiles and walks on.)
> *Kingfish*: Hey, that gimme an idea. You know, I see them boys up there at Sather Gate, saying Karmels over and over again, and people be putting coin into their hats. (Strokes chin) You know, Andy, I think it's about time we went in the Karmel bizness [*LDLR* 113].

In due course, the two turn up at Sather Gate, dressed in pink robes and sandals, their heads shaved, Andy still, however, wearing his derby, shaking tambourines and chanting, "Karmels! Karmels!" (*LDLR* 117). When their scheme fails, they resort to burglary, breaking into Amos's house, where he confronts them and has them arrested. Amos has sold out, become "bushwa," no longer sympathetic to these oppressed peoples. In a parody of the "Free Bobby Seale" campaigns of the late '60s, Minnie and the Moochers will initiate a mail campaign to have these two "political prisoners" released from jail.

That Amos escapes from the stereotypical representation while Andy and Kingfish cannot does suggest that something more than fate or karma, past events, determine the future. The stories mostly track, but not perfectly. There always seems to be room for revision. In this case, Etiocles and Polynices still kill each other, though Creon himself sees to the burial of the brothers and then rescues Antigone from death rather than condemning her to death for violating his orders to leave Polynices unburied. The story could, perhaps, be tracking an earlier Egyptian version, or it might be playing against an alternate ending in the Greek tradition, but the influence of past events on present possibilities is open to interpretation. The use of astrology in the novel seems to reinforce this idea. Astrology seems significant, at some level. Berkeley is an Aries town (*LDLR* 5), Ed Yellings a Pisces (*LDLR* 10) as is Blue Coal (*LDLR* 176), and one of Ed's first assignments is to retrieve the papers of a dead New Orleans astrologer, Doc John, whose notes included an astrological theory of disease which Ed deciphered and which led to his success in formulating a cure for cancer (*LDLR* 164). The four Yellings children all seem to be astrological accidents, in a way, that Ed "didn't want children, but she [Ruby, his wife] was always miscalculating her 'phase of the moon'; she was always talking that way as if influenced by forces in the remote universe" (*LDLR* 11). In her case, the forces at work are more biological than occult. If Ed's passionate Pisces nature led him to fall in love with Ruby in the first place, he quickly fell prey to her sexual allure: "It was all passion and no intellect that made him take her home to his italianate cottage on Milvia and succumb to her clamping squeezing sensual techniques. Before he knew it he was in her vice" (*LDLR* 10). Astrology is both akin to hoodoo spiritualism, an affront to Western empirical science, and a '60s Age of Aquarius cliché. With regard to the mystery of Ed Yellings's murder and the subsequent havoc wreaked on the Yellings family, the explanation is perfectly prosaic. PaPa LaBas, largely after the fact, has worked out the details, that having found a cure for cancer, Ed was on the verge of developing a cure for heroin addiction, a cure which would have severely cut into the profits of the drug trade. Or, as Ms. Better Weathers sums it up in their conversation with Sister, "What he's saying ... is that your family was destroyed not by fate but by a conspiracy. Not *Que sera, sera*, whatever will be will be, but plain old niggers and white front men up to ugly" (*LDLR* 165).

Astrology, as such, seems more metaphoric than not, whereas the conspiracy is real. Louisiana Red is figured as a corporate structure, as organized crime, as animal instinct/appetite, a death-dealing Darwinian force, nature red in tooth and claw, powered by greed and self interest. In fact, biology is, curiously, a driving force in the book, especially the biology of sexual attraction as Ruby's power over Ed demonstrates. The book is insistently sexist in ways meant, it seems, to parody the radical, militant feminism at the time, though even this element proves troubling, for instance, the cartoonish lesbian feminazi Reichsfuhrer, dressed in her Wonder Woman costume, discovering the pleasures of (forced) heterosexual sex with a real man, thereby repairing a fault in her character. But what can be potentially excused as bad taste in passages like these becomes even more troubling when PaPa LaBas takes up the conspiracy angle, arguing first that women use their sexuality to manipulate men, and second that black women, in particular, irresistible to white men, have conspired with those same men to subjugate black men. The language is particularly outrageous. After telling Minnie that Moochism is just another name for the philosophy of slavery, he then turns to the ways she has used her sexuality as a means of enslaving men:

> "Have you ever heard the term 'pussy-whipped,' or 'pussy-chained'? These expressions may be crude, but they smack of the truth. A woman uses her cunt power to threaten and intimidate, even to blackmail—to cause brother to kill brother. We're still expected to pick up the bill and do the tipping, even though you say we're the same" [*LDLR* 126].

LaBas continues on, over Minnie's objections, adding in the "benefits" that accrue to black women in a world controlled by white men:

> "O, you're denying the very lucrative benefits that go along with being a black woman in a white man's country? One of our Business people, Zora Neale Hurston, had an informant in Georgia say, 'White men and black women are running this thing.'"
> "What lucrative benefits are you talking about—rape?"
> "You say it was all rape, huh?" LaBas turns from the window where he has been standing with his hands behind his back, gazing out over the bay towards Alcatraz. "A lot of you begged for him and fought over the trinkets he threw at you, nursed him and taught him how to fuck, loved the bastard children he gave you more than your own. You are defiling the truths of history when you deny this" [*LDLR* 127].

LaBas here indulges in the same prejudices that appear in standard histories, typical, for instance, of accounts of Thomas Jefferson's children with Sally Hemings. The interracial children, "illegitimate" children of an illicit union, are never accounted among the "real" children these white men and black women otherwise produced. Somehow these children are not the woman's "own," just as Jefferson's children with Sally Hemings never count as his. In some ways, LaBas seems unprepared to accept some aspects of the black woman-white man conspiracy that he is otherwise claiming to be real.

When LaBas first appears in the story, he is investigating the figure of Minnie the Moocher in the Cab Calloway song, a "special type of psychic crook" (*LDLR* 34), not the victim of history as the "liberal social-worker line" would have it, but "a dedicated agent of the sphinx's jinx, an acolyte of an ugly cause" (*LDLR* 35). We might be able to write this whole business off as "antediluvian bullshit," as Minnie puts it (*LDLR* 126), the sexism inherent in the hardboiled tradition emerging as a flaw even in the psychic detective, were it not then reinforced in LaBas's conversation with the messenger, "the messenger standing on the right-hand side of Osiris" (*LDLR* 135), who provides the back story of Doc John and the origins of Louisiana Red. Louisiana Red is the work of a beautiful woman, Marie, Doc John's Business rival, who has him killed and then uses her feminine wiles to escapes prosecution: "Well, Marie got her powerful connections to spring her, and nothing was ever made of it after that. Marie had too much power, and that was the end of the first attempt by a brother to run the 'Business' in America; it was mama before and it's been mama ever since" (*LDLR* 141). The dominance of black women who use their sexual powers to acquire their positions of privilege in (white) society not only goes unchallenged but, in fact, gets written into the alternate mythology that Reed develops in these books.

The general movement here again seems to confirm Strombeck's argument that the conspiracy-theory "generates masculinity wherever it lands" (303), or, perhaps, arguments like those Maureen T. Reddy advances in *Traces, Codes and Clues: Reading Race in Crime Fiction*, that in the hard-boiled mystery, a white, male, heterosexist perspective prevails, and that insofar as "the ideology and the fiction are inseparable" (35), there is no possible way "to read that fiction 'innocently'" (38). With regard to the prevailing sexism inherent in the genre, Reed seems, even in his post-modernist revisions of the form, to perpetuate rather than contest masculine values. In the end, LaBas himself proves to be susceptible to female charms, first conceding to Ms. Better Weather's request that he petition the Board of Directors to release Minnie's soul, and then, having accomplished that task, finding himself "stirred" by her embrace. Having been kicked out of the spirit world, literally, by Blue Coal,

> [Minnie] got up and started towards him. She was beautiful in the bright red light. The star music played in the background. You won't believe this but it was harp music, too. She moved as if on air, in slow motion. She headed straight towards LaBas and cuddled up to his chest. There was nothing underneath her

nightgown and the warm youthful flesh stirred the old man. "It was like a world of endless blackness."

"I know," LaBas said, putting his coat about her, She began to sob. LaBas had won her an out [*LDLR* 169].

We might read this moment "innocently" as suggesting a possibility of rapprochement between Creon/LaBas and Antigone/Minnie, of old animosities being put to rest, revising the Sophoclean drama. Given that Louisiana Red has not been fully defeated, as the novel's final chapter makes clear, on the other hand, we might be looking at business as usual:

> Had the presence of Solid Gumbo Works meant the complete end of Louisiana Red as Ed wanted? Never, thought LaBas, who subscribed to the viewpoint that man is a savage who does the best he can, and so there will always be Louisiana Red. No, Ed wouldn't go down as the man who ended Louisiana Red, but only one of many people who put it into its last days. But like the tough old swaggering pugnacious vitriolic cuss Louisiana Red was, it would linger on until it was put out of man's mind forever [*LDLR* 175].

Holding the thinly-clad Minnie against him, even LaBas is "stirred," a biological reflex, part of that savage nature over which man has no control. LaBas said earlier in his conversation with his housekeeper that he had done "what he had to do," perhaps, the best he could do under the circumstances. Clearly, in the end, there is only so much one man can do.

Going Up

There is something, in the end, not perfectly satisfying in Reed's work, the whole business seeming to fall prey, especially in its unabashed sexism, its white-man-black-woman conspiracy theories, to the same forces it seeks to satirize. After forty years, these books seem less interesting and potentially less powerful than when first published; if they retain the ability to shock, and parts of these books are truly shocking, it's the coarse, masculinist elements in the books that give pause, not their revolutionary engaging of literary and social conventions and historical constructions that may have seemed so remarkable at the time. By contrast, Colson Whitehead's *The Intuitionist*, published in 1999, is a far more engaging, more fully satisfying work on every level. Whitehead's book is clearly akin to Reed's in a number of ways, Signifyin(g) on and ultimately surpassing Reed's books.

The Intuitionist tells the wholly unlikely story of Lila Mae Watson, the first "colored" female Inspector of Elevators, one of only two African American inspectors in the department, working in a 1960ish, New York–like city.

5. Entr'Acte

She has come north to attend the Institute for Vertical Transport and then to find employment in this city of tall buildings. She is a devout Intuitionist, representing one side in the philosophically divided world of elevator inspection, a world still dominated by old-school Empiricists in spite of the fact that the Intuitionist inspectors' assessments prove to be ten percent more accurate than those produced by empirical methods. In the racial allegory of the novel, the elevator will provide a means for social uplift, with the Empiricists proving to be rational, scientific sorts acting on surface appearance, on "skin color," following established paradigms and protocols, whereas the Intuitionists commune with the elevator, in touch with the spirit of the machine, not, as it were, subject to superficial and/or stereotypical judgments. Intuitionism is the brain-child of James Fulton, whose visionary work, *Theoretical Elevators*, laid the foundation for their practice and which in its later volumes, the final notebooks left unpublished at his death, promised to unveil the "black box," the perfect elevator that will enable the second elevation. That James Fulton turns out to be a mixed-race man—"colored" in terms of the racial codes of the time—who is passing as white clearly informs the vision and colors the text, that is, if the reader knows where to look, his or her reading informed by the knowledge of Fulton's racial identity. By the end of the novel, Lila Mae will be in possession of Fulton's notebooks and his family secrets, poised to complete Volume 3 of *Theoretical Elevators* and, perhaps, to usher in the brave new world promised in his work. *Perhaps*, however, seems to be the operative word here, given the uncertainties that remain at the novel's end. If nothing else, the Intuitionist Lila Mae, now self-appointed literary executor to the Fulton estate, seems ironically linked through her surname to Dr. Watson, the physician chronicler of Sherlock Holmes's acts of observation and ratiocination, and perhaps to the wearers of the Watson Cross in Reed's *Last Days of Louisiana Red*, in both cases, something of a mixed blessing.

The mystery in this case arises when an elevator in the newly constructed and not yet opened municipal building, an elevator Lila Mae has just inspected and given a clean bill of health, goes into total freefall, an all but impossible, unimaginable failure. The elevator's failure is even more remarkable in that Lila Mae "is never wrong" (9), or at least has never been wrong before, and at least when we're talking about elevators. She suspects sabotage, that she has been set up, and that the whole business is politically motivated to ensure that the current Chair of the Elevator Guild and as such, by default, the director of the city's Department of Elevator Inspectors, is re-elected. Director Chancre, an Empiricist, is backed both by corporate forces and organized crime, the elevator mishap seemingly designed to embarrass his Intuitionist rival. She is equally sure that Pompey, the other African American inspector in the department, an obsequious, servile character, is the culprit. Lila Mae's suspicions, to all appearances, seem perfectly reasonable. In fact, they will prove to be wrong.

In "The Second Elevation of the Novel: Race, Form, and the Postrace Aesthetic in Contemporary Narration," Ramon Saldivar seems to have perfectly captured the qualities that differentiate and ultimately elevate Whitehead's book over earlier efforts, Reed's among them. Whitehead's work is "post-racial," part of a "post-postmodern, post–Civil Rights moment" (Saldivar 3). "Postrace" in this usage does not imply that we have moved beyond the racism inherent in American history and society, only beyond its most overt forms. In fact, the rise of so-called "genre fiction" among ethnic minority authors "represent[s] and mediate[s] the crisis of the contemporary" (Saldivar 3), a persistent register of these authors' anxiety over our inability to achieve a full sense of equity and social justice. The response of authors like Whitehead has been to develop a "postrace aesthetic," a form that "is in critical dialogue with the aesthetics of postmodernism," in general, and with ethnic literature in the United States, more specifically; that "draws on the history of genres and typically mixes generic forms"; that "is invested in speculative realism," what Saldivar defines as "a hybrid crossing of the fictional modes of the speculative genres, naturalism, social realism, surrealism, magic realism, 'dirty realism,' and metaphysical realism"; all of which results in an aesthetic that "explores the thematics of race in twenty-first-century American" (Saldivar 4–5). The resulting work, in all these ways, supports a "distancing reading," "the kind of critique that attempts to remain immune to the logical and rhetorical traps and dead ends that its own analysis reveals" (Saldivar 7). *The Intuitionist* proves to be paradigmatic in all of these ways, the novel's postmodern heritage clear, as is its relationship to earlier ethnic literature, at the same time that the book mixes narrative modes and genres in ways that allow it to move beyond the conceptual and aesthetic limits of its predecessors.

Most striking, for instance, is the way the novel mixes fictional forms. *The Intuitionist* is and is not, at least in any conventional sense, an historical novel. In its evocation of the past, it both situates the reader in a place that is fully recognizable, that has the solidity of historical artifact, but which is also utterly fantastic. The unnamed city of tall buildings and the elevators which made the vertical landscape possible is like New York but isn't New York, just as the action, marked by the beginnings of integration in a still overtly segregated world, suggests a late 1950s, early 1960s timeframe, though one that remains impossible to date precisely on the basis of internal evidence. The sense is cinematic, at once evocative of a specific time and place and yet recognizable as a fictional construct, a Hollywood fantasy of the past fully in keeping, for instance, with modern standards of hygiene. Elevator engineering is grounded historically in the technical achievements of Elisha Otis introduced at the 1853 Exhibition of the Industry of All Nations set in New York's Crystal Palace, a scene the novel describes. This much is historically accurate. On the other hand, Whitehead inserts a quote into this scene from a speech purportedly presented by "the Vice-President of the United States," a "man with the lungs of a bear" (80); given the racist attitudes still prevalent in the novel's present, the speech offers an ironic comment on the exhibition's promise to "soften, if not eradicate altogether, the prejudices and animosities which have so long retarded the happiness of all nations" (80). The scene is perfectly convincing, though on several accounts, utterly false. At the time of the exhibition, the United States was without a vice president, William R. King, Franklin Pierce's vice president, having died of tuberculosis on April 18, 1853, roughly six weeks after being inaugurated. And the speech itself is a mash-up of lines taken with only slight changes from *The Art Journal Illustrated Catalogue of the Great Exhibition of the Industry of All Nations* (1851) (the opening sentence of the purported speech) and from a speech Prince Albert delivered at the Lord Mayor's Banquet, London, 1849, which was then printed in *The Illustrated London News* on 11 October 1849 (Black et al. 859–861).[4] The subject of these lines is the 1851 London Exposition whose success inspired the 1853 New York event. The history imagined in the novel, if not made up out of whole cloth, is still very much a mixed bag, what more than one commentator on the novel has identified as Whitehead's "steampunk" aesthetic, a science fiction fantasy composed of repurposed elements of Victoriana. (Saldivar hedges, referring to "Whitehead's not-quite-steampunk, alternative history" [7].) In this case, the description seems apt.

Whitehead's mixing of genres in this case becomes a good example of what Saldivar terms "speculative realism," the "fantasy-based realism that undergirds the narrative of *The Intuitionist*" (12). *The Intuitionist* describes, Saldivar writes, "a parabasis of *constant* and *complete* rupture between delightfully comic psychic facades that bar the way to memories of a traumatic past and the equally persistent ironic impulses toward the utopian desires that remain impervious to the real" (12, emphasis original to the text). And it is this characteristic rhetorical stance that distinguishes the postrace novel, lifting it over the obstacles earlier postmodern treatments stumbled over:

> This double impulse toward and against history and utopia is what makes postrace fictions as transformative rather than merely different from previous kinds of ethnic literature even as they try to retain the force of the real in the object world. That is, in postrace fiction neither literary realism nor modernist estrangement nor postmodern play nor magical-realistic wonder can suffice as

formal stand-ins for the concrete *content* of justice [Saldivar 12, emphasis original to the text].

The double consciousness typical of African American literature, in general, and of detective fiction written by African American authors, specifically, is transformed and proves transformative in works like *The Intuitionist*.

In the novel itself, James Fulton seems to perfectly capture the movement from the postmodern to the post-postmodern, postrace moment that Saldivar describes. *Theoretical Elevators* and Intuitionism were, in the beginning, a joke, a joke perpetuated on the unsuspecting white world by the mixed-race, colored man passing as white. White people, in general, are Empiricists, "slaves to what they could see," as Mrs. Rogers, Fulton's colored housekeeper, puts it (239). "They looked at the skin of things," Lila Mae adds (239). Or, as the narrative says, channeling Lila Mae's thoughts, "White people's reality is built on what things appear to be—that's the business of Empiricism" (239). Intuitionism, as such, at least in the beginning, was a joke, a kind of postmodernist goof recognizing and then playing with the conventional constructions, revealing the conventionality of the construction. An early laudatory review, the first to refer to Fulton's philosophy as "Intuitionist," describes Fulton's work as "postrational," "innate," that Fulton, "the field's greatest visionary since Otis," represents "hope's last chance against modernity's relentless death march" (238). This first movement deconstructs modernist, materialist, Empiricist constructions, allowing a glimpse of the innate through the cracks in the façade, something not so much seen as intuited. Had Fulton ended here, satisfied with the joke, his work would be merely postmodern. That he moves beyond the joke makes his work post-postmodern. As Mrs. Rogers tells Lila Mae, "Yes, he was having a joke on them at first, but it wasn't a joke at the end. It became true" (236). Fulton moves from the postmodernist joke to speculative realism, to a kind of conceptual engineering, moving beyond the limits and capacities and tolerances of contemporary methods and materials, much as conceptual architects might do in designing a mile-high building, imagining a future possible if not yet achievable.

Moreover, passing represents a postmodernist condition, another kind of game, one that explores generic conventions of behavior. But again, Fulton at least seems to embody the potential to move beyond a postmodernist toying with conventional constructions to a postracial realization. He seems to exemplify Saldivar's four defining properties of the postrace aesthetic, a biracial man (mixing of genres) posing as white (in critical dialogue with postmodernism, in general, and the traditions of ethnic literature, specifically), invested in conceptual engineering (speculative realism), and all in ways that explore the thematics of race. Fulton has not escaped racism or racial constructions, but, unlike PaPa LaBas, he is fully capable of moving beyond the conceptual and aesthetic limits of his predecessors.

This larger pattern is repeated in minor moments in the novel, Whitehead Signifyin(g) on postmodernist themes. After the Mr. Gizzard and Hambone minstrel act at the Funicular Follies (154–56), a scene that reflects Reed's appropriation of *Amos and Andy* in *The Last Days of Louisiana Red*, Whitehead reverses the action. Where Kingfish "collectivized" the tip left on an adjoining table, Freeport, Lila Mae's one-night stand soon after her arrival in the city, carefully anchors his tip with a water glass, in spite of the fact that they are in the bar of the "famous and fabulous Chesterfield Hotel" (174):

> Freeport extracted a bill from his gold money clip and set her still half-full glass atop it. His eyes shifted about the room, searching for thieves. "You never know with white people around," he said, chuckling [178].

Shifted, a somewhat unusual word choice, shifts the suspicion from the always shifty and wholly stereotypical Kingfish—Reed's joke—to the middle-class colored man's distrust of white society—Whitehead's ironic reversal. And much the same thing happens again when Whitehead depicts Ben Urich, the reporter, pursuing his favorite pastime, coin flipping. Tom Stoppard had used coin flipping and the improbable run of heads in *Rosencrantz and Guildenstern Are Dead* to explore the arbitrary physics of on-stage realities. In Whitehead's book, physics reasserts itself: "Ben Urich on a Saturday night: ambling quickly down the street, a blur in his favorite powder blue seersucker. He's flipping a dime as he walks—heads, he always bets on heads and is correct about half the time" (69). Whitehead moves us beyond these postmodernist moments to the more fully imagined if no less speculative reality of *The Intuitionist* and all in ways that let the reader recognize even here the limits of the reality. Lila Mae discusses the weather, for instance, with Mr. Reed (the name cannot be wholly accidental), after being offered safe haven at Intuitionist House: "He [Mr. Reed] looks up at the sky for a long moment. 'It looks like it's going to rain, but it's not. Not today'" (64), spoken like a true Intuitionist. The narrative, again channeling Lila Mae's reaction, two short paragraphs later, responds: "This slow debate about the rain: it's not about the rain at all, but the fragility of what we know. We're all just guessing" (64). As it happens, the story returns ten pages later to Lila Mae sitting in the garden: "A slow hour passed, distracted by intermittent drops of moisture from above, as if the sky were conducting a feasibility study on the implications of rain. Of committing to a course of action. Lila Mae left the garden and resumed her scheming in her room" (77). Forecasting the weather is an empirical science yielding an educated guess, playing the probabilities, that seems to be right about half of the time.

The uncertainties here seem to speak to the "persistent ironic impulses toward the utopian desires that remain impervious to the real," as Saldivar puts it (12). Lila Mae proves to be one such persistent ironic impulse. We are told early in the novel that Lila Mae "is never wrong" (9), except, of course, when she is, which proves to be the case consistently through the novel, the fall of the Fanny Briggs elevator only one instance when her intuitions prove to be mistaken. She consistently misreads people, her assumptions almost always wrong. Pompey, Natchez, Mrs. Gravely, the Intuitionist House cook, and Marie Claire Rogers, Fulton's housekeeper, all prove to be different from the people she imagines them to be, a blind spot that even extends to herself, "how little self-perception she has" (187). Moreover, Lila Mae, we are told, had been "a practicing solipsist since before she could walk" (235); with regard to religion, "She has always considered herself an atheist":

> She has knelt beside her mother and father in church and said the words she was supposed to say, but she never believed them, and when she came North she stopped going. She has always considered herself an atheist, not realizing she had a religion. Anyone can start a religion. They just need the need of others [241].

In fact, Lila Mae's solipsism, manifested in her consistent problems reading other minds and understanding others' intentions, combined with her atheism, her paradoxical inability to place her faith in things unseen, seem to mark her as a touch autistic, if not literally, at least metaphorically. Lila Mae's fixation on elevators, on mechanical mechanisms with which she seems to have an intuitive bond is perhaps the most obvious manifestation of her autistic tendencies; she "understands" elevators while interpersonal relationships mystify her. Words consistently fail her, whereas she "communicates" with elevators wordlessly, their internal workings appearing to her in geometric forms, a kind of abstract expressionism. Inspecting an elevator in the opening pages of the book, Lila Mae leans against the wall of the elevator, concentrating on the vibrations of the motor transmitted through the cable into the cab:

> She's trying to concentrate on the vibrations massaging her back. She can almost see them now, an aqua-blue cone. Her pen rests in her palm and her grip loosens. It might fall. She shuts out the sound of the super's breathing which is a low rumble lilting into a wheeze at the ultimate convexity of his exhalation. That's noise. The elevator moves. The elevator moves upward in the well, toward the grunting in the machine room, and Lila Mae turns that into a picture, too. The ascension is a red spike circling around the blue cone, which doubles in size

and wobbles as the elevator starts climbing. You don't pick the shapes and their behavior. Everyone has their own set of genies. Depends on how your brain works. Lila Mae has always had a thing for geometric forms [6].

She is socially awkward, and she is clearly fond of routines, comfortable in her uniform, one for each weekday, her uniforms lined up in order in her closet. In the end, she takes up Fulton's journals, adopting his voice, her language a self-conscious imitation of his. She seems to be composed in equal parts of Temple Grandin, with her intuitive understanding of animals, a high-functioning autistic woman who thinks in pictures, not in words, and of Donna Williams, another high-functioning autistic woman, whose impressive acts of mimicry disguise her own innate wordlessness. Lila Mae seems, much as Grandin describes herself in her interviews with Oliver Sacks, an "anthropologist on Mars," an alien observer trying to make sense of the rituals and values and ways of knowing characteristic of the subject culture she is attempting to understand (Sacks 259).

In the end, Lila Mae is not the person we expect her to be, not the protagonist, the hero of genre fiction but a character who, if anything, seems somewhat delusional in the end. The cryptic remark in the margins of Fulton's journals that "Lila Mae Watson is the one" turns out to be little more than a random note, the answer to Fulton's question about the name of the colored girl living in a room off the gymnasium (253), of no more meaning than the string of numbers also recorded in the margins of the notebook that proves, finally, to correspond to his dry cleaning bill (248). Nevertheless, she persists in seeing the remark as prophetic. In this way, the novel's critique remains "immune to the logical and rhetorical traps and dead ends that its own analysis reveals" (Saldivar 7), a point that the catastrophic failure of the Fanny Briggs elevator reinforces, that there are always more things in heaven and on earth than are dreamt of in your philosophy, the anomalous data, the noise in the system, the outlier in the results. This seems to be the point:

> A catastrophic accident. The things that emerge from the black, nether reaches of space and collide here, comets that connect with this frail world after countless unavailing ellipses. Emissaries from the unknowable.... She is never wrong when it comes to Intuitionism. Things occur to her. What her discipline and Empiricism have in common: they cannot account for the catastrophic accident [227].

The failure makes no sense, the whole thing "beyond calculation" (228).

As a work of anti-detective fiction, *The Intuitionist* doesn't so much solve the mystery as confront the essential mystery at the center of existence, something of a dark vision. The figure of the Screaming Man (94ff), a character who at first seems to be but turns out not to be Ben Urich, proves to be emblematic here, a descendant of Conrad's Kurtz, a variation of Edvard Munch's *The Scream*, a nightmare image that cannot otherwise be explained or assimilated into the novel. We can no more identify the screaming man than we can explain the catastrophic failure of the Fanny Briggs elevator, which, in the end, seems to be the point.

6

Falling into History
Easy Rawlins and the Arc of African American Experience

Anxiety Revisited: Intransigence and Opportunity in the Post-Civil Rights Era

Easy Rawlins first appears in print in 1990 in *Devil in a Blue Dress*, following the rejection of an earlier "literary" novel that Walter Mosley had written, the story of nineteen-year-old Easy and Mouse back home in Texas, the novel Mosley eventually publishes as *Gone Fishin'* (1997). The series seemingly concludes with *Blonde Faith* (2007), with the now 47-year-old Easy Rawlins driving his car off an embankment. Were the story not told in the first person, we might assume that this accident would prove fatal, but these stories, all told in the first person and all inflected by comments—"at that time," "in those days," "that was before"—that place the telling of the story well after the fact, suggest a future yet to unfold. Still, Mosley has commented (Hahn) that he has no intention of continuing the Easy Rawlins saga, the stories left—almost literally—up in the air, a cliff hanger, much as happens when a television series of several seasons is cancelled; the unresolved action of this season's installment is simply suspended, a conclusion in which nothing is concluded. After a total of eleven books—nine mystery novels, one set of loosely linked short stories, and the initial coming-of-age adventure in Pariah, Texas—the story is over, at least for now.[1]

The series has proved to be both critically and commercially successful, something of a mystery in itself, given, first, the critical prejudices against popular literature, something Theodore O. Mason, Jr., notes in his 1992 *Kenyon Review* article, probably the first critical response in the journal literature to Mosley's work, and, second, the somewhat accidental nature of Mosley's movement into detective fiction and the relatively slim number of minority authors in this field in 1990. Daylanne K. English, in one of the more recent articles examining the series, has considered the possible reasons why an African American author writing in 1990 would, first, adopt the hard-boiled novel as his particular medium, and, second, set those novels as they develop in the twenty years moving from the end of World War II through the 1960s. The answers, she rightfully suggests, turn on the character of the times in which the books were being written, on the ways in which the historical period being considered, as it mirrors contemporary concerns, provides a means for examining them, and in the conventions of a genre, the hard-boiled novel, that seems tailor-made for examining political systems and the distribution of power in society. The late 1980s, early 1990s—the Reagan/Bush I years—were clearly anxious times, a point when the promises and limited progress of the Civil Rights Movement were beginning to erode. As English notes, the 1991 beating of Rodney King and the 1992 riots that erupted following the acquittal of the officers responsible for the beating bear a striking resemblance to the 1965 Watts Riots, showing just how little has changed. On the other end of the series, the devastation wrought by Hurricane Katrina in late August 2005 and the inept, inadequate federal response of the second Bush administration to the disaster displayed quite clearly how little things have changed in the United States for people like Easy Rawlins.

In that regard, Jonathan Kozol's landmark studies of the ways in which educational resources are distributed in the United States, *Savage Inequalities* (1991) and *The Shame of the Nation: The Restoration of Apartheid Schooling in America* (2005), provide a means for measuring the failures of school and social reform in the post–Civil Rights era that seem one of the underlying impulses behind these novels. The Supreme Court's 1954 ruling in *Brown v. Board* clearly acknowledged the ways in which segregated schools were inherently unequal, a ruling that led slowly to the integration of the public schools in this country, first through forced busing, then through voluntary transfer programs centered around the creation of magnet schools in urban areas. While these programs resulted in modest improvements through the late 1960s, early 1970s, any movement had stalled by the late 1980s. In the preface to *Savage Inequalities*, "Looking Backward: 1965–1991," Kozol remarks how surprised he was, returning to the public schools after being away for twenty-five years, to find how much segregation had "intensified" (3) and how little interested in the problems posed by segregation public officials proved to be:

> What seems unmistakable, but, oddly enough, is rarely said in public settings nowadays, is that the nation, for all practice and intent, has turned its back upon the moral implications, if not yet the legal ramifications, of the *Brown* decision. The struggle being waged today, where there is any struggle being waged at all,

is closer to the one that was addressed in 1896 in *Plessy v. Ferguson*, in which the court accepted segregated institutions for black people, stipulating only that they must be equal to those open to white people. The dual society, at least in public education, seems in general to be unquestioned [4].

A paragraph later, Kozol reiterates this point:

Liberal critics of the Reagan era sometimes note that social policy in the United States, to the extent that it concerns black children and poor children, has been turned back several decades. But this assertion, which is accurate as a description of some setbacks in the areas of housing, health and welfare, is not adequate to speak about the present-day reality in public education. In public schooling, social policy has been turned back almost one hundred years [4].

Insofar as school funding systems continued to depend upon property taxes, educational funding in property-poor districts, those typically populated by low income and minority peoples, lagged behind funding in property-rich districts, sometimes by a factor of three to one. In most cases, these differences in funding were not offset by state aid, the foundation formulas used to distribute money to local schools often awarding more money *per capita*, not less, to wealthier school districts, exacerbating, not ameliorating, the problem. The racism of low expectations was clearly expressed in foundation formulas that set low thresholds for educational attainment; cost-benefit analyses suggested that moneys spent on the economically advantaged, on the reasonably well-to-do, would likely yield higher returns in tax dollars than spending money in inner-city areas.

Returning to the story fifteen years later in *The Shame of the Nation*, little has changed, in spite of a great deal of hand-wringing over the achievement gap between white and black students and the requirements of No Child Left Behind that states establish standards and assessment systems capable of demonstrating that all schools are achieving adequate yearly progress figures. The net effect, if anything, seems to have been to make an already impoverished education worse through the institution of canned programs like Success For All and the focusing of instructional time and effort on test preparation, not real learning, and often only in those areas being tested—math and language skills—deemphasizing the study of history, literature, art, science, music. That the school systems remain largely segregated goes without saying. That these measures do little to improve student retention—some critics suggest just the opposite, that the emphasis on testing and test prep increases dropout rates—is also clearly the case.

The inequitable distribution of educational resources in the United States is an old story, but one that is consistently cited as one of several underlying causes fueling racial unrest and the periodic riots that result. Kozol's books document conditions in South Central Los Angeles, among other urban areas, in the neighborhoods that Easy Rawlins works in as supervisor of maintenance at Sojourner Truth Junior High School in the middle books of the series and where his adopted children, Jesus and Feather, attend school. In *Bad Boy Brawley Brown*, set in the winter of 1964, just prior to the Watts Riots of summer 1965, Jesus seeks Easy's permission to drop out of school (*BBBB* 76–77). He is frustrated by the teachers' low expectations of him, by teachers who don't really believe that the black and Latino/a children in their charge are truly educable. Easy acquiesces, on condition that Jesus devote himself to building the sailboat he has started and that he pursue a course of reading, anything with a boat in it, that he discusses with Easy on a daily basis. This home-schooling regimen proves to be both progressive, academic content conveyed through preferred learning styles and centered on student interests, and traditional, recalling the advice of Easy's mentor, the carpenter Melvin Price, one of several people who "raised" Easy following the death of his parents and who had always insisted on the virtues of skilled manual labor, of learning to use tools, a kind of capital investment that could never be taken away. The aging and ill Price appears in *Black Betty*, providing something of a counterpoint both to Easy's investigations as he searches for a figure from his past, Elizabeth Eady—the Black Betty of the title—and to his real estate investments, as his attempts to develop a shopping center collapse, taking with it all of the money he has invested in plans and permits, attesting to the wisdom of Price's philosophy.

Moreover, education has been an issue in these books from the beginning. Easy begins the series as an illiterate nineteen-year-old, having had access to little or no formal schooling as a child, a problem he rectifies in the period between *Gone Fishin'* and *Devil in a Blue Dress*. He has completed a GED at Los Angeles City College and continued to take courses on a part-time basis, most notably in literature and history. As one of the few working-class African Americans on staff at Sojourner Truth, Easy often acts as a mentor and tutor to the children and an interpreter/liaison for their parents, people who can more readily identify with him than with the school authorities. In his unofficial capacity, Easy remarks that he has read every curriculum guide for every subject at the school so that he can properly assist the children with their work.

The story of the Easy Rawlins books, however, is not so simple or unambiguous as it might seem. While these books clearly explore the lack of meaningful social and educational reform in the United States, the ways that entrenched, often institutional prejudices continue unabated, the very existence of these books also attests to the expanding opportunities available, at least in publishing, to minority authors. Clearly, someone somewhere believed detective fiction featuring a minority detective to be commercially viable, something that English says relatively little about. Mosley's books supply content for an expanding market for multicultural, multiethnic literature. In 1990, apart from Tony Hillerman's long-running Leaphorn and Chee novels and Joseph Hansen's equally well established Dave Brandstetter series, a series featuring a gay detective—Hansen's and Hillerman's first novels both appeared in 1970—few if any series being actively written by minority authors or featuring minority figures existed. By 2005, the market was flooded. Of active authors and series, only Gar Anthony Haywood's Aaron Gunner seems to predate Easy Rawlins, debuting in 1988. Between 1992 and 2005, some 24 additional African American authors emerge, including Eleanor Taylor Brand, Charlotte Carter, Steven L. Carter (a professor of law at Yale University), Evelyn Coleman, Margaret Cuthbert, Christopher Darden (the prosecutor in the first O.J. Simpson trial), Nora DeLoach, Grace Edwards, Ardella Garland, Robert Greer, Terris Grimes, Barbara Hambly, Jake Lamar, Penny Mickelbury, Barbara Neely, Gary Phillips, Judith Smith-Levin, Pamela Thomas-Graham, Nichelle Tramble, Blair S. Walker and Hugh B. Price, Valerie Wilson Wesley, Chassie West, and Paula L. Woods. The list is almost certainly incomplete. Mystery series by Latino/a authors or featuring Latino/a detectives also appear (Rudolfo Anaya, Edna Buchanan, Lucha Corpi, Carolina Garcia-Aguilera, Rolando Hinojosa, Jose Latour, Manuel Ramos, Marcos McPeek Villatoro); by Asian American authors or featuring Asian American detectives (Naomi Hirahara, Leonard Chang, Dale Furutani, Chang-rae Lee, Gus Lee, Sujata Massey, Ann Wingate), by Native American authors or, more often, by Euro-American writers featuring Native American detectives (Sherman Alexie, Margaret Coel, James D. Doss, Jean Hagar, James W. Kunetka, Dana Stabenow, Aimee and David Thurlo). Lesbian authors also turn in droves to genre fiction, in general, and crime fiction, specifically. In some cases, the mystery form is being used for "literary" purposes, as in Chang-rae Lee's *Native Speaker* and Sherman Alexie's *Indian Killer*; in other cases, established authors of literary fiction and/or poetry—Rudolfo Anaya and Lucha Corpi, for instance— cross over into detective fiction, in part, we have to imagine, because of the commercial potential of this genre. In a few cases, the work in question seems intended merely to exploit the commercial potential of this particular market, the detective fiction something of a sideline for authors whose primary occupation is writing Harlequin Romances.

 The appearance of so many new series and authors exploring multiethnic American experience corresponds in popular literature to the simultaneous push to create truly inclusive curricula in schools, curricula that reflect an understanding of the multicultural nature of the population. The National

Association of Multicultural Education, significantly, was also formed in 1990, specifically to address the needs of ethnic minority students and educators in the United States. But the development of a popular literature exploring multiethnic experience is not the only or even most visible or most commercially viable art form in this period to explore urban, African American experience. The emergence of rap and hip hop, along with its distinctive style of dress, clearly transformed youth culture. This music, especially in its "gangsta" forms, provides a parallel expression, albeit one aimed at a different generation, to the noir novels' investigation of African American concerns and subjectivities. In that respect, the emergence of rap and hip hop in the late 1980s, early 1990s, and the ways it transformed youth culture are analogous to the ways jazz in the early twentieth century and rock and roll in the 1950s, building on black roots, also transformed American culture. The early novels in the Easy Rawlins series will track this shift in musical taste in the black clubs from jazz to rock and roll. The cultural transformations of the latter decades of the century seem to parallel mid-century events, at least with regard to popular music and youth culture.

The combination of opportunity and intransigence and the anxiety that both produce seem to be part of the historical condition that African American authors of crime fiction explore, from Hopkins to Fisher to Himes to Mosley. In *Plan B*, Chester Himes comments that racial conflict in the United States results specifically because whites and blacks (implicitly) acknowledge the equality of the races, a notion other white-dominated societies don't necessarily share:

> While Americans suffer guilt over black segregation and restriction, in other white societies the assumption of black equality is summarily dismissed. This is why other white majorities treat their black minorities with greater consideration and politeness. They do not fear that blacks will ever attain equality or that they will even request it.
>
> Strangely enough, American blacks don't know this, and probably most whites don't either [*Plan B* 144].

Bonnie Shay, Easy's Caribbean-born companion, an Air France flight attendant, echoes these sentiments in *Bad Boy Brawley Brown*, that white Europeans do not discriminate against their black minorities in the ways white Americans do because white Europeans do not see blacks as their equals. French men don't lynch blacks, she says, "but that's because in France they aren't afraid of blacks, just certain that we are from a lesser culture. We are interesting, but in the end just primitives" (*BBBB* 249–250). Easy reveals in the conversation that he had once considered emigrating to France. In other conversations, particularly in *Six Easy Pieces* following Bonnie's assignment to an extended diplomatic mission in Africa on which she meets a Sengalese prince fighting to liberate his country, she points to her own Caribbean experiences and to the experiences recounted by her Sengalese prince as instances of unrelieved oppression, something that African Americans have gotten beyond. Easy remembers his father escaping a lynching and comments on occasion that his own behavior, his insolence with police, his dealings with white women, a generation ago, would have earned him the same fate. The stories of *Six Easy Pieces* all occur in 1964. While the color barriers are still securely in place, as the 1965 riots that form the backdrop of *Little Scarlet* clearly attest, conditions have changed. Easy now has a white woman principal at Sojourner Truth who appreciates what he does and respects his opinion; he interacts with an LAPD detective, Sgt. Suggs, who does not automatically assume he is a criminal, extending to him the constitutional assumption of innocence until proven guilty; and he has daily interactions with white people, including some who work under his supervision, who accept him as a person. Change, however slow, seems possible.

Much of the critical discussion of the Easy Rawlins books has turned on their conflicted relationship with the hard-boiled genre, the degrees to which the books emulate or depart from the conventions of this form, and on seeming inconsistencies and/or ambiguities in Easy's attitudes. Critics have additionally noted conflicts and inconsistencies in the stories he recounts of his childhood and adolescence in Texas, in particular the circumstances surrounding the disappearance and deaths of his parents, or the exact nature of the incidents in Pariah and Mouse's killing of daddy Reese. Easy is often of two minds, literally, a "voice" speaking to him at times of stress, telling him what to do, advice he sometimes takes and sometimes resists. He aspires to be a middle class homeowner, working a steady job, coming home in the evening to his family, sitting with Feather on his lap, watching *Hazel*, her favorite show, on television; on the other hand, he is constantly being drawn back to the streets, with all the danger and disruption that life implies. What is central here is the sense of conflict, the divided consciousness—of being an African American in a white dominated society, but also recognizing, simultaneously, both the historical vestiges of racist attitudes as old as slavery and the possibilities of change—that seems to be a constant in African American experience. Still, Watts, whatever its limitations, seems better than Harlem, as the investigations into the Watts Riots point out (Governor's Commission).

In fact, *Little Scarlet,* the book set during the 1965 riots, marks something of a turning point in the series. The conclusion of *Little Scarlet*, in spite of the riots and the devastation done to the African American community, is curiously optimistic, especially when compared to the books that immediately precede and follow it. While the book is always clear as to how deep and damaging the history of African Americans is—the bipolar homeless man, Harold Ostenberg, who is responsible for the murders of young black women, both in this book and in "Amber Gate," is a case in point—progress seems possible. Easy emerges from the adventure a little worse for the wear, but he has been effective in small ways: He has saved Benita Flag from her attempted suicide, following her rejection by Mouse, a small if significant act, one black person rescued from her own self-destructive despair. In the books that follow, Benita will become Jesus's common-law wife and bear Easy's first grandchild. Easy has also taken money from Mouse and turned it into LACC tuition for Juanda, a young woman he meets on the streets and who assists with his investigation. Easy poses as a reference, albeit a fraudulent one, for Jackson Blue, who is pursuing employment as a computer technician in a bank; Jackson is hoping to support Jewelle, who has formerly supported him, until her real estate development plans, which have eaten up her capital, begin to pay off. Again, in future books, Jackson will appear as a corporate vice president in charge of information technology for the LA branch of a French reinsurance corporation, and Jewelle's real estate dealings will include a lavish estate overlooking the Pacific. Easy works with Sgt. Suggs to solve the mystery; while Suggs is clearly an exception, something of an outsider in the LAPD, he does seem genuinely interested in seeing justice done, and he does take Easy's theories seriously, something the police failed to do in "Amber Gate." This failure led directly to the death of another African American woman.

And Easy is working with a white woman, the principal at Sojourner Truth, who respects Easy and listens to him and his explanation for, among other things, one of the historical roots of the riots: "Every child is brought up thinking that only white people make things, rule countries, have histories" (*LS* 78). Harold's self loathing is a product of that history, the direct result of his treatment at the hands of a light-skinned mother passing as white, a woman who has rejected him and dark-skinned men to take a white husband. She has done everything possible to preserve the fiction that she is white, including passing off her dark-skinned child as the child of her African American maid. Her own sense of self loathing is an old story. Easy sums up the problem:

> It wasn't the first time I had met someone like her. And I didn't hate her for hating herself. If everybody in the world despises you, sees your features as ugly and simian, makes jokes about your ways of talking, calls you stupid and beneath contempt; if you have no history, no heroes, and no future where a hero might lead, then you might begin to hate yourself, your face and features, your parents, and even your child. It could all happen and you would never even know it.

And then one hot summer's night you just erupt and go burning and shooting and nobody seems to know why [*LS* 255–56].

At least one point of these books is to tell that story, to make the formerly invisible history visible and provide a means both of coming to terms with the past and, finally, a means of moving forward.

Falling into History

The Easy Rawlins series traces the arc of African American experience through the middle decades of the twentieth century, from Easy's emergence from his service in the army during World War II and his settling in California following the war through the twenty years that follow, from 1946 in *Devil in a Blue Dress* to 1968 in *Blonde Faith*. The prequel, *Gone Fishin'*, provides a glimpse into Easy's pre-war life in Houston in 1939, when, at the age of 19, he accompanies Mouse on a trip to his hometown of Pariah, Texas, a small town of black sharecroppers working land owned by a white woman, Miss Dixon. Mouse is after his abusive step-father's money, at least part of which he believes is owed him, an inheritance from his mother, all so that Mouse can afford to give EttaMae Harris the wedding she deserves. It is conventional to point out that Easy's movement from the Deep South to California following the war recounts the history of the Great Migration, the movement of African American people, 90 percent of whom lived in the Deep South at the beginning of the twentieth century, through the United States, a movement of about 10 percent per decade, spurred in part by the two world wars and the employment opportunities that resulted. Following his term of service in the Jim Crow army fighting the Second World War, Easy settles in California, an Edenic world, a "promised land" (*DBD* 27) of economic opportunity, where African Americans could, at last, live the American Dream. Albright's snaky handshake, the handshake of the very white man who appears in the opening paragraph of *Devil in a Blue Dress* and who offers Easy an opportunity to earn the money he needs to pay his mortgage following his dismissal from Champion Aircraft, suggests how short lived this sojourn in Eden will prove. Wage slavery is the principal result of home ownership for everyone but the very wealthy. When EttaMae appears in Easy's house in *A Red Death*, having gathered the fruits and flowers from his yard, it is significant that the lemonade she offers him has been made from the fruit of a neighbor's tree (*RD* 19). As Mouse's estranged wife, she is as much forbidden fruit as the lemons from the neighbor's yard. Easy's attempts to pay the mortgage on his first house (*Devil in a Blue Dress*), to create through his real estate holdings a sense of economic self-sufficiency (*A Red Death*), to develop a shopping center, Freedom Plaza, on land he owns (*White Butterfly, Black Betty*), to protect his property managers Mofass (*Black Betty*) and, later, Jewelle ("Silver Lining") from the predatory practices of Jewelle's Aunt Clovis, even his uneasy relationship to these property holdings and his felt need to hide them from the government, his wife, and his friends, a secrecy that, in part, costs him his first wife (*White Butterfly*)—property ownership proves to be as much problem as promise, sometimes more trouble than it's worth. In *A Red Death*, Easy clearly understands that his real estate holdings and the tax liability they represent make him a "slave" (*RD* 124) to IRS Agent Lawrence and FBI Agent Craxton, that he "suffered all this [i.e., the events of the story] because I'm not my own man" (*RD* 203). The promises tied to home ownership and real estate investment, projected by the American Dream, prove to be a mixed blessing at best.

In this regard, Theodore O. Mason, Jr.'s 1992 article, "Walter Mosley's Easy Rawlins: The Detective and Afro-American Fiction," seems particularly prescient, especially his use of Lukacs's and Bakhtin's theories of the novel in the analysis of Mosley's first two books. For Lukacs, the novel portrays a fallen world. As Mason puts it:

> Lukacs consistently reads the novel as the epic of a fallen world. In one of his earliest published works, *Theory of the Novel* (1920), Lukacs conceives of the novel in the following terms: "The novel is the epic of an age in which the extensive totality of life is no longer directly given, in which the immanence of meaning in life has become a problem, yet which still thinks in terms of totality" (56).... The wholeness of the epic world sharply contrasts with the inherent brokenness of the novelistic universe. While this brokenness may well be seen as the result of a Fall, it is a fortunate Fall (in a limited sense) into the realm of history. From Lukacs's perspective, the absence of *totality* in the novelistic world provides the novel with its fundamental impetus—the desire to reform some version of epic totality, even if that version is historical and contingent, rather than transcendental and necessary [175–76].

This fall into the social world foregrounds epistemology, something that is not a problem in the epic.

Clearly, the Easy Rawlins novels trace this first movement, the fall into history away from the epic narrative of *America*, a land of limitless possibility, a promise seemingly held out even to African Americans following the Emancipation Proclamation and the passage of the Fourteenth Amendment. California represented that promised land following the Second World War. Thrown out of work, the vision of home ownership imperiled, Easy is forced into the role of detective, an epistemologist trading in information. At one level, the movement is clearly a negative one, the series tracking the collapse of an intact African American community built on country values of mutual respect and assistance, on the doing of favors, not for pay, but future considerations, much as the giving of gifts, the offers of assistance in *Beowulf*, for instance, represent a mutual-assistance pact. Because of kindnesses his father had received in his time of need, Beowulf will return the favor, offering Hrothgar assistance when he needs it. In the brutal, uncertain world of *Beowulf*, or Houston's Fifth Ward before the war, favors and the systems of indebtedness they represent function as real capital.

While Easy Rawlins never loses sight of the brutality and uncertainty of life in these earlier times, and so never casts over them a sense of nostalgia, the series will track the fracturing of that once intact community. In *Devil in a Blue Dress*, Watts represents a closed community in which everyone, transplanted from the South, knows everyone else. The fabric of life is densely interwoven at this point, but this sense of community progressively frays through the series, even as Easy continues to insist that he is dealing in favors, a "country" way of doing things. In *A Little Yellow Dog*, having taken the position as supervisor of maintenance at Sojourner Truth, Easy recognizes that the country-way of doing things is breaking down. Talking with Grace Phillips's elderly landlady, a woman Easy knows from the old days, he remarks to the reader how little time he now has to chat with her, that in the old days he would have come by periodically—unbidden—to do chores around her house (*LYD* 238). In *Little Scarlet*, Easy confronts the beginning of the end, seeing, at least in retrospect, that the Watts Riots represented both the historical frustrations of the African American community and the possibilities of its end:

> Even though I didn't know it at the time, that was the beginning of the breakup of our community. It was the first time you could see that there was another side to be on. If you identified with white people, you had a place where you were welcomed in [*LS* 77].

Where once all minority peoples had been treated as "black," providing a basis for unity—Easy's relationship with Primo is a case in point—by the end of the series, inter-racial tensions have erupted, driving the African American and Hispanic communities apart. In *Blonde Faith*, Primo tells Easy that he is going to move out of the little house, Easy's first real estate purchase, to East LA, into a Mexican American community, because of the problems his children and grandchildren confront as Hispanics in a black neighborhood (*BF* 178).

The negative movement, however, represents only half of the story. Mason cites Bakhtin and his sense that this fall opens up possibilities not previously available:

Rather, Bakhtin sees in the very fluidity of the world a set of conditions perfect for representation by the novel. Throughout the pages of "Epic and Novel," he celebrates the novel's very incompleteness, a condition mirroring the condition of "reality" the novel takes as its field of representation. "The novel comes into contact with the spontaneity of the inconclusive present; this is what keeps the genre from congealing. The novelist is drawn toward everthing that is not yet complete" (27). This incompleteness mimics and is mimicked by a similar condition in the representation of characters, particularly the "hero." As Bakhtin states it, "one of the basic internal themes of the novel is precisely the theme of the hero's inadequacy to his fate or his situation" (37). The combination of a highly unstable "field" of representation and the instability of the hero's relation to the task before him or her underscores the novel's status as a highly problematized project.

But where Lukacs may have seen this condition as defective (if perhaps inevitable), Bakhtin embraces this instability as a site of multiple possibility. Part of this enthusiasm we can grasp as a recognition of the understandable indeterminacy or indeterminateness of historical existence. Unlike the epic world, the novelistic world's absence of "totality" causes reality to be always in process, always somehow unequal to our categories of understanding [176].

For Bakhtin, again, epistemology becomes a dominant concern when the novel becomes the dominant form.

The Easy Rawlins novels, as historical novels, are clearly concerned with history and historiography, interested as much with the how as the what, with the ways stories are told and the possibilities inherent in them. Bakhtin and his general insights into the novel and literacy, as well as his discussions of discourse and heteroglossia, all seem immediately applicable to the movement in these novels. Literacy, storytelling, the construction of historical narratives, Easy's dual roles as an agent of history and as author of these histories, and the emphasis throughout on epistemology, all function as important themes in these books.

As Easy's comments in *Little Scarlet* make clear, the riots represent both a historical frustration and a frustration with history, at least as it is conventionally constructed, that "if you have no history, no heroes, and no future where a hero might lead, then you might begin to hate yourself, your face and features, your parents, and even your child. It could all happen and you would never even know it" (*LS* 255–56). That wordless frustration translates directly into the inarticulate rage of the riots. The antidote is history, heroes, and a future. In that regard, the novels set a course that begins in Easy's learning to read, the acquisition of a functional literacy, between the end of *Gone Fishin'* and *Devil in a Blue Dress* and then progresses by stages through the following books, through his growing understanding of narrative function, history, and epistemology: (1) his stated interest in history in *A Red Death*, even though he claims it is not "real" (*RD* 223); (2) in *Bad Boy Brawley Brown* (264 ff), his discovery of what Jackson Blue refers to as "black history," the untold stories of Isaac Newton's alchemical investigations, his heretical Arianist beliefs, and his activities as head of the National Mint, overseeing, among other things, the meting out of capital punishment; (3) Easy's claim in *Cinnamon Kiss* that evidence is not always empirically verifiable (*CK* 269). These elements signpost an argument that is otherwise framed by Easy's service in World War II and the discovery of Nazi connections at the center of his investigations in *Cinnamon Kiss*. Additionally, the introduction of Christmas Black in the later books and the ways his family history and his participation in the major military engagements of mid-twentieth century history, especially the war in Vietnam, lead us to reimagine a history that has been inadequately imagined, move the discussion forward.

In *Gone Fishin'*, Easy promises himself that he will learn to read. He has been impressed by Domaque's ability to read and, more importantly, to reshape the material he has read, making the biblical stories he has read his own. Easy recognizes, implicitly, the conventionality of the written word, something one can see in print that remains invisible in oral culture, and in seeing its conventionality, its historical contingency, he also understands its plasticity, that stories can be reshaped. Easy is haunted by Mouse's shooting of daddy Reese's dogs, an image he cannot get out of his mind. At that moment, he realizes that if he could read, he could escape from those images into another world, into the stories available in print, stories that he could reshape and make his own, if need be:

> I looked at those papers [newspapers sitting on a bedside table] and thought that if I could read what was in them I wouldn't have to think about those dogs; I thought that if I could read I wouldn't have to hang around people like Mouse to tell me stories, I could just read stories myself. And if I didn't like the stories I read then I could just change them the way Dom did with the Bible.
> That was a big moment for me. And I'd say that the whole trip was worth it just for that, but I can't say that because I lived to tell about it and not everybody else did [*GF* 133].

Easy does learn to read, and he takes a particular interest in history, but he does not "believe" in history, in the reality of what he reads. In the midst of his current investigations, Easy finds that he "doesn't have any heart" for the history of Rome he has been reading, that it doesn't "move" him in the ways it has in the past (*RD* 223). This material doesn't seem real to him:

> I didn't believe in history, really. Real was what was happening to me right then. Real was a toothache and a man you trusted who did you dirt. Real was an empty stomach or a woman saying yes, or a woman saying no. Real was what

you feel. History was like watching TV for me, it wasn't the great wave of mankind moving through an ocean of minutes and hours. It wasn't mankind getting better either; I had seen enough murder in Europe to know that the Nazis were even worse than the barbarians at Rome's gate. And even if I was in Rome they would have called me a barbarian; it was no different that day in Watts [RD 223].

Easy is still living wholly in the present; real is what is immediately felt, empirical experience, arising in the moment. Easy had earlier in the novel turned to Jackson Blue for information and had learned an important lesson, that the library is open and it contains information that can challenge the received wisdom, what you have always been told (RD 184–85). He clearly understands the fictive forces operating in nonfiction forms, and he is aware of the ways that these stories can be ideologically deposed. Still, immediate experience and historical constructions occupy separate spheres of experience, the "real" and the "fictional," because immediate and constructed, respectively. Easy's positivist epistemology, what might be described as Mississippi mud realism, needs to be complicated. Things are not always as simple or obvious as they seem.

Newton, however odd an example, proves to be an object lesson. In *Bad Boy Brawley Brown*, Easy consults Jackson Blue, as he often will in these books, availing himself of the autodidact's wealth of information. Jackson's current interest is Isaac Newton. Newton's story is one we think we know, one that entails his discoveries of gravity, the postulating of a series of fundamental laws of physics, the development of calculus. This is the official history, the authorized account. What Jackson Blue is fascinated by is the history that has been suppressed, Newton's interest in alchemy, his heretical theological beliefs, and his overseeing of public executions as director of the National Mint. These are the things that we don't know, that if known, would complicate the picture, this heroic figure of the Enlightenment still operating under the influence of an outworn belief system. Easy doesn't quite understand the relevance of all this information or Jackson's interest in it:

"So what, Jackson?"
"So what? This is black history we talkin' here, Easy."
"So now you sayin' Newton was a black man?"
"No, brother. I'm sayin' that all they teach in schools is how a apple done fell on Isaac's head and that's it. They don't teach you about how he believed in magic or how he was in his heart against the Church of England. They don't want you to know that you can sit in your room and discover things all by yourself that nobody else knows. I'm down here collectin' knowledge while some other Negro is outside someplace swingin' a hammer. That's what I'm sayin'."
"Swingin' a hammer is more than you do," I said out of reflex. I didn't really

believe it. Jackson Blue's rendition of Isaac Newton reminded me of me, a man living in shadows in almost every part of his life. A man who keeps secrets and harbors passions that could get him killed if he let them out into the world [*BBBB* 266].

The application is a bit odd, as odd as the example itself, but apt, at least in terms of Easy's engagement with history and with the "official" channels of knowledge running through these books.

The narratives are always more complicated than they seem, the "public" face masking the private satisfaction of self interest, particularly the operations of sex and greed, and the systems of power that preserve dominance. The list is a long one. Just in the first several books, the catalogue might include the pederasty of a mayoral candidate (*Devil in a Blue Dress*), Agent Lawrence's use of IRS investigations and access to tax records to further his own private lusts and Craxton's similar use of tax records to cover his own inept handling of security matters (*A Red Death*), the use of eminent domain to wrest Easy's shopping center development from him, the land, itself, initially a repayment for recovering a Japanese American's lost property (*White Butterfly* and *Black Betty*). Historically, eminent domain was used in California to seize land owned by minorities so that it could be reassigned to white developers, just as the internment of Japanese Americans during the Second World War, an event alluded to in these novels, allowed their properties to be stolen and "reassigned." Cain's use of Commander Styles to blackmail his African American maid, Betty, into a sexual relationship in *Black Betty*, and the mixed-race children it produces, simply repeats a practice passed down from slavery. Moreover, the corrupt systems of power, a convention of the noir tradition, becomes an apt metaphor for African American experience in almost every way.

It is in *Cinnamon Kiss* and *Blonde Faith*, however, that the full outline of Easy's engagement with history becomes clear and the ways that Mason's early suggestions, particularly his reference to Lukacs and Bakhtin, prove particularly prescient. Easy is identified from the start as a veteran of World War II, having enlisted to escape his own immediate past, his life in Houston with Mouse. Initially relegated in the segregated army to a desk job, he enters into combat as a volunteer at the Battle of the Bulge, where his actions prove conventionally heroic; he saves "a white major's ass" (*GF* 242) and he is part, finally, of the force that liberates the concentration camps. He also becomes part of the brutality of the conflict, a "killing machine" as he calls himself (*DBD* 54), capable of wringing the life out of German soldiers, hardly more than boys themselves, with his bare hands. That he and other African American soldiers served honorably, however, doesn't protect them from the racist attitudes of the white troops after the armistice when, in Paris, "there were gangs of white American soldiers roaming the streets, killing solitary black enlisted men" (*GF* 243).

This seeming off-hand reference immediately disrupts the "heroic" image of the war, the "greatest generation" a generation of racists. In this regard, the discovery in *Cinnamon Kiss* that the substantial fortunes of several prominent San Francisco families can be traced to their earlier dealings with the Nazis brings the story full circle. The plot seems, in some ways, reminiscent of the Fox television network show *24*, where the true threats are ultimately traced, not to external agents of terror but to self-appointed protectors of American corporate interests. ("America" and "corporate interests" are always synonymous.) The totalitarianism of the white perspective and of European-American constructions of civilization form a backdrop to the Easy Rawlins series. From the German point of view, the war represented an epic struggle, in almost Bakhtinian terms, to impose a unified vision on the West, to enforce a mythos of white supremacy, one where racial and cultural and epistemological differences were not tolerated, as epic a struggle as that of the Allies to defend democratic traditions against Hitler and his vision of Aryan supremacy. What this epic vision disregards are the historical continuities, that Nazi genetics arguing the racial superiority of Aryan peoples is built on British and American theories of eugenics. Easy discovers that the crimes he is investigating are the direct result of much earlier criminal enterprises, of corporate interests working in collusion with the enemy. Mosley opens a trapdoor into history into which we fall.

In all these ways, the Easy Rawlins series offers an alternate history, one that disrupts the "master" narrative of Euro-American history. Easy represents himself as a patriot at this time, as someone who believes in the popular vision of the war. He is just as clearly aware of the ironies of his service in the Jim Crow army that fought that war, and he is still haunted by the atrocities he committed in the service of his country. The introduction of Christmas Black in *Cinnamon Kiss* and *Blonde Faith* will finally disrupt any lingering notions of the nobility of military service. A retired career Army officer, Christmas Black descends from a revolutionary-era American family of free blacks, a family "more American than most white peoples": "They had been at every important moment in America's tumultuous attempt at creating democracy. They had been at every victory and every massacre, their heads wreathed in glory and their hands drenched with blood" (*BF* 46). Christmas had seen service in World War II, Korea, and Vietnam, where he carried out covert operations resulting in My Lai–like massacres, acts of brutality that even he could no longer participate in in good conscience. The very existence of Christmas Black, his family and experiences, destabilizes the officially-sanctioned, conventional stories of the textbook traditions. And the agents of unrest in *Blonde Faith*, all ex-military men, represent an unprecedented level of brutality, something that even Easy is shocked by, enough to lift him out of his current crisis, Bonnie Shay's engagement to her Senegalese prince:

> ... I was shocked out of the melancholy that had settled in on me. I remembered what it was to be a man living in the cracks: a slave, nigger, jigaboo, coon, spade, spear-chucker, darky, boy. Walking down the streets of white gentility, I was always a target. And a target couldn't afford roots or a broken heart. A target couldn't fire back on the men who used him for sport.
> All a man like me could do was to wait for the sun to go down, move through darkness and hope.
> The validity of this litany of the past was fading, but it had not gone away. It is true—I was an American citizen too; a citizen who had to watch his step, a citizen who had to distrust the police and the government, public opinion, and even the history taught in schools [*BF* 163].

The list of racial epithets echoes a very similar list from the black man's lament in *Hair*, attesting both to the pervasiveness of such terms and attitudes in popular culture and the attempts of the counter-cultural movement to disrupt that legacy. History proves to be suspect terrain all the way through these books.

For Easy, these cases require him to rethink his epistemological assumptions of the early books. The Mississippi-mud realism of the early books is replaced by a more nuanced sense of the complex histories that emerge in the course of his investigations. In *Cinnamon Kiss*, Easy describes the evanescent nature of "evidence":

> Proof is a funny thing. For policemen and for lawyers it depends on tangible evidence: fingerprints, eyewitnesses, irrefutable logic, or self-incrimination. But for me evidence is like morning mist over a complex terrain. You see the landscape and then it's gone. And all you can do is try to remember and watch your step [*CK* 269].

The so-called "hard evidence," the tangible results that forensic science depends on like fingerprints and eyewitness accounts, proves to be far less reliable than initially believed, the stated evidence subject to interpretation; fingerprint analysis is no more an exact science than are eyewitness accounts wholly without bias. The truth is always more complicated and never as clear as it seems.

While these books trace the larger dramas of mid-century American history, the larger patterns of experience, they also locate them within the domestic circumstances and smaller details of description running through the series. Alva, John's partner in *Bad Boy Brawley Brown*, can no more escape her family history, try as she might, than can Harold, the bi-polar serial killer of "Amber Gate" and *Little Scarlet*. When Easy finally locates Pericles Tarr in *Blonde Faith*, he sees in his face the mixed histories and heritages, the geology of the African American experience:

> His face and body were a hodgepodge of the true Afro-American experience. There were northern European features to his bulbous nose and cheeks, Slavic influence in his Asiatic eyes, serflike economy to his compact bone structure and wide hands. His hair was kinky and his lips full. He was the jambalaya of the New World, a dozen or more European and African races competing for a piece of his body's geography [*BF* 231].

Easy is more fully aware of the complex tectonic forces that have shaped Pericles Tarr and more capable of reading them in his face, in much the way that trained geologists can read in the exposed rocks of a road cut the complex forces that have shaped the local environment, than he was at the outset of the series when he looked at Daphne Monet and saw a white girl.

The personal consequences, the cumulative effects, like everything else here, are mixed. Family, for Easy, is both precious and precarious, his less-than-legal adoption of Jesus and Feather, children who do not look like him in any way, always subject to exposure. His taking in of abandoned or orphaned children recalls his own "adoption" by Odell following the deaths of Easy's parents, a communal practice that finds its own roots in the conditions of slavery, the selling of parents and partners apart from their children. The problem, however, truly arises in *Cinnamon Kiss* when Feather is diagnosed with a rare and typically fatal blood disorder. A Swiss clinic that has had some success with treating this condition represents the only hope Easy has of saving Feather, but it is an expensive and exclusive establishment, only accepting a limited number of cases, and only after a substantial down payment. Easy will raise the money, enough to allow him to send Feather in Bonnie's care to Switzerland. What he doesn't immediately recognize is that Bonnie has secured Feather's admission to the clinic through her connections to Jogaye Cham, the Senegalese prince introduced in "Lavender" to whom she will be engaged in *Blonde Faith*. (The spelling of his name also changes, from *Jogaye* in "Lavender" (*SEP* 119) to *Joguye* in later books.) Bonnie is staying with Joguye in Switzerland during the course of Feather's treatment.

The symbolic import of this rare and usually fatal blood disorder is obvious enough, recalling a long history of racial debate over blood, its "purity," the effects of one drop, and so forth. Feather is a mixed-race child who is not related to Easy by either blood or marriage, his adoption of her lacking any legal ground or sanction. That he loves her and would do anything for her, as will Bonnie, whose connection to her is even more tenuous, poses the problem. The family drama pits personal loyalties and commitments against each other

6. Falling into History 153

in ways that ultimately lead to the collapse of Easy and Bonnie's "civil" union, a common-law arrangement built on personal commitment alone. Bonnie's personal loyalty to this child and the man who loves that child requires her, at the least, to violate a trust, to prove unfaithful to some higher, ideal image Easy has of her. Joguye's intercession secures Feather's admission to the clinic and her possible survival but at the cost of Bonnie's relationship with Easy. The problem is clearly his, a problem he wrestles with through the pages of *Blonde Faith*. When a possible resolution appears, it proves too late to undo the damage already done. As always, Easy is left to live with the consequences.

Cinnamon Kiss produces a complicated mix of over-lapping, if not quite parallel themes, playing on questions of family loyalties, loyalty to one's country, loyalty to one's ideals. Axel Bowers, an idealistic lawyer, discovers the source of his family's money, his grandfather part of a corporate venture, a chemical company trading with the Nazi high command. He loses his life attempting to make reparations for the crimes committed by these earlier generations. Christmas Black, a descendant of a family of military men tracing their heritage back to Crispus Attucks, "the son of a prince and a runaway slave" (*CK* 230), a family dedicated to the service of this country, is attempting to atone for the atrocities he has committed in the name of his country, having adopted a Vietnamese child, the sole survivor of a village he massacred. Easy recognizes the problem and his complicity in it, that his taxes are paying for the murder of women and children in Vietnam by men like Black:

> All those years our people had struggled and prayed for freedom and now a man like Christmas, who came from a whole line of heroes, was just another killer like all those white men had been for us.
> Is that what we labored for all those years? Was it just to have the right to step on some other poor soul's neck? Were we any better than the white men who lynched us in the night if we killed Easter Dawn's mother and father, sister and brother, cousins and friends? If we could kill like that, everything that we fought for would be called into question. If we became the white men we hated and who hated us, then we were nowhere, nowhere at all [*CK* 243].

That the story unfolds in 1966, a year after the Watts Riots, and takes Easy into the counter-cultural communities of Oakland and Haight-Ashbury in San Francisco, into a world preaching peace and free love and questioning American materialism, its military incursions into Vietnam, the dangers posed by the military-industrial complex, is appropriate. That the book was being written at a time when U.S. forces had invaded Iraq, a venture immediately compared to Vietnam and producing its own tales of atrocities, an adventure in which corporate interests seemed the only real beneficiaries, also seems significant.

Telling Tales

In "Amber Gate," Easy recounts a conversation with Mouse in which Mouse explained his theory of "the luck of the black man," that a black man must be luckier than any white man, a product of natural selection. As Mouse explains it:

> "Well you know white men had it easy. They had jobs and guns and the western plains for them. All we had was chains and nooses and shit like that. For a white man's father's father to survive was nuthin'. But if one of our people lived it was only because of the best luck. Jackson Blue said it to me. He said that this scientist, Derwin I think, said that you got things from your ancestors through the blood. I got luck from mines."
>
> That didn't explain why Mouse thought he was luckier than other black men, but I didn't question his beliefs because he was the luckiest man I had ever known [*SEP* 251].

The comment, coming from a resurrected Mouse, shot in *A Little Yellow Dog* and reported dead by EttaMae in "Silver Lining," picks up on a conversation from earlier in *Six Easy Pieces* from "Crimson Stain." Easy is talking with Moms, the madam of a Compton brothel and a former resident of Fifth Ward Houston. Easy is following a lead, one of Moms's women having seen a man matching Mouse's description in Richmond, a lead passed to Easy by Jackson Blue. The mention of Fifth Ward elicits a response from Moms:

> "Oh, honey," Moms sang. "I remember Fifth Ward. The cops would leave down there on Saturday sunset and come back Sunday mornin' to count the dead."
>
> "That's the truth," I replied, falling into the rhythm of her speech. "The only law down there back then was survival of the fittest."
>
> "An' the way Jackson tells it," Moms added, "the fittest was that man Mouse and you was the fittest's friend" [*SEP* 42–43].

As it turns out, Mouse did survive, largely through the insistence of EttaMae and the magic of Moma Jo, the herbalist/witch Mouse knew as a child in Pariah and who has since relocated to the Los Angeles area.

These references to Darwin and evolutionary theory—in "Crimson Stain," Easy will refer to himself as "a black man down at the bottom of the food chain" (*SEP* 56), and he will describe Reverend Winters as a "whole new species of man" (*SEP* 64)—speak to the conventional naturalism of the hard-boiled genre, the mean streets always a violent place, "red in tooth and claw," where only the fittest survive. Biology is destiny, at least metaphorically. This same naturalism, especially inflected by the lingering effects of eugenics theory, underwrites racist ideas of white supremacy. Significantly, 1967, the year in which *Cinnamon Kiss* takes place, also marks the Supreme Court decision in *Loving v. Virginia*. The Loving Decision overturned the Racial Integrity Act of 1924, a Virginia law forbidding interracial marriage, one of two eugenics laws passed that year; the other required the sterilization of "feeble-minded" people held in state institutions. These ideas have a long history, which, curiously, is still being played out as conservative forces sponsor "defense of marriage" amendments and acts to prevent the legalization of same-sex marriages. The Loving Decision is often cited in this debate, but that is another story.

Biology, like history, however, is never far from the discussion. Easy's comment in *A Red Death* with regard to the unreality of history, for instance, also challenges nineteenth-century notions of evolutionary progress:

> History was like watching TV for me, it wasn't the great wave of mankind moving through an ocean of minutes and hours. It wasn't mankind getting better either; I had seen enough murder in Europe to know that the Nazis were even worse than the barbarians at Rome's gate [*RD* 223].

As most commonly portrayed, evolution is depicted as tracing a path of improvement, the so-called "ascent of man," our biological ancestors having climbed out of the oceans onto dry land—"moving through an ocean of minutes and hours"—at which point humankind proceeded to evolve, in even increments, from quadruped to biped to white man, finally, at the end. The image, of course, represents a misreading of evolutionary theory, assuming that evolution equates with progress, teleological in construction, and always with a white man at the end of the line. This picture is remarkably persistent, however, part of the popular imagination. The actual operations of random mutation, adaptation, and natural selection, or of the degrees to which symbiosis, not competition, represents the better bet, or of the path that leads to modern humans, with all it dead ends and evolutionary cul-de-sacs, are not so easily depicted, or even, at this point, so clearly understood. Whatever happens, it's not a story of "mankind getting better." In that regard, Jesus, whom Easy always refers to as "the better man," is equally often noted as a direct descendent of the indigenous peoples of this place, part of that ancient, prehistoric race that originally populated this part of North America. Everyone else is an immigrant, an invasive species, environmental opportunists who have altered the native ecosystems, and not necessarily for the better.

The insistent colorism in Fisher and Himes gives way in Mosley to a more subtle reading of racial construction, especially as the series progresses. Pericles Tarr, for instance, isn't just a black man. He is a hybrid product whose mixture of features represents a complex genetic heritage which, in turn, is itself embedded in history. And his name is as ironic as the man, as hybrid a construction as he is. He has been named both for the Athenian orator responsible for deposing the aristocracy and instituting democratic government and, it seems, for the proverbial Tar Baby of African American folklore to whom everything sticks, an altogether common man. Genetically-determined traits like eye and hair and skin colors are read as historical markers in these books, a product of complex forces only dimly understood, which is just what Easy says of evidence in *Cinnamon Kiss*: "for me evidence is like morning mist over a complex terrain. You see the landscape and then it's gone. And all you can do is try to remember and watch your step" (*CK* 269).

Trying to remember seems to be the point here. Easy is both a historical agent and a historian, a teller of tales. The stories are clearly layered, the actions presently being recounted told from a future vantage point, never itself identified but always placing things in perspective. Easy notes changes in the landscape, how at the time of the story, certain sections, now fully developed, retained a rural character, just as he notes changes in the social landscape, changes in race relations. When Sgt. Andre Brown responds to Easy's questions in a civil fashion, for instance, he places the event in perspective:

> That was my first experience with the second half of the twentieth century; the first time a man, black or white, holding a professional office, had given me the benefit of the doubt. He wasn't running a scam. He wasn't trying to get back at the police department. He simply saw my value and believed in my character [*SEP* 34)].

This comment, in turn, is echoed in *Little Scarlet*, that the riots marked "the first time you could see that there was another side to be on" (*LS* 77).

In *Bad Boy Brawley Brown*, a story set in the winter of 1964 only months before the riots erupt, the narrative seems densely foreshadowed, already fully aware where this story will go. When Detective Knorr asks Easy for his assistance, the riots are clearly anticipated, more clearly, perhaps, than he can understand, as are a number of other developments in the series:

> "There's blood boiling under the surface of Watts," he said.
> The subtle hiss of the gas jets accented his words with a sinister edge.
> "What's that supposed to mean?"
> "The Negroes are getting anxious for some changes," he said. "They want an end to de facto segregation. They want better jobs. They want to be treated like war heroes after coming home from World War II and Korea. Some even question going into the army and fighting for their country" [*BBBB* 104].

Set in the midst of discussions of the Urban Revolutionary Party and the possibilities of armed insurrection (*BBBB* 49) and of discussions of constitutional rights (*BBBB* 106) and of police violations of civil rights, the foundation for the riots is all in place. Liselle, another figure from Easy's Fifth Ward days who now operates a boarding house in Watts, expresses her fear that any fires, once started, will burn indiscriminately:

Men been comin' by with com'unist leaflets and rough talk about killin' and burnin' down the street. I asked 'em was they gonna burn down my house and they said no, but how you gonna start a fire an' ask it to skip the houses you want to save? Once the flames get goin', they burn down everything [*BBBB* 169].

Liselle's fears, as it turned out, were well founded.

The narrative plays back and forth in time, placing these actions in perspective, aware of the narrative function. This attention to storytelling is equally accented by the frequent recounting of dreams that, often as not, recall events from Easy's past, providing another layer to the story. Curiously, the details of these accounts change in the course of the books. That the details change, as does the spelling, for instance, of *Jogaye/Joguye*, might simply be attributed to editorial oversight, to problems of maintaining continuity in a long-running series. (Even the critics have had trouble keeping narrative detail straight. In one case, Mouse's formal name is given as "Raymond *Navrochet*," not *Alexander*, and he is said to have been shot by daddy Reese when, in fact, it was Navrochet, Mouses's step-brother, who wounded Mouse in an exchange of gunfire [Young 147–48]; another critic identifies Feather as being the child of a dead black stripper and white father, Jesus as autistic, and Pariah as being in Louisiana, not Texas [Whall 194, 196, and 198, respectively].) On the other hand, these discrepancies do seem to serve some possible purpose. Alice Mills, for instance, has noted some of these problems in "Warring Ideals in Dark Bodies: Cultural Allegiances in the Work of Walter Mosley," connecting the shifting accounts Easy offers of his father's disappearance to the myths of the trickster Esu:

> According to Geoffrey Hartman, indeterminacy "acts as a bar between understanding and truth" (Gates, *Signifying Monkey* 25). Easy's strategies are in a way reminiscent of the myths of Esu, whose preferred forms of expression are ambiguity and the co-existence of opposites. Throughout Mosley's entire series of detective stories, the more closely Easy's words relate to his intimate feelings, the more they manifest themselves through the process of modified repetition that is considered essential to the African principle of expression. For example, the disappearance of Easy's father is related in fragments which are constantly remodeled. Was his father killed in a fight? Was he lynched? Was he arrested and imprisoned? Did he remarry and forget his child? Or, was his disappearance due to some even more mysterious cause? All these reasons are advanced by Easy at one point or another in accordance with the trickster's dialectical process [29].

The answer may, in fact, be somewhat simpler, that these discrepancies attest to the fact that these stories are being actively constructed, a remembering of the past. They speak in part to the problems of memorial reconstruction and in part to the shifting character of the truth. Following a conversation with Sam Houston about the Urban Revolutionary Party, Easy decides to go see things for himself:

> I decided to go down to the First Men's storefront and see what it was that they were all about. Sam had his point of view and I was sure that he had told me the truth as far as he saw it; but truth, as my uncle Roger used to say, is just one man's explanation for what he thinks he understands [BBBB 42].

Truth depends on perspective, on how the story is told, on the vantage point from which the events are observed.

These inconsistencies are no more mistakes than the anachronisms in Shakespeare. In Mosley's case, they create a sense of self-consciousness, a sense that the stories are relative and shifting, that Easy is still, to a degree, trying to figure out how to tell the story. Easy isn't a "natural" storyteller like Mouse, whose "lies" always seem true, no matter how preposterous. Mouse's shooting of Navrochet is a case in point, his first feigning fright, then pissing on Navrochet's boots and shooting him four times when he leapt out of the way (DBD 33), a tall tale that ends with the wounded Mouse confronting and threatening the figure of death himself. Easy's stories, by contrast, are more self-consciously told.

Even Mosley seems to play the same kind of game, certainly in the color-coding of his titles, and, perhaps, in the puzzling title of his one volume of Easy Rawlins short stories, *Six Easy Pieces*, a book that includes seven stories, all, of course, told by Easy and about his investigations. The apparent miscount, however, seems to refer to a more basic point about these stories and the effort required to prepare this book for publication, and not to the number of stories themselves: Six of the stories had been previously published as bonuses in the latest paperback editions of the first six books in the series. Collecting them for this edition was presumably easy. "Amber Gate," by contrast, a new story, would have required more effort, not so easy as the others. In "Miscounts, Loopholes, and Flashbacks: Strategic Evasion in Walter Mosley's Detective Fiction," Elisabeth Ford notes the miscount, diagnoses a sense of exhaustion in "Amber Gate" that separates it from the earlier works in the series (1074–5), and then goes on to offer a sophisticated analysis of the various "strategic evasions" Mosley uses and that seem to be characteristic of African American fiction. "Amber Gate" is unusual, though not unique in the series, in that the final paragraph positions the narrator at a distinct time and place, not some unidentified vantage point in the future:

> I still work at Sojourner Truth Junior High School and see Raymond now and then. Bonnie and I are still together. I read the newspapers a little closer nowadays. Looking for the deaths of young black women and reading between the lines [SEP 278].

He notes that he has spent the previous six months looking for Harold, but to no avail. In the books that follow, he will find Harold, leave his job at Sojourner Truth, and lose Bonnie.

The ending of "Amber Gate," summing up present circumstances, repeats, in a way, the ending of *Gone Fishin'*, the narrative again positioned in a specific time and place, a hotel room in Paris following the armistice, before Easy ships out for home. Easy has just finished recounting the events in Pariah and Houston that led to his enlisting in the army and his service in the war, and he has just been speculating on what may have become of Mouse. The book ends "There's no way for me to tell the future from this room in Paris. All I can do is follow my footsteps, not at all like my father, and go back home" (*GF* 243–4). These books end, but always short of a conclusion. In *Gone Fishin'* and "Amber Gate," these present-tense moments anticipate a future yet to unfold. In the other books, told from an undetermined point in the future, we're always left hanging. The first-person narrative particularizes the point of view, creates a sense of historical perspective, self-consciously reflects on narrative function, and, finally, refuses a sense of closure, and with it, any sense that justice has finally been achieved.

7

Our Kind of People
Stephen L. Carter and the Mysteries of the Black Bourgeoisie

Counter-Conspiracy

Lemaster Carlyle, former professor of law, listens to rap music, an odd choice for an otherwise conservative university president. Carlyle, who plays a minor role in Stephen L. Carter's debut novel, *The Emperor of Ocean Park* (2002), returns in *New England White* (2007) after a short stint as a federal judge and then as White House counsel to take the presidency of Carter's Yale-like university. Rap seems an odd choice for the otherwise very proper Carlyle, a man of Jamaican stock, Ivy-league educated, a highly-respected law professor, a one-time divinity student and a practicing Anglican, the college-roommate of both the current conservative president and his liberal democratic challenger. The taste seems somewhat eccentric, but potentially appropriate, perhaps telling. Carlyle might, for instance, have been listening to Kanye West's *The College Dropout* (2004), and *Late Registration* (2005), the first two albums in a projected tetralogy dealing with educational themes and both winners of the Grammy Awards for Best Rap Album in their respective years; *Rolling Stone* named *Late Registration* the best album of 2005. The third installment of the planned four-album series, *Graduation*, appeared in 2007. Several of the songs on *Late Registration* appeal to personal or social issues that Carlyle might relate to: "Heard 'Em Say," for instance, "talks about being honest with yourself in a world that is not" (Hess 573), while "Diamonds from Sierra Leone" takes up the issue of the "blood diamonds" used to finance the civil wars in West Africa. He might, also, however, have found the interpolated skits about joining a fictional black fraternity, "Broke Phi Broke," at least modestly amusing. The members of the fraternity "pride themselves on living a life without money or worldly possession" ("Late Registration"). According to Mickey Hess, the skits explore "a contradiction at the core of contemporary American life: the need to belong, to fit in, with your fellow humans versus the Darwinistic mad grab at material things, success in the latter being the very definition of success in our culture" (574). While the former divinity student might have appreciated the abstemious impulse of the fraternity, the wealthy owner of Hunter's Heights, a new and impressive estate dominating the rural landscape of the very white and now fashionable Tyler's Landing, would have been alive to the conspicuous consumption that speaks success.

Carlyle's tastes, however, run to "the more rebellious and edgy and less commercial end of the hip-hop spectrum" (*NEW* 12).[1] In that regard, Jay-Z's 2003 release, *The Black Album*, might be more in keeping with his perceived tastes and with themes that will come to dominate this novel and *Palace Council*, the novel that follows and which provides the family and social history for present characters and concerns. In fact, hip-hop's obsession with the Iluminati, first identified as the source of African American oppression in the mid–1990s and then seemingly appropriated by Jay-Z and others in a counter-conspiracy in the following decade, provides an analog for the action of these novels, in particular for the actions and influence of the Empyreals, a seemingly minor Harlem's men's club to which Lemaster belongs.

In a 1997 *New York Times Magazine* article entitled "Bound by Suspicion," Michiko Kakutani comments on the new paranoia operating as a leitmotif in much of popular culture, that while "paranoia is nothing new in American politics," "millennial anxieties seem to have fanned the flames of conspiracy thinking":

> No doubt the new paranoid style in American arts reflects the national mood: Watergate taught us to be suspicious, and later investigations (from Iran-contra to Whitewater) further fueled those suspicions. As for the demise of the Communist threat, it left us not with a new sense of security but with a flurry of free-floating suspicions.

Kakutani identifies this new paranoia as the driving element behind everything from "The X-Files" to Joan Didion's *The Last Thing He Wanted* and notes that it has resulted in competing tendencies:

> We are once again on the brink of a new century, faced with mind-boggling changes like the breakdown of cold-war politics, the proliferation of new technologies and growing tensions among the races and sexes. One reaction—apparent in rap music and avant-garde fiction—has been to push discontinuity further, to celebrate incoherence. Another reaction, the paranoid reaction, has been to embrace an esthetic that does not mirror indeterminacy but defines it.

Indeed, "nothing is unexplained in the paranoid's universe; nothing is incoherent." Such will clearly be the case in Carter's fiction where the Empyreals seem to be calling the shots, the driving force behind much of what is happening in contemporary politics. In short, the Empyreals provide an African American version of groups like the Illuminati, a group arising in the European Enlightenment that is associated with Freemasonry and dedicated to the development of a New World Order, at least according to contemporary conspiracy theory, all of it providing an alternate theory of history. Everything is part of the plan.

The Internet, in general, seems to be the primary repository for conspiracy theorists' paranoid speculations. Jeffrey E., for instance, provides a brief overview of the common conspiracy theories surrounding the Illuminati on *illuminatiarchchives.org*. "Rumor has it," he writes, "that the Illuminati actually consists of several secret societies and fraternal orders compartmentalized into a pyramidal hierarchy of need-to-know and initiation." These organizations communicate through "occult symbols and rituals," through "arcane codex which they [the members] have sworn an oath never to reveal." Such is true of the Freemasons, not a "secret society" but "a society with secrets," a group to which many American presidents have allegedly belonged and one of whose symbols, the all-seeing eye topping a pyramid, appears on the back of the dollar bill. Associated groups include Yale's Skull and Bones Society, which includes "once presidential contenders George W. Bush and John Kerry, whom [sic] are both cousins related by blood," and the Bohemian Grove Club:

> The Bohemian Grove club is an organization which includes some of the most powerful men in the world. The Bohemian Club meets each year in private campgrounds located in Sonoma County California. Bohemian Club's elite members include Presidents Ronald Regan, Richard Nixon, George Bush, Sr., and Bush Jr., as well as many media and entertainment industry executives. The culmination of this event ends with a ceremony in which a human effigy is ritualistically burned at an altar beside a forty-foot concrete statue of an owl. The owl itself is said to be connected to wisdom and the occult symbolism of the Illuminati. A depiction of an owl figure can be seen within the architecture of the streets surrounding the United States Capital in Washington, D.C.

Such conspiracies proliferate on the Web.

Carter's various plot devices mirror these paranoid delusions almost exactly: The exclusive "fraternity" of the four college roommates at his Yale-like Ivy League College—including the scion of a wealthy family, a sitting conservative president, his democratic rival, and Lemaster Carlyle—proves to be central to the plot of *New England White*, which begins to reveal the forces shaping contemporary affairs. The Empyreals emerge as the keepers of the official secrets and consequently the real power behind the throne. In *Palace Council*, the Empyreals intersect with other groups. They are present at a meeting of twenty powerful men, twelve white, including then sitting Vice-President Richard Nixon, eight black, who meet on Martha's Vineyard in 1952 and conspire to create a new world order, to shake the throne; their plan is encoded in a language and images drawn from Milton's *Paradise Lost*. Moreover, everything that happens in *Palace Council* and the twenty years from *Brown v. Board* to Nixon's resignation, a period that Carter refers to as the Sixties, the period of the story, seems to hark back to this meeting and the forces that emerge there. Though minority members of "The Project," as it is known, the African American members of the plot, in general, and the Empyreals, specifically, not a secret society but a society with secrets, seem to be calling the shots. Carter's plots parallel the kinds of conspiracies that run rampant through the blogs and which attribute contemporary events to the unseen operations of the Masons, to the members of secret societies hatching plans at clandestine meetings. The only distinction appears in the interracial composition of Carter's groups, with the African American members proving themselves disproportionately responsible for the course of contemporary history.

The revisionary movement Carter effects here seems to parallel developments in rap from the mid–1990s, where the Illuminati are identified with the forces oppressing black people in the ghetto to Jay-Z's appropriation of the power of the Illuminati as a countervailing force in contemporary America. In "Naming the Illuminati," Christopher Holmes Smith and John Fiske have analyzed the references to the Illuminati that emerge in rap music in the mid- to late 1990s. "Many rappers," they write, "have chosen to document the existence of a multidimensional array of power operating upon black bodies through the tenets of the Illuminati" (607). Moreover, "one of the conditions of postmodern oppression is a regularity of material effects whose originary source is so immaterial as to appear to be absent" (607). In the case of lower-class blacks, those effects are all too clear in rates of poverty, incarceration, educational attainment, infant mortality and life expectancy in the African American community, while the causes remain veiled. Smith and Fiske write:

> Two of the phantasmatic, formless entities that are so diffused that they can be perceived only dimly if at all yet whose power effects constitute the imperative materiality of life in the ghetto are, to name them simply, whiteness and global capital. And maybe the two entities are, in the final analysis, one. The unreality of global capital is partly a function of its electronic mobility, its being everywhere and nowhere, always absent as it is inescapably present, and partly in its ever increasing distance from the pauperized pavements of the ghetto from where it appears like a shower of meteorites forever circling the globe, forever out of reach and growing more so—and yet, and yet—someone, somewhere,

somehow can access it, control it, and milk it—the Illuminati. Pauperization is the process that widens the gap between the haves and the have-nots to the extent that it appears to put the haves and the having out of reach, out of touch.

The globalization of capital puts wealth into orbit and localizes poverty into anchored, grounded, immobile fixity. Gravity ties poverty down while wealth flies freely [208].

These are the strains of imagery that appear in Mobb Deep and Goodie Mob, that "Illuminati wants my mind, soul, and my body/Secret society, trying to keep an eye on me," a lyric Mobb Deep quotes from LL Cool J (qtd. in Smith and Fiske 612).

Talcott Garland, the central figure of Carter's first novel, would appreciate this analysis. His work in semiotics, his investigation of his father, dubbed "the Emperor of Ocean Park" by *Time Magazine*, and the references in the book to Noah's indiscretions, to being found drunk and naked in his tent, all seem to coalesce in Smith and Fiske's comments about the Illuminati:

Calling the black knowledge of the Iluminati "paranoid" may be more delusionary for whites than the belief it labels for blacks. The Emperor has clothes as long as people can avoid seeing his nakedness. Power is real as long as the signs of its nonexistence are as real as those of its effects [610].

To develop the point they quote from Jean Baudrillard's *Simulations*:

Power ... produces nothing but the signs of its resemblance. And at the same time, another figure of power comes into play; that of a collective demand for *signs* of power—a holy union which forms around the disappearance of power.... This has already given rise to fascism, that overdose of a powerful referential in a society which cannot terminate its mourning [qtd. in Smith and Fiske 610].

Oliver Garland's excess of mourning over the death in a hit-and-run accident of his younger daughter leads him to enter into a pact with Jack Zeigler, a sign of power that clearly results in the disappearance of power, in the abnegation of his democratic judicial functions, and in his final descent into a strident conservativism, his own fascist response. Talcott will be forced to know his father's sin and to recognize the distance between sign and signified in *The Emperor of Ocean Park*.

In rap, however, in what appears an act of appropriation, Jay-Z seems to align himself with the Illuminati, not against it, proposing an alternate history. Music blogs have speculated about Jay-Z's connections to the occult for years, many of those rumors apparently finding confirmation in his 2010 recording, "Run This Town." References to Freemasonry, to Satanism, and to the Five Percenters all find their way into his work, with conspiracy theorists linking references to Lucifer, "the bearer of light," to the Illuminati; the references to the rebellious angels are in keeping with the Illuminati's humanist agenda to overthrown existing governments and religions to be replaced by a new world order.² Such references seem equally appropriate to Carter's Empyreals and their references to Milton's portrayal of the fallen angels in *Paradise Lost*. In Carter's case, the forces of darkness emerge from "the darker nation," the term Eddie Wesley coins in his novels (*Palace Council*) and which is used through all of Carter's novels to refer to Americans of African descent; blackmail is their preferred means of exerting influence. References to Freemasonry and the Illuminati, to Lucifer, and to the occult practices and beliefs of the Five Percenters, a group based in Harlem that "believe that the black man emerging from the Asian continent is God and that all men are God in potential" (Raz) all swirl through Jay'Z's lyrics and music videos. Rather than being the victims of Illuminati-led conspiracies, of the forces of whiteness and global capitalism, Jay-Z and company have insinuated that they are part of the conspiracy, working toward a new world order. In his fiction, Carter is working the same angles.

Sins of Our Fathers

The early announcements and reviews of Carter's first novel, *The Emperor of Ocean Park*, made a great deal to do about the $4.2 million advance this first-time novelist received for *Emperor* and a second novel and about the depiction of an affluent African American community few Americans, white or black, seemed to know much about. As a Yale law professor, Carter had published seven books during the previous decade, studies of affirmative action (which drew on his own personal experiences), of the role of religion in government, and of the judicial nomination and approval process, among other topics, but he had never published any fiction. That he opposed affirmative action and supported a role for religion in public life generally placed him right of center, clearly conservative; that he has also identified the Republican Party as offering safe haven for racists and racist sentiments and that he stops short of fully embracing conservative religious principles somewhat tempers that perceived conservativism.³ Still, the combination of a book describing an affluent African American community, their wealth and lineage generations old, often predating emancipation (and thus, negating arguments in support of affirmative action); written by a conservative African American author, in a relatively conservative form, the murder mystery, especially in the ways Carter handles the genre; at just the moment that George W. Bush was ushering in a new conservative administration—all of these elements taken together must have suggested the financial viability of this project and justified the advance.

To date, Carter has published five novels: *The Emperor of Ocean Park* (2002), *New England White* (2007), *Palace Council* (2008), *Jericho's Fall* (2009), and *The Impeachment of Abraham Lincoln* (2012), a work of historical fiction. The first three novels tie together. Set in the twenty years between 1952 and 1972, *Palace Council* provides background history for characters and events we have already met in the first two books. *Emperor* is told in a first-person present-tense narrative contemporary with the book's publication; *New England White* takes place some three years later. Both novels are set in the same New England Ivy League town, and they do share a number of characters, people whose family histories emerge in *Palace Council*. The fourth novel, *Jericho's Fall*, is more spy thriller than murder mystery, is set in a Colorado town far distant from the New England settings of the earlier novels, and employs a cast of characters, aside from two relatively minor characters introduced in *Emperor*, distinct from the other books. Each book, in turn, has garnered less critical notice than its predecessor; *New England White* received approximately half the attention *Emperor* generated, *Palace Council* perhaps a third as much, and *Jericho's Fall* less still. While the reviews of the first three novels were largely positive, responses to *Jericho's Fall*, the story transpiring wholly outside of the affluent African American community at the center of the first three books, were decidedly tepid. Jan Stuart, for instance, notes that while Carter had been "heralded as the Dreiser of the black bourgeoisie" following the publication of *Emperor*, with *Jericho's Fall*, "this assiduously middle-brow new suspense novel, he makes his bid to be the Sidney Sheldon of post-racial America," and not all that successfully. A short piece in *Kirkus Reviews* finds the book "turgid and redundant," and concludes, "Let's hope the real Stephen L. Carter reappears soon, displacing this unsatisfying Robert Ludlum clone." While Carter's study of the African American elite in the first three novels proved largely successful and satisfying, his movement away from that material in *Jericho's Fall* proved far less so. Even so, the reappearance of Maxine, first introduced in *Emperor*, provides possibilities for connecting these story lines in future novels. Maxine's mere presence deepens the plot, suggesting the existence of unseen and unsuspected forces moving beneath the surface of the story. Her inclusion is a small thing, easily overlooked by readers who have not come to this book after reading Carter's earlier works, but it immediately lifts this book out of the category of generic thriller, connecting it to the vastly more complicated and compelling political realities of the earlier work.

By far and away, Carter's portrayal of an affluent African American community, not of nouveau riche athletes, rappers, and movie stars but of old families and old money capable, in some cases, of tracing their ancestry back to the colonial period, has claimed the greatest amount of attention in the early reviews. In a review of *Emperor* published in *The New York Review of Books*, K. Anthony Appiah considers and then dismisses the idea that the novel is a *roman à clef* at the same time that he argues that the novel does clearly explore contemporary realities: "If the novel is a portrait of imaginary places, embedded in real ones, it is also an exploration of an imaginary family, equally embedded in the actualities of our country and age" (4), specifically the families and the places of the affluent African American community. "Even in novels that no one would think fictionalized portrayals of real events," he writes, "the world of the novel is very often close to the actual world" (5):

> And the reality that many Americans will find most interestingly available in *The Emperor of Ocean Park* is, pace its author, exactly that of upper-middle-class black America. Long before its publication, Carter's novel received a good deal of attention in the press because of the singularly intense competition for the manuscript among publishing houses (it received a record advance for a first novel), and, indeed, movie studios. In his mastery of atmosphere and the intricacies of plot, Carter deserves comparison with such successful practitioners of the crime novel as Scott Turow, but what sets *The Emperor of Ocean Park* apart is the sense it provides of introducing us to a world within a world. It is the world of the black elite that has connections in Washington's Gold Coast and in Oak Bluffs, and that was once centered academically on Howard University but now has outposts at Stanford and the Ivy League. Many of its members have served both the nation and the black community with honor and distinction, as Thurgood Marshall—for whom Mr. Carter clerked—did, and as Oliver Garland once sought to do [5].

The portrayal in *Emperor* of the Gold Coast community in Washington, D.C., with their favored summer retreat in Oak Bluffs, Martha's Vineyard, and in *New England White* and *Palace Council* of the Harlem elite with their Sugar Hill addresses, occupying the high ground overlooking "the valley," the scene of Chester Himes's books, is drawn from life.

The world that Carter explores is clearly that portrayed by Lawrence Otis Graham in *Our Kind of People: Inside America's Black Upper Class*, first published in 1999. In the introduction to the 2000 Harper Perennial edition, Graham remarks on the controversy generated by the first edition:

> Although I have spent six years researching *Our Kind of People*, I could never have been prepared for the controversy that it elicited from various groups upon its initial publication. Although there is a constant cry for diversity in our media, our literature, our history books, and in our communities, it became obvious to me that there are certain narrow stereotypes—even within an integrated society—that people are simply unwilling to relinquish. The stereotype of the working-class black or impoverished black is one that whites, as well as blacks, have come to embrace and accept as an accurate and complete account of the

black American experience. *Our Kind of People* upset that stereotype. And it upset many people—particularly blacks—who have been taught never to challenge a stereotype that we have been saddled with since slavery [ix].

In part, the book grew out of Graham's interactions in the late 1980s with Reginald Lewis, a graduate of Harvard Law and, at the time, the wealthiest black man in America, who, in spite of his great wealth and accomplishments, was not native to the traditions of the affluent African American community, not in the ways Graham proved to be, and was struggling at the time to find ways to raise his daughters in what seemed disparate worlds, that of the affluent and of the authentically black. Graham realized that "there needed to be a chronicle of a community that was hidden from so many people":

> Although it's a world I've known all of my life, and although it's an important part of our nation's history, it's a world that is filled with irony and conflict. This book was an opportunity to reveal a rarely discussed aspect of American history. It is an opportunity to capture the stories and lives of people like Lewis and many others, who have lived at the boundary of two worlds and been misunderstood by both [xviii].

This is the world from which the Garland family, Julia Carlyle, and Eddie Wesley emerge in Carter's novels, and whose conflicts are most clearly embodied in Talcott Garland.

The rampant colorism in the novels of Rudolph Fisher and Chester Himes remains an obsession in Carter's early books, though clearly entertained from the perspective of the privileged class. Graham comments that such concerns were "a color thing and a class thing" and that "for generations of black people, color and class have been inexorably linked together" (4). He was aware, even as a child, of the dichotomies of class in the black world: "At the age of six, I already understood the importance of achieving a better shade of black," a lesson his younger brother was just learning:

> Unlike my brother, I already knew that there was *us* and there was *them*. There were those children who belonged to Jack and Jill and summered in Sag Harbor; Highland Beach; or Oak Bluffs, Martha's Vineyard; and those who didn't. There were those mothers who graduated from Spelman or Fisk and joined AKA, the Deltas, the Links, and the Girl Friends, and there were those who didn't. There were those fathers who were dentists, lawyers, and physicians from Howard or Meharry and who were Alphas, Kappas, or Omegas and members of the Comus, the Boulé, or the Guardsmen, and there were those who weren't. There were those who could look back two or three generations and point to relatives who owned insurance companies, newspapers, funeral homes, local banks, trucking companies, restaurants, catering firms, or farmland, and there were those who couldn't. There were those families that made what some called "a handsome picture" of people with "good hair" (wavy or straight), with "nice complexions"

(light brown to white), with "sharp features" (thin nose, thin lips, sharp jaw) and curiously non-Negroid hazel, green, or blue eyes—and there were those that didn't. I had a precious few of the above, while many I knew and played with were able to check off *all* the right boxes. In fact, I knew some who not only had complexions lighter than that paper bag, and hair as straight as any ruler, but also had multiple generations of "good looks," wealth, and accomplishment. And, of course, I also knew some black kids who could claim nothing at all [4].

For those in the African American elite, at least through the middle decades of the twentieth century, class distinctions were marked by place of residence, school affiliations, attendance at specific summer camps, membership in specific organizations—Jack and Jill for children and teenagers, one of several college fraternities or sororities while in school, and then one or more civic or social organizations thereafter—preferred vacation spots, preferred churches, preferred funeral homes, specific families, introductions into society at one of the debutant balls sponsored by various local and national organizations. Membership in many of the organizations, Jack and Jill, the Links, and Boulé, for instance, is by invitation only, the whole process of nomination and selection a carefully guarded secret. In some cases, the Boulé is one example, these organizations have only recently emerged from the secrecy that prevailed for much of their early histories (Graham 133).

For members of these affluent African American communities, such were the vernacular experiences of the group; for those outside these communities, this world remained largely invisible, unknown, unsuspected. Few people in the United States have not heard of Harvard, Yale, and Princeton. On the other hand, few of those same people have heard of Phillips Exeter, Andover or Peddie, the elite boarding schools that have historically supplied significant numbers of students to the Ivy League and select liberal arts colleges. They would be equally unaware of application procedures and largely baffled as to how they could ever afford the $40,000 annual price tag of such an education, or why it might be even worth the cost. Elite institutions like Exeter remain something of a well-kept secret outside of certain social circles. That elite black institutions tend to be equally unknown outside of a narrowly prescribed circle should hardly be surprising.

Several immediate impressions arise from reading Graham's study of the black upper-class. One is of the tightly interwoven fabric of this community, the network of connections supported by the relatively small size of the community and by multiple and overlapping memberships in these key social groups—Jack and Jill, college fraternities and sororities, civic and social organizations. For Oliver Garland's generation, people who were educated and came of age prior to *Brown v. Board*, such connections were particularly strong. Graham lists the names of prominent members of such organizations, noting in particular the participation of nearly every prominent African American—member of Congress, Cabinet secretary, big city mayor, ranking military officer, judge, doctor, lawyer, corporate executive—in one or more of these groups. It is also true that integration and the expanding range of educational, employment and housing options it offers has led to some erosion in these tight-knit networks. While Lemaster Carlyle and Julia belong to fictional equivalents of the Boulé and Girl Friends, respectively, and Talcott and Mariah Garland are alumni of Jack and Jill, certain rifts begin to appear, first in their Ivy League educations, one of the historic paths taken by affluent African Americans for generations but one that does not offer the advantages of a Howard or Spelman education, and in Mariah's marriage to a white man. Graham quotes a member of an old-guard Washington, D.C., family who would certainly not have approved of the Garland children's choices in spouse or schools:

> "Sometimes I honestly believe that segregation was better for us," says a grandmother who thumbs through a photo album filled with graduation pictures of herself and other family members. "This is me when I was graduating from Dunbar, and here I am again when I finished Howard. Do you notice the difference between these pictures and the ones from my grandkids' graduations?" [Graham 244].

The difference, it hardly need be pointed out, is in the racial composition, her grandchildren surrounded "by a sea of white faces." She clearly feels that her grandchildren are at a disadvantage:

> "Where are my grandkids' role models? Where is their support system? Where is their tie to our people?" The woman paused. "At Dunbar and at Howard, we had examples to follow and black classmates that we connected with. They were people with background—people we'd know for a lifetime. My grandkids don't know about fraternities or black roommates. They never even had a black teacher. They grew up in the best city in the country for rich blacks—and I feel like we somehow let them get away" [Graham 244–45].

In some ways, the drama that plays out here is analogous to the history Walter Mosley tells in the Easy Rawlins series, of an early tight-knit Watts community, with a shared history in Houston's Fifth Ward and a sense of community values still intact that steadily erodes through the books. While some changes are for the better, others are not.

In Mosley, the conventions of the hard-boiled mystery, of the noir novel, become a metaphor for African American experience in post–World War II Los Angeles. In Carter, the tightly interwoven character of the affluent African American community essentially supports the worlds of power, privilege and political intrigue central to these novels, of an organization, not so much a secret society but a society with secrets, communicating in a coded language, conspiring together to create a new world order. The political dramas of *New England White* and *Palace Council* provide a clearer representation of this world than does *Emperor* and the more domestic drama that unfolds there; Oliver Garland's use of Jack Zeigler to pursue a private revenge is essentially different from the Empyreals' plot to manipulate public policy. On the other hand, Talcott's highly ambiguous relationship with his father and his father's politics, with his own privilege, reading of race, troubled marriage, and religious beliefs seem completely representative of the irony and conflict Graham finds at the center of life in the affluent African American community. Talcott can only solve the mystery of the "arrangements" by coming to know his father's failings. Oliver, the Judge, had demanded a retributive form of justice, an Old Testament exchange of an eye for an eye, and to achieve it, he had availed himself of Jack Zeigler's services, entering into an unholy pact that would result in his own public humiliation and very nearly in the death of his son. Talcott comments in the course of the narrative on the extravagance of this society, on the obsessions over skin color and family connections still in play, and on his own moments of rage, his "seeing red" when his own black sensibilities are confronted. He is clearly a product of his environment.

While Carter's world is obviously distinct from that of Fisher, Himes, and Mosley, his novels are often marked by concerns similar to theirs: the exploration of a black vernacular experience; a recognition of the double-consciousness that being African American always seems to entail; some consideration of the alternative ways of being in and knowing the world, what Soitos identifies as the Hoodoo element, that prevails historically within the African American community; and in the ways he engages historical and generic constructions, creating alternative constructions of both. Talcott's seeing red is generically equivalent to the inner voice Easy Rawlins hears periodically. His embracing of his Christianity, especially of more evangelical expressions of the religion, seems to place him in traditions alternative to those prevailing in the secular academic world of the law school and, to a degree, to the Anglican traditions favored by the affluent African American community; his is an alternative way of knowing, one that is alive to the ambiguities and uncertainties of knowledge in this world. Talcott comments at the end of *Emperor* that his sister, Mariah, true to the tenets of her training as an investigative journalist, will continue to search for evidence that will confirm her hypothesis that the Judge was murdered. He, however, has called off his personal search:

> Let Mariah continue to try to prove the Judge was murdered; that is her way of coping, and, with her journalistic tenacity, she may yet uncover a further

unhappy truth. I admire her search but will not join it. I have long been comfortable living without perfect knowledge. Semiotics has taught me to live with ambiguity in my work; Kimberly has taught me to live with ambiguity in my home; and Morris Young is teaching me to live with ambiguity in my faith. That truth, even moral truth, exists I have no doubt, for I am no relativist; but we weak, fallen humans will never perceive it except imperfectly, a faintly glowing presence toward which we creep through the mists of reason, tradition, and faith [*EOP* 653].

Talcott's use of the present perfect in the first two cases—that of his work and his home—that he "has learned" to live with these ambiguities, seems a bit premature, perhaps. That he is moving beyond the forensic investigations of his sister and away from the retributive justice prevailing in his father's legalistic mathematics, an Old Testament formula, to some more spiritual reality, however, is also the case.

Structuralist Poetics

Carter's first four novels tend to be nothing if not self-conscience in construction and rather repetitive, in general, in terms of plot. All four novels begin with a prologue which establishes, in suitably auspicious tones, a point of departure for the story. In *Emperor*, the question concerns Oliver Garland's death and Mariah's suspicion that the causes were other than natural. In *New England White*, "you"—the address is second person—are sufficiently unsettled by Vera Brightwood's gossipy assessment of both recent events and her African American neighbors that you head out of town as quickly as you can go, heedless of potential speed traps; Vera is the proprietor of the local sweet shop in Tyler's Landing and a notorious busybody. In *Palace Council*, we attend and then escape a clandestine meeting of powerful men. We're centered inside the consciousness of an unnamed lawyer who, in spite of his relief at this moment, will be dead within thirty months (*PC* 6). Chapter 1 then opens with Eddie Wesley's discovering that dead man, a short reprieve, indeed. And in *Jericho's Fall*, the prologue briefly sketches the week about to happen: "On the Sunday before the terror began, Rebecca DeForde pointed the rental car into the sullen darkness of her distant past…. By Friday, Rebecca DeForde would be running for her life" (*JF* 3, 5). The reader has some sense of the story's arc, the detailed account of which will cover the next 350 pages in *Jericho's Fall*, 550–650 pages in the other three.

Similarly, each novel ends with an "Author's Note." Having told the story, Carter then steps forward to address possible issues and inaccuracies in the text. He is at pains to explain that the story just read is a fictional construction, not a *roman à clef*, the events and people all products of the author's imagination (*EOP* 655). At the same time, he also points out minor discrepancies of fact, that he has omitted "the hideous public boathouse" that now obscures a certain view of a particular Martha's Vineyard beach (*EOP* 655), that he has returned the Brooks Brothers to its former L Street address, not the current Connecticut Avenue location (*EOP* 656). In *Palace Council*, he notes a number of discrepancies, both small and large. While many—most—of the events that form the historical backdrop of this period are historically accurate, for instance, Carter remarks that

> I have not, however, been entirely true to the record. The opening chapters of this novel rest on a slight anachronism. The Harlem society in which Eddie Wesley moves was more characteristic of the 1940s than the 1950s, and of the 1950s than the 1960s. By the time Eddie Wesley began to come to prominence as a writer, the trickle of middle-class families out of Sugar Hill and into midtown Manhattan and the suburbs had become a flood [*PC* 574].

Of smaller issues, he has dated the Official Secrets Act to spring 1961, not winter 1962; introduced Virginia Slims into the market prior to their debut in 1968; and placed a minor character in a Subaru two years before Subarus were first sold in the United States (*PC* 575). The historical and social contexts are all drawn from life though Carter admits that he has altered some details in order to support the narrative. He has, in all these ways, created a "true story."

Internal divisions in the novels are as self-conscious as these framing devices. *Emperor* and *New England White* use chess problems and economic terms, respectively, to title the larger movements of their stories. In *Palace Council* and *Jericho's Fall*, the sections are labeled by time and place or the day of the week, respectively, emphasizing chronology, either the larger history of the two decades running from the *Brown v. Board* decision to Nixon's resignation or of the rapid unraveling of Rebecca DeForde's week. The emphasis is on the construction of these stories, on narrative or thematic devices, on the structural elements that have gone into the making of these pieces. Individual details are subsumed in these larger structures.

And within these four books, each story follows the same basic plot outline. The first three stories all turn on a suspicious death, a cryptic reference to a document that promises to explain the circumstances behind that death, and a race to decode the clues that will reveal the whereabouts of the document in question; in each case, the race is hotly contested, though the exact identity of the contestants and the people they represent are also cloaked in mystery. In *Jericho's Fall*, the actual death is replaced by an impending death, that of Jericho Ainsley, former intelligence agent/head of the CIA, who is rumored to have classified documents that, if leaked, would prove highly embarrassing, all part of his personal insurance policy, a kind of "get-out-of-jail-free" card protecting him from prosecution. At one level, all of the stories are the same story, part Golden Age puzzle box, part post–Watergate paranoia/conspiracy, a neo-conservative kind of fiction. Oliver Garland's "arrangements," Kellen Zant's "capital"—a diary kept by a local police detective unsatisfied with the official resolution of a crime committed thirty years earlier—Castle's "testament," and Jericho's purloined documents all promise to reveal the underlying and potentially destabilizing truths behind some set of current affairs, if the appointed executor—Professor of Law Talcott Garland, Deputy Dean Julia Carlyle, novelist Eddie Wesley, former mistress Rebecca DeForde—can solve the chess problem, explicate the economics or veiled references to *Paradise Lost*, or decode a former lover's cryptic remarks with regard to events in a shared past that never, in fact, happened. That the resolutions often turn on utterly improbable events—the appearance of an elderly, gun-toting Supreme Court justice in the midst of violent weather in *Emperor*—or that the story depended on some improbable relationship to begin with—the Jericho Ainsley/Rebecca DeForde affair of *Jericho's Fall*—only reinforces how artificial these constructions are.

At one level, it might be easy enough to dismiss these kinds of things as flaws in the formulas of genre fiction or as Carter's less-than-skillful handling of his material. Genre fiction is frequently formulaic, especially in the hands of its less accomplished practitioners, and the representations of criminals, criminal behavior, and crime investigations are often stereotypical and/or utterly unrealistic. On the other hand, what can seem absolutely implausible in Carter's books, in *Palace Council* the intermixture of fictional and historical figures, of Eddie Wesley's interactions, for instance, with the Kennedys and Richard Nixon and Langston Hughes, may not be as farfetched as it first seems, given the closely interwoven nature of affluent African-American society, a world where anyone of substance seems to know everyone else of importance, a community closely connected to the seats of economic and political power. As the son of a prominent African American pastor of a Boston church and as an accomplished writer at home in Sugar Hill society, Eddie Wesley might have known and mixed with such people.

On another level, however, these elements seem to be part of the plan, not a problem in this fiction. Language and representation, signs and signification are often central to these books. Talcott Garland's undergraduate training was in semiotics, a fact that is frequently repeated in the book and which comes into play when a dead man, for instance, his body identified by fingerprints and dental records, comes back to life. The "official" story, based on official records, often proves to be a convenient fiction. Signs and signification may not align as neatly as expected. In this regard, Bentley Garland's, Talcott's son, delayed language development does seem significant, as does Vanessa Carlyle's, Lemaster and Julia's teenage daughter, facility with word games. In Bentley's case, his "Dare you," sometimes a question, sometimes a statement, and never clearly explicated or fully understood, seems a nervous questioning of appearances, his version of the *fort/da* game played by Freud's grandson Ernst. "Dare you" seems to translate into "There you," as in "Are you there?" or "There you are." Bentley seems to be uncannily aware of his parents' marital difficulties, of the mysterious disappearances of his mother, of his father's tenuous existence, and of the inherent difficulties in connecting appearances and realities, signs and signification; his "dare you," like little Ernst's "da," becomes a means of symbolically controlling his own anxieties.

The repeated plot structures, centered on mysterious deaths, carefully concealed documents, cryptic clues and their decoding, all embedded in a field of social and political forces, play out as variations on a theme, expressions of contemporary anxiety, of the "new paranoia" Kakutani describes, but also, literally, as linguistic expressions, plots that embody underlying rule-governed systems of signification, a structuralist poetics. Each book provides a variant expression of a particularly contemporary conspiracy mytheme that appears throughout popular and literary fiction, in television shows and movies, in rap music and on Internet blogs. In *Emperor* and *New England White*, the structuring devices of chess problem and economic theory both suggest this concern with the rules of engagement, with game theory. Learning the rules of the game, learning to see the underlying principles that structure and explain contemporary events is the point. If nothing else, Talcott will benefit from the rules, that neither he nor his family can be hurt, a promise that Jack Zeigler will see enforced.

In the end, however, the Double Excelsior chess problem that Oliver Garland obsesses over and that has been so central to Talcott Garland's efforts to locate the arrangements and to unravel the mystery of his father proves to be a red herring. The chess problem, with black and white pieces collaborating in the mating of the black king, may adequately characterize the action of the book in some ways, but it has little to do with the actual location of the "arrangements," a computer disk with records of those parties who have benefited from Oliver Garland's appellate court decisions, the results of his indebtedness to Jack Zeigler and of his collusion with a second member of the three-judge panel whose assistance was necessary to ensure the verdicts in these cases. The computer disk is hidden in a stuffed bear, once the property of Talcott's younger sister, the bear named after the boyfriend of Angela Davis. The reference is more crossword-puzzle clue than chess problem.

The world that Carter chronicles proves similar in many ways to that of *24*, one of two television shows that Jericho Ainsley watches, with the threats being as much internal often as external. And, as in *24*, even the election of an African American president in the early seasons and of a woman president in the later ones is not sufficient to change the rules of the game. The affluent African American community is subject to the same forces and attitudes as the white community. Talcott notes as much upon entering the lobby of the D.C. hotel he is staying in where he is confronted by a gathering of affluent African Americans. Dressed as he is in a plain grey suit and disheveled from his latest encounters on the street, he does not look, as his mother "used to say in the old days" as "our kind of Negro" (*EOP* 266). He continues:

> The lobby reels redly about me for a moment, and I find myself wondering, as I did in my nationalistic college days, who the real enemy is, for those of us who considered ourselves the radical vanguard of the battle for a better future used to sit up half the night cursing the black bourgeoisie. E. Franklin Frazier was right: I see my father and his cold intellectual amusement at "the other Negroes," I see my mother and her elite sororities and social clubs as living a dark imitation of white society, ultimately mimicking, in their desperate quest for status, even the racial attitudes of the larger world. So stunned am I by the visions pulsing angrily through my mind that I am, briefly, unable to move or speak or do anything but watch these beautiful people swirl around me [*EOP* 266].

In *New England White*, the Empyreals will attempt to justify their trafficking in secrets and peddling influence as a "distributive" form of justice, not a "retributive" one, a means of taking from the rich and white and giving to the poor and black. The rationalization is less than convincing, proving only how complicit they are in the same systems of oppression responsible for the current inequitable distribution of wealth. As Oliver Garland has said, we need to draw a line and put the past in the past. Carter's books simultaneously demonstrate the wisdom of that advice and the impossibility of following it.

Some discussion has arisen in the reviews generated by *Jericho's Fall* as to Rebecca DeForde's race, whether she is white or black. While some readers have simply assumed she is black, nothing in the narrative marks her as such. In a *USA Today* interview, Carter claims that he left the question of DeForde's race open intentionally:

> I wanted it to be intriguing. I never mention her race in the book. With at least some of my early readers—editors and booksellers—the automatic default is that she's white. For me, it's intriguing to have a protagonist whose race I don't specify. In today's America, it shouldn't matter what race the character is, and I shouldn't have to say [Donahue].

The clear implication is that in the post-racial era ushered in by the election of an African American president, race need not be considered a defining feature. On the other hand, in the very white world of Colorado where the novel transpires, where the one African American in the community, Ms Kelly, the local librarian, is clearly distinct, Carter's comment seems a bit disingenuous. If anything, Barack Obama's election seems only to have refocused attention on matters of race, not moved us securely beyond them. Clearly, the election of an African American as president—Carter remarks that "most black people did not think that they would see it in their lifetime" (Donahue)—is a game changer in many ways. On the other hand, racial sensitivities in the White House and the racist remarks of Tea Party conservatives seem only to suggest how far we are from the post-racial society, one where "it shouldn't matter what race a character is," which the election of a black president seemed to portend. As seems always to be the case, at least where racial attitudes in the United States are concerned, the more things change, the more they stay the same.

8

Detecting Difference?

> A man's actions are defined by history, my father told me a hundred times before he went off to be swallowed whole by the Struggle. Men are bullets shot from an unpredictable and inexhaustible Gatling gun. You may not be able to foresee where they'll end up, but they are always on their way there.
> —Walter Mosley, *When the Thrill Is Gone* 28

> "I learned when I was at sea," he continued, "that a black man don't need to let his head hang down, he could have just as big dreams as any white man or Brahmin, Aztec princess or Gypsy king. I gave my children the kind of dreams they could live by, but dreams are like oceans, Mr. McGill. If they're worth a damn, they're bigger than the dreamer, and sometimes, when the one dreaming wants to be as big as what they imagine, the wave pulls 'em down."
> —Walter Mosley, *When the Thrill Is Gone* 100

> If you fight a war, terrible things will happen. If you do not want terrible things to happen, do not fight any wars, but bear in mind the risk that the rest of the world might not mind doing terrible things quite as much as you do.
> —Stephen L. Carter, *The Violence of Peace* kl547–53

In 2008, just on the eve of the historic election that brought a black man into the office of President of the United States, Walter Mosley published the first volume of the Leonid McGill mysteries, *The Long Fall*. That book, followed by *Known to Evil* (2010), *When the Thrill Is Gone* (2011) and *All I Did Was Shoot My Man* (2012), is set in contemporary New York and focuses on the life and investigations of private detective Leonid Trotter McGill, 54 years old, born in 1954 or 55, the son of Tolstoy, a self-educated, well-read Marxist revolutionary and one-time union organizer, who leaves the family when Leonid is 11 in order to join some revolution in Central or South America. Tolstoy never returns, Leonid's mother dies, apparently of a broken heart, and Leonid is left to make his way in the world. After the better part of a life working as a "fixer" for crime bosses, adept at derailing official investigations and criminal prosecutions by planting evidence that shifts blame from the guilty party to someone innocent of that particular crime though almost always guilty of others at least as reprehensible, Leonid is now trying to reform, to go straight, to find redemption, to do (private) penance for the harm he has caused. Leaving the life behind is anything but easy, but he perseveres.

Any devoted reader of the Easy Rawlins series, coming to this new character, will find similarities, recurring motifs, things that feel familiar. Like Easy, Leonid lost his father early on and largely raised himself, though with help from an older man, a member of the community, in this case, Gordo, a boxing coach, the owner and operator of a Manhattan gym who offered the young Leonid a place to be and thereafter instruction in boxing. Leonid's family life is easily as complicated as Easy Rawlins's was. Leonid is married to a woman, Katrina, of Scandinavian descent and has three children, though only one, Dimitri, is his biological offspring; a second son, Twilliam, and daughter, Shelly, are the products of Katrina's affairs. Ironically, Twill and Shelly are as loving as Dimitri is disdainful of their father. While Dimitri and Shelly seem to be successful in school, Twill drops out, truly Leonid's son; Leonid devotes almost as much time and attention to monitoring Twill's illegal activities as he devotes to his various investigations. These investigations are assisted by a computer geek, a later-day Jackson Blue, albeit white and overweight, and Leonid does occasionally call on a retired hit man, Hush, a man as sociopathic as Mouse, if far less colorful, when muscle is required. Leonid remains devoted to his family, to the children who need him, whether his or not, though he long ago gave up on the woman he is married to, a woman who never understood him and whom he doesn't love.

A number of points, even in this brief delineation of character, stand out as significant. That Leonid is 54 in 2008 means that he was born in the year of the *Brown* decision (or the year thereafter), born into a United States at just that moment when state-sponsored segregation had been declared unconstitutional and the slow movement to dismantle the apartheid institutions our segregated society depended on had begun. It would be another thirteen years before laws criminalizing interracial marriages were finally declared unconstitutional in the 1967 *Loving* decision, and 54 years before a bi-racial man would run for and be elected President, a half century in which a number of things obviously changed. That Leonid's early experience was shaped by his politically radical father, a Communist devoted to the cause, running clearly contrary to the Red Menace/Cold War fifties, marks him as doubly dislocated. While Leonid is no Communist, he has never forgotten his father's teachings. He fully understands that, as his father has taught him, "a man's actions are defined by history," that we are embedded in time; he also knows, as Gordo and his experience as a boxer have taught him, that "time is always running out" (*Thrill* 2). It, whatever *it* is, ain't over 'til it's over, but any reprieve, any remission, is likely a temporary state.

The immediate problem is that we are defined by history, and that we cannot escape that history, try as we might. Leonid is a man burdened by his history who is now seeking redemption. The problem is that he is no more capable of redeeming the past than he is of repairing his marriage to Katrina, a civil-enough union that persists even in the face of mutual distrust and repeated betrayals on both sides. It is not difficult to imagine a more perfect union; it is just as clear that time has all but run out on this one. The unrelieved anxiety of this situation is compounded by the sense of belatedness hanging over the action, that we have arrived too late to effect meaningful change, that the more things change, the more, somehow, they stay the same.

Such seems to be the case in current events, one of the underlying causes of contemporary anxiety, and seemingly the foundation for these books. After a period of time when school integration made progress, for instance, trends have reversed, segregation increasing, not decreasing, in the schools. The persistent achievement gap between white and minority children prompted the Bush-era No Child Left Behind Act, requiring states to set standards for grade-level proficiency and then to assess progress toward its achievement, with all students required to be operating at or above proficiency in mathematics and reading by 2014. While recognizing that all children can learn and that all children are equally worthy of a rigorous education, the project was doomed from the start by the requirement for universal grade-level proficiency, a requirement that seemingly only set schools up to fail, thereby leading to restructuring, furthering school choice, and weakening teachers' unions. The use of standardized tests to assess "adequate yearly progress" seemed to result in modest gains (though critics like Diane Ravitch are quick to point out that such gains represented a drop compared to the improvement rates posted in the years immediately before NCLB was implemented [Ravitch 110]), but it also resulted in schools teaching to the test, focusing curriculum and instruction on the materials being tested, and in states lowering their standards to make achieving grade-level proficiency possible. There is some argument that NCLB may even have accelerated drop-out rates, a side effect of impoverished curriculum and administrative interest in raising average scores by eliminating the lowest scoring students.

The immediate problem—and the source of some anxiety—is that the Obama administration has not significantly changed course, at least with regard to education. In *The Death and Life of the Great American School Sys-*

tem, Ravitch argues that educational policy has largely remained unchanged from the Regan-Bush administrations through Obama, the general programs more alike than different (20–22). While NCLB has not been re-approved, the Obama administration has stressed the use of test scores to evaluate teacher performance, for instance. Things have changed but not in ways that are likely to change much. Children like Dimitri, aka Bulldog, and the compliant Shelly, not unlike Feather Rawlins, will get a somewhat more adequate education in contemporary New York than Jesus Rawlins encountered in mid-century Los Angeles, though the obviously bright and very street smart Twill will still find school a waste of time, nothing that speaks directly to his needs, interests, or experience. Progress, if one can call it that, achieved by programs designed to improve test scores, not real learning, has been halting at best.

While the election of a black man campaigning on the premise of hope was largely regarded as a game changer, a watershed moment in American politics, the change has been slow in coming. The Obama administration's pursuit of the wars in Iraq, Afghanistan, and against terror, for instance, has stayed the course established under the Bush administration, something that Stephen L. Carter discusses at length in *The Violence of Peace*, his extended analysis of Obama's Nobel Peace Prize address and Obama's invocation of just war theory in that speech. The "man many considered the peace candidate was transformed into a war President," Carter writes, "largely adopt[ing] the policies of his predecessor" (k137). Under Obama, Carter notes, the news media report that the practice of rendition has increased (k801–7), as has the use of Predator and Reaper Drones (k912–17) and the use of targeted assassination those tools make possible. Obama seems to have discovered what President Bush discovered: "there are forces in the world," forces of evil, "that must not be allowed to triumph. Sometimes matters really are that simple" (k262–67). Carter voices his misgivings in places but clearly approves of the ways the Obama administration has stayed the course in the current wars. By contrast, Leonid McGill's references to these wars and the fact that war has become the normal state of affairs in the United States suggest a less than positive appraisal of U.S. foreign policy, an opinion, perhaps, all the more remarkable coming from a man whose offices in the Tesla Building provide a view down the Hudson "to where the World Trade Center used to stand" (*Thrill* 8).

Carter's discussion of Obama's Nobel address highlights the distinction between law and morality, or, to change his terms slightly, between law and justice, a point that is central to detective fiction, especially written by African American authors. Obama invoked just war theory and not international law in his speech, Carter argues, because Obama "was not interested in what is legally ordained but what is morally ordained" (kl524–29). The killing of bin Laden and the prevailing public sentiment that "justice has been done" is a case in point. The killing of bin Laden may represent a retributive kind of justice, but it had nothing of the judicial about it. From the violation of Pakistan's national sovereignty to the killing itself, unconvincingly justified as an act of self defense—bin Laden was reportedly holding a gun—this was clearly an extra-legal operation. One might have hoped for a better outcome, especially from a country championing national sovereignty and civil and judicial rights. But Carter is clear from the start:

> War is not the same as law. The two are antitheses. Law is what the nation does at its leisure, battling titanically from the safety of its living rooms and laptops and congressional offices over whether to raise or lower the capital gains tax half a point or so. War is how the leisure to engage in robust democratic argument is protected [kl26–32].

That the very state we expect to protect us from violence perpetuates violence in war is, however, only an apparent contradiction:

> It is the commission of violence that protects us from violence. The police go armed; our soldiers, more so. The world of laws, whether national or international, survives because it is enforced on dissenters at the point of the gun. But war is not law enforcement. War is not, contra Hegel, a continuation of the dialectic, the battle over abstract ideas. War is the work of a more primitive urge, an aspect of humanity older than the state but also necessary to its existence: the determination to kill them before they kill you [kl343–49].

In the McGill mysteries, Mosley seems to be trying to turn the corner, to move beyond the kill-or-be-killed realities that obtained historically in American society where legal and moral imperatives, especially with regard to people of African descent, were different. What has been clear from the start is that justice is very much a work in progress, that in the hands of most minority authors, the end of detective fiction is to demonstrate how far short of justice current systems fall, not to repair some rift in the social order and reinstate an essentially just society. The problem is that we have come too late to this attempt, weighed down by too long a history for trends to be easily reversed, if reversed at all.

Many things remain unchanged in the McGill mysteries. The rampant colorism that has been a traditional piece of both white and black understandings of the world and that runs through detective fiction by African American authors continues here, too ingrained in a man of Leonid's age and experience to vanish, suggesting just how far we are from a post-racial period. Leonid, like Easy Rawlins before him, operates as a metaphor for contemporary African American anxiety. Where the conventions of noir fiction, of the hard-boiled novel in the Rawlins series operated as a metaphor for African American experience through the middle decades of the twentieth century, from the end of World War II through the Red Scare, Cold War, Civil Rights movement, Watts Riots, and Vietnam, McGill represents, in almost allegorical terms, contemporary anxieties over the possibility of redeeming the past, of moving beyond the historical determinants that have propelled us into the present. In *The Long Fall*, the primary plot turns on a grieving mother's belated attempts, seventeen years after the fact, to visit retribution on the four men she believes responsible for the death of her son. Seventeen years was a lifetime ago, and the death was the result of youthful ignorance and indiscretion. To seek vengeance at this point is thus doubly pointless, pursued by a mentally unbalanced woman with the financial means to prosecute her desire. *Known to Evil* similarly plays out another woman's vendetta—again propelled by the loss of a child, mental illness, and wealth—against Alphonse Rinaldo, Special Assistant to the City of New York, who has refused to help her win the zoning variance she needs in order to build a commercial building bearing her son's name. The object of her vengeance is a young woman, Tara, a former diner waitress that Rinaldo has "adopted"; Tara is aware of her extraordinary run of luck—an uncanny ability to win scholarships, grants, and even find affordable, below-market-rate apartments—but not the fact that she owes her luck to this official, the ultimate bureaucrat and real power in New York City government, an official who is not elected and whose existence is unguessed by the population at large. Tara is as unaware of the cause of her success as she is ignorant and innocent of the reasons she is being pursued.

Leonid is far more self aware, aware of his long fall away from the revolutionary idealism of his father into the evil world of organized crime, the life he is trying at this stage of his life to leave behind. His is the long fall; he is the one known to evil seeking redemption here, a representative experience. In that light, *When the Thrill Is Gone*, as a title, and in this case a title that is not immediately connected to the central action and/or mental states of the characters in the book, suggests how much work remains to be done in spite of recent advances, the elation of electing a black man President giving way to the hard realities of government. The difficulties are formidable, especially in a world populated by evil forces and unforeseen and unsuspected powers, shadowy figures like Alphonse Rinaldo, a figure reminiscent of the power brokers and intelligence operatives populating Carter's crime fiction.

The McGill mysteries are complicated pieces, always involving multiple cases transpiring simultaneously, with large casts that are frequently hard to keep track of. The action always, as well, involves the evolving family drama of McGill's marriage and of his sons' activities, by turns gallant and immensely clever, at least where Twill in involved, and usually criminal, and always the source of considerable anxiety. The solutions of the central cases that Leonid is hired to investigate typically, for all their complexity, reveal pedestrian motives like revenge or greed, enabled by privilege and abetted by mental illness, and often, as noted above, turning on events that transpired years earlier, a lifetime ago. Leonid is always careful to vet his clients and cases, to determine motives and assess possible consequences before he accepts an assignment, but nothing ever turns out to be simple or as straight forward as appearances suggest, and Leonid will typically be unpleasantly surprised in the process. Against this background, it is the minor details that seem significant, both generically and historically, Leonid's attempts, for instance, to control his anger, that "more primitive urge" that emerges in war, through Zen meditation, or his marriage to Katrina, a dysfunctional relationship which, in spite of their mutual infidelities and emotional distance and even occasional separations, both partners remain curiously committed to, Katrina cooking family dinners, Leonid a loving and supportive father.

The interracial marriage and blended family have played a role in African American detective fiction since the beginning, central to the action of Hopkins's *Hagar's Daughter*, the action of the book taking root in St. Louis at the time of the *Dred Scott* decision, the book itself being written in the immediate aftermath of *Plessy v. Ferguson*; the decisions in both cases cite colonial-era laws criminalizing interracial marriage. Historically, interracial marriage was both a target of eugenics and the political policies it spawned and of Ku Klux Klan "family values" campaigns in the 1920s, campaigns that seem to have established a foundation for and to have been as successful as contemporary family-values campaigns favored by social conservatives, Glen Beck among them. The eugenics-inspired legislation, built on the theories of biological determinism that Rudolph Fisher seems at some levels to be satirizing in the rite of the gonad in *The Conjure-Man Dies*, was not finally repealed until the 1967 *Loving* decision, issued at the height of the Civil Rights movement. Both Chester Himes, in the Harlem domestic series, and Mosley, in the Easy Rawlins books, will track marriage trends as their stories move through the 1960s; moreover, Daphne Monet, a mixed-race woman, was the object of Easy Rawlins's first assignment as a detective in *Devil in a Blue Dress*. Easy Rawlins's comments in later books about the intermixture of features in a black face speaks to a mixed genetic inheritance reaching back into slavery. In popular culture, prohibitions against the depiction of interracial dating and marriage on television and in film have only recently fallen by the way, an indication of how long in coming public acceptance of unions between people of different races has been. Add to this particular mix the issues surrounding family in the African American community, from the historical conditions under slavery to contemporary issues over absentee fathers, and Leonid McGill's peculiar marriage and family seem significant, an object lesson in African American history and sociology. McGill and Katrina's marriage, preserved at the moment because of the economic collapse and banking scandals transpiring just before the 2008 beginning of the series—Katrina was poised to leave Leonid for her investment banker boyfriend when the industry collapsed and he was implicated in irregular financial transactions—is a civil union, in almost every sense of the word, an uneasy compromise. Initiated out of physical attraction and stubbornly preserved perhaps because of Leonid's need to amend his own family history, to give his children, even if they are not his, what he had been denied, the marriage persists even in the face of emotional and physical estrangement. Leonid returns home most nights and Katrina has dinner on the table, preserving the forms and the essential functions no matter how dysfunctional the underlying relationship has become. This is not, perhaps, where either one wants to be, though Katrina does seem to be making an effort to repair the damage she has done, at least through the course of *The Long Fall*, but each, for the time being, seems to have acquiesced in their compromised relationship. In general, their relationship seems a fitting image of black-white relations.

Equally telling in some ways is Leonid's frequent recourse to Zen-inspired breathing exercises and meditation to rein in his desire to do violence, a response to stress and threat, the fight response once flight has been eliminated as a possibility. In Leonid's case, the possibility of flight was eliminated long ago, a course of action determined by his father's leaving the family to join the Struggle, requiring Leonid to "step up," by Leonid's entry into the boxing ring, by his eventually joining forces with organized crime. The recurring nightmare Leonid experiences in *The Long Fall* of being trapped in a burning building with no means of escape registers Leonid's existential plight and the very long fall, a fatal plunge from an upper-story window, that represents his only means of escape. For Easy Rawlins, self-preservation appeared in the form of a voice telling him to kill, a voice that first spoke to him in the war and which continues to appear throughout the earlier books in the series. As a foot soldier enlisted in the ranks of organized crime, something of a black ops agent, McGill has certainly been imbued with the kill-or-be-killed ethos of the war. The race war that breaks out in Himes's *Plan B* and the attempt to win equality by any means necessary seems another variation on this particular theme. Self preservation and the higher moral values associated with achieving equality under the law seem to necessitate and to a degree legitimize this guerrilla action, echoing Carter's discussion of just war theory and the higher moral imperatives Obama has invoked, even in violation of international law, to justify actions in the war on terror, in Iraq, in Afghanistan. Terrible things happen in war, and the only way to avoid those unfortunate outcomes is not to fight, as Carter remarks, recognizing the very real hazards that not fighting, in turn, represents. Once the war starts, the only real question is "what we are willing to become to protect ourselves," the question Carter raises with regard to torture, "the scariest subject in the War on Terror" (k680–85). Given the critical role intelligence plays in defeating terrorism and the near impossibility of extracting information through typical means and channels, torture seems the only option. Leonid will play out this scenario and choice in enlisting the services of a South American colleague to extract information from a hit man in the course of *Known to Evil*.

This is the mindset, however, that Leonid seems to be trying to leave behind, his answer a mindfulness born of Zen-inspired meditation exercises as an antidote to the mindless violence he engaged in in his past life. The sociopathic Hush, now retired but once New York's most professional and proficient hit man, joins Leonid in these exercises. Generically, such exercises seem to have a touch of the hoodoo tradition about them, one of those elements Soitos sees as a common thread in the blues detective, an alternate epistemology. For Leonid, fully steeped in his father's Marxist philosophy, the exercises are more mechanical than mystical, a means of short circuiting an automatic physiological response. The physical discipline and the rules of boxing provide the aging, short, paunchy detective with the ability, when necessary, to respond to threatened violence, a proportional and disciplined show of force, typically a measure of last resort, echoing the terms of just war theory. The taking of human life in war is justified if the war being fought is for a just cause, is a measure of last resort, is undertaken by a legitimate authority (i.e., state sponsored and not perpetrated by a private party), has a reasonable hope of success, is proportional in its use of force (not using more force than necessary to achieve its just end), and exercises discrimination (targeting combatants and military targets, not civilians) (Carter k476–82). At some levels, Leonid's attempts to go straight perfectly parallel the criteria Aquinas delineates to ensure that a war is just.

But Leonid goes beyond, invoking a tradition associated with nonviolence, with resistance, an attempt to move beyond war to legal action. War is not law, and the principal result in McGill's investigations involves his divulging what he has discovered to the appropriate authorities so that the guilty parties can be duly prosecuted. In *The Long Fall*, for instance, Leonid intervenes in Twill's resolve to kill the abusive father of one of his classmates.

Earlier in his life, Leonid would have done much the same. Now he breaks into the man's apartment, finds the incriminating evidence of sexual abuse documented in the man's collection of pornographic images, and has these images posted to a website created by McGill's computer-geek colleague for just this purpose. The police are duly alerted to the website, and the law takes its course. In *Known to Evil*, a similar solution is worked out to protect Dimitri's girlfriend, Tatyana, a victim of human trafficking, from the traffickers reluctant to release her from the sex trade. Though McGill's earlier activities have earned him a permanent place as a person of interest to the NYPD, a man subject to being detained and questioned for almost any reason, he has developed a working relationship with Detectives Carson Kitteridge and Bonnie Bonilla, whose honesty and integrity he can count on. Their relationship is a work in progress, mutually beneficial if also marked by mutual suspicion and distrust on both sides.

As a measure of anxiety and a representation of social and historical conditions, detective fiction by African American authors from Hopkins to Mosley consistently registers dismay with the failure of social systems and official channels to deliver justice, to achieve meaningful change. Television crime drama provides one point of comparison, a means of measuring current concerns and majority attitudes. Significantly, many of the detectives in continuing series seem to have been the victims themselves of crime, crimes that have gone unsolved and which they obsess over. Olivia Benson from *Law and Order SVU*, the product of a rape, is one example; Detective Kate Beckett in *Castle*, whose mother was murdered, and Patrick Jane in *The Mentalist*, whose family was murdered by a serial killer known as Red John, are others. All of them, when it comes to the investigation of these crimes, are willing to bend the law, something Benson and Beckett, at least, are otherwise careful to uphold. But the limitations of law enforcement are clear as the reliance of law enforcement agencies on "consultants," investigators not fully bound by the laws, indicates. Patrick Jane, a former carnival psychic/mind-reader who vehemently denies any paranormal powers, contending that close observation alone and deduction provide the supposed ability to read minds, and Rick Castle, a mystery novelist who uses his imagination, sense of plot, and research into forensic science to piece together the crimes he and Beckett investigate, are two examples. In these instances, the police alone, hamstrung by civil rights, rules of evidence, and the need to observe protocols, and hampered, as are Beckett and Jane, by superiors who prove to be corrupt, require outside assistance to bring criminals to justice. Legal and judicial channels may not be up to the task of doing justice, at least in these cases.

For the most part, however, in the 2010–11 season, the good guys are good and the system is winning. Forensic science, in particular, seems to be triumphing over higher powers and sheer intuition, with crime scene investigators (three *CSIs*, two *NCISs*), profilers (two *Criminal Minds*), and various pathologists (*Body of Proof, Rizzoli and Isles*, among others) accounting for a disproportionate number of collars. Police procedurals like *Chicago Code* and *Blue Bloods* portray dedicated and sympathetic civil servants rooting out crime and corruption in the midst of on-going family dramas. *Chicago Code*, which Fox cancelled at the end of its first season, focuses on Teresa Colvin, a bi-racial woman, the first female Superintendent of Police, and the widow of an African American officer killed in the line of duty. Played by Jennifer Beals (who appeared as Daphne Monet in the film version of *Devil in a Blue Dress*), Colvin's stated intention is to bring down a wholly corrupt African American Alderman. A product of the city's public housing projects and now potentially the most powerful political figure in the city, he is both alive to the needs of his constituents and in league with the Irish Mafia. Colvin's former partner and now lead investigator into corruption in the city, Jarek Wysoki, is Polish American, his brother a policeman killed in the line of duty (who we also discover was not fully the honest cop he appeared to be); his niece is also on the force, a young patrol woman who is involved in an affair with her African American partner. If nothing else, the racial politics prove to be interesting. *Law and Order*, still active in Los Angeles, the United Kingdom, and New York's Special Victims Unit in 2010–11, the original New York series and *Criminal Intent* having just closed up shop, continues to police and prosecute crimes, sexually-based offenses in New York and violence associated with Latino street gangs and Mexican drug lords in LA their primary foci. Crime and its prosecution, at least on television, seem as relentless as ever, business as usual.

In reality, it does seem more like business as usual than the long hoped for period of peace and prosperity and the beginning of a post-racial era. The promise of hope held out by the Obama campaign has gone the way of most campaign promises. The United States is still waging the war against terror, an extremely expensive war, with troops still on the ground in Afghanistan, if only as advisers. Recent Supreme Court decisions, particularly with regard to corporations and campaign finance, have favored moneyed interests. More importantly, a conservative court repeatedly ruled in the 2010–11 term to limit the ability of consumers, employees, and criminal defendants to seek redress for their grievances in court (Chemerensky B1). Noting this trend in a July 2011 op-ed article, Erwin Chemerensky argues that these rulings go beyond the typical pro-business, pro-prosecutor attitudes of a conservative judiciary, that they evince the high court's distrust of the lower courts and court system in general. The immediate result is to prevent injured parties from seeking redress: "The Supreme Court is closing the courthouse doors to those who have claims that should be heard" (B4). Problems in the schools persist. Most educators recognize that the schools are far better at perpetuating the status quo than at enabling upward mobility. Conservative fiscal policies are resulting in reduced funding for education and social services. Crime rates are down, but the prisons are still overpopulated in most places, with inmate populations disproportionately poor, under-educated, and minority. It's hard not to feel anxious at times like these, to feel the weight of history as a constraint on change. Mosley's Leonid McGill, given his past life and crimes and current efforts to change his ways, seems perfectly positioned to appreciate the ways the past weighs heavily on the present.

The murder mystery has always operated as a barometer of contemporary anxieties, even more so when the author is a member of a racial minority group. It is clear that social justice is very much a work in progress and achieving racial equality still very much a part of that process, as several recent Supreme Court decisions suggest. In the 2003 University of Michigan affirmative action decisions, *Gratz v. Bollinger* and *Grutter v. Bollinger*, the Supreme Court upheld its earlier approval of affirmative action programs to encourage racial diversity so long as the methods used were narrowly tailored to achieve that effect and only that effect, but the decision also noted that it hoped such measures would not be necessary in twenty-five years. By contrast, the Court's 2007 ruling in the Louisville and Seattle school desegregation cases struck down the use of race in school assignments, arguing that the original intent of the Reconstruction Congress in adopting the Fourteenth Amendment was to create a color-blind Constitution, a claim that James D. Anderson argues is based on a fictive history, a "myth" (256), that is not justified by a close reading of the historical record. Clearly the debate continues, over contemporary measures to foster diversity and over the reconstruction of history and the ways it directs current policies and programs. The murder mystery, in general, and Mosley's Leonid McGill, in particular, continue to engage history and the debate over social justice.

Chapter Notes

Chapter 1

1. The eventual total included six separate shows: *Law and Order* (1990–2010), *Law and Order: SVU* (1999–present), *Law and Order: Criminal Intent* (2001–11), *Law and Order: Trial by Jury* (2005–06), *Law and Order: LA* (2010–11), and *Law and Order: UK* (2009–12), the locus of activity set in London.

2. In "Mr. Monk Is on the Air," originally broadcast on 12 February 2007, a shock-jock radio host's wife asphyxiates in her bedroom while he is on air; she is in a locked house showing no signs of forced entry. As it turns out, she has been murdered by her husband, who has trained the neighbor's dog to enter the house through a basement window and to turn on the gas logs in the bedroom in response to a specific catch phrase. Monk follows clues—a missing loafer from the shock-jock's closet—works out the means, and then convenes a meeting in the bedroom of all of the involved parties, where he presents the solution. In "Mr. Monk and the Really, Really Dead Guy" (23 February 2007), a doctor commits a second, elaborately-staged murder, promising to repeat the performance in 36 hours, in order to conceal an earlier murder, delaying the investigation and autopsy long enough to allow for the first victim's stomach contents—including a unique dessert that will connect her to a specific restaurant and to a specific meal with the perpetrator—to fully digest.

3. In the second case noted above, the doctor's first murder is never really explained. The red herring not only distracts the investigation, pursued by clownish FBI agents, themselves parodies of the all-too-serious profilers of *Criminal Minds* and who come equipped in this instance with all of the high-tech tools of *CSI*, but also distracts the audience from looking too deeply into the matter. In this case, Monk's low-tech methods work, the 36-hour period specified by the seeming serial killer the key to the solution, something the technologically-sophisticated FBI agents discount.

4. *Medium*, which began on NBC in January 2005, ended its run on CBS in January 2011.

5. *Raines*, a mid-season replacement introduced by NBC in the spring of 2007, mediates between the two poles that Monk and Alison Dubois describe. Like Alison, Raines, played by Jeff Goldblum, talks to dead people, the victims of the crimes he is currently investigating. In his case, however, the concerns are not psychic but psychological, the figures he sees projections, the aftereffects of the trauma he suffered when he was shot and his long-time partner killed in a recent investigation. The device is interesting, allowing Raines to progressively interrogate the ways he reads the crime and the character of the victim. He starts with a conclusion, the dead body, and something of a narrative, albeit a narrative filled with gaps, gaps he fills based on his notions of gender, race, class, and crime. He then proceeds to interrogate these assumptions, to progressively test, refine, discard as the investigation moves

forward. In one early episode, "Meet Juan Doe" (March 22, 2007), a dead young man, an undocumented Mexican in the United States illegally who seems to have been stalking a local politician, a city councilman, himself a former illegal immigrant who now talks a hard line on illegal immigration, turns out to be the son of that same councilman, his former girlfriend having been pregnant all those years ago when he left the country. The young man, recently married and with a child of his own, is here to present his child to his grandfather, not to take up residence or to assassinate the councilman. Believing himself to be imperiled, the councilman kills the young man, his son, when he appears on the street outside of the councilman's home. The paranoia, perhaps legitimate, results in an overreaction which the councilman immediately attempts to conceal by disposing of the body rather than pleading self-defense and trusting the system to exonerate him.

Chapter 2

1. The seven-year sentence seems interesting, perhaps biblical in origin, equal to the seven years that Jacob labors, twice, to win Rachel's hand in marriage (Gen. 29:15–28).

2. Sumner was, in fact, the victim of a vicious beating on the Senate floor by Preston Brooks, a member of the House of Representatives from South Carolina who felt he had been insulted by Sumner in his "Crime Against Kansas" speech, May 19, 1856. The specific targets of Sumner's response were Stephen Douglas, Dem., Illinois, and Andrew Butler, Dem., South Carolina, both supporters of legislation to admit Kansas as a slave state. It is this beating that Hopkins refers to in the novel.

3. The story of the Massachusetts Fifty-fourth is not, perhaps, often told. Walter Dean Myers does include it and the siege of Fort Wagner in *Now Is Your Time: The African-American Struggle for Freedom*, a history written for young readers. In it he points out the extraordinary threats that African Americans serving in the war faced, that the Confederates had announced that they would not accord prisoner-of-war status to captured African American soldiers, that they consequently faced immediate execution if taken in battle (155). Myers also notes that following Lee's surrender at Appomattox, Northern newspapers credited the entrance of 180,000 soldiers of African descent into the war with shortening the war by as much as a year (179). The siege of Fort Wagner required extraordinary bravery, as Smith's narrative suggests.

Chapter 3

1. "John Archer's Nose," a short story also featuring the physician and detective, opens on a despondent Archer who has lost a young patient when the parents turned to the services of a traditional healer rather than avail themselves of the x-ray treatments that Archer, and Fisher, a roentgenologist, know will quickly and efficiently cure the problem. In this case, modern medical science fails in the face of local superstition and ineffectual folk remedies. In other instances, Fisher's short fiction will examine the ways that recent arrivals in Harlem, a supposed city of refuge, will find themselves exploited, unequal to life in this alien urban environment. In either case, these traditional practices seem maladapted to life in the big city.

2. Bubber Brown, his partner Jinx Jenkins, and parts of the Harlem streetscape, including Patmore's Pool Hall, appear in Fisher's earlier novel, *The Walls of Jericho*. Brown and Jenkins represent "stage-type Harlemese-speaking" African Americans, in the words of *The Dictionary of Literary Biography*, a role that they reprise here.

3. See, for instance, Charles Helgar's discussion of Fisher's novel and its influence on Chester Himes and Walter Mosley, "Rudolph Fisher and the African American Detective."

4. Somewhat more obscure, though potentially interesting, are the eugenics theories that developed following the discovery of blood types, both in Germany and Japan, the latter in active circulation in the

late 1920s. Such theories claimed that blood type determined character, personality, individual destiny. Given Frimbo's interest in determinism and his claims, based on Herbert Spencer's work, that psychology should be classed among the biological sciences as a study of "the physiology of the nervous system"(214), the possible connections are tantalizing if unprovable.

5. An Internet search, for instance, reveals two listings for *Buwongo*, one a place in Uganda, the other as a language spoken in the Democratic Republic of the Congo. *Malindo* is listed as the plural of *lindo*, Swahili for "guard post," "lookout," or a cylindrical box made out of bark (Kamusi Project).

6. Jack Kaminsky's entry for Herbert Spencer in *The Encyclopedia of Philosophy* provides a useful overview of Spencer's work, of the role evolution played in his thought, his defense of individual rights, the strengths and the limits of his work. A number of issues Frimbo and Archer discuss seem to echo matters of interest to Spencer.

Chapter 4

1. They do make a cameo appearance on p. 74, a random reference in a list of seemingly unrelated events all occurring during the celebration of Nat Turner Day in Harlem: "Eleven black nuns came out of a crumbling, dilapidated private house which had a sign in the window reading: FUNERALS PERFORMED. They were carrying a brass four-poster bed as though it were a coffin. The bed had a mattress. On the mattress was a nappy, unkempt head of an old man, sticking from beneath a dirty sheet. He lay so still he might have been dead. No one asked." The reference seems to come out of nowhere and goes nowhere.

Chapter 5

1. In "The Conspiracy of Masculinity in Ishmael Reed," Strombeck argues that the anti-feminist *Reckless Eyeballing* finds its roots in the inherent sexism of the conspiracy theory form central to *Mumbo Jumbo*: "In *Mumbo Jumbo*, the secret-society conspiracy theory generates masculinity wherever it lands. For Reed, something about the theory's form itself leads inevitably to masculine dominance and exclusion. Closely associated with the reified character of PaPa LaBas, and reinforced by its metaphysical attack on western cultures, the secret-society conspiracy theory limits the postmodernist deconstruction of *Mumbo Jumbo*. The form itself reflects and reinforces masculine desire, a desire consistent with the historical origins of the secret-society conspiracy theory" (303).

2. An Internet search for these various materials leads to company websites and online encyclopedias tracing the development of these materials: Acrylic glass is developed in 1928 and first marketed as Plexiglas in 1933 by the Rhom and Haas Company and as Lucite in 1938 by DuPont. Polystyrene, while first discovered in 1839, does not appear on the market until 1937, the result of work at Dow Chemical in the '30s. BoPET film, of which Mylar is one example, is developed in the 1950s, and Teflon first appears in commercial products in 1946

3. Some part of this particular conflict arises in the character of George Jefferson, who first appears as Archie Bunker's neighbor in Norman Lear's *All in the Family* (1971). After turning an insurance settlement into a chain of dry cleaning stores and consequently moving up from working- to middle-class status, George Jefferson and family are spun off into *The Jeffersons* (1975), Norman Lear moving the family from Queens to the East Side. The upwardly mobile George Jefferson is never fully comfortable with his economic status and what it represents. Reed's characters here reflect both the pop cultural representations and the conflicts embedded within them playing out on television and in movie theaters during the first half of the 1970s.

4. While much of the language is taken verbatim from the original, some slight changes do appear. For example, Prince

Albert describes the ways that modern inventions have facilitated travel, bringing the nations of the world closer together: "The distances which separated the different nations and parts of the globe are gradually vanishing before the achievements of modern invention, and we can traverse them with incredible ease" (Black et al. 859). In Whitehead, *gradually* becomes *rapidly* and *ease* is transformed into *speed* (Whitehead 81). Prince Albert addresses only the gentlemen in the audience whereas Whitehead's fictitious vice president speaks to ladies and gentlemen.

Chapter 6

1. In fact, the series doesn't end in *Blonde Faith*, Mosley having now published two additional books in the series, *Little Green* (2013) and *Rose Gold* (2014), the twelfth and thirteenth installments, no obvious end in sight.

Chapter 7

1. Driving home from a university function at the beginning of the book, Lemaster tunes the satellite radio away from the channel playing Broadway show tunes, his wife's, Julia's, preferred music, to a hip-hop station, "his own secret passion." The screen identifies the band as "Goodie Mobb" (*NEW* 12). *Goodie Mobb* seems to be a blending of *Mobb Deep*, a hard-core New York rap duo best known for its second album, *The Infamous*, released in 1995, and an Atlanta, Georgia, group named Goodie Mob, which debuted in 1995 with an album entitled *Soul Food*. "Fighting," one track on the album, explains the origin of their name: "the GOOD Die Mostly Over Bullshit" ("Goodie Mob"). While their first two albums were generally well received, by 2004–05, the group had declined. Similarly, Mobb Deep's early success—they are credited with transforming East Coast rap in the mid-'90s—had also waned at the time the action in the novel takes place, their 2001 album *Infamy*, a more commercial product leading to accusations that the duo had "sold out"; *Amerikaz Nightmare*, released in 2004, was generally perceived as a weaker release ("Mobb Deep"). While Carter's Goodie Mobb seems a fictional creation, a generic rap group, Mobb Deep and Goodie Mob reflect recurring themes in hip-hop that will speak to issues in the novel. Mobb Deep and Goodie Mob, for instance, are both cited in Christopher Holmes Smith and John Fiske, "Naming the Illuminati," both groups representative of a mid-'90s movement in rap to attribute the oppression of African Americans to an occult conspiracy they identify with the Illuminati.

2. For one account of the history of the Illuminati, see William H. McIlhany, "A Primer on the Illuminati," *The New American* 22 June 2009: 31–36. *The New American* is a publication of the John Birch Society. McIlhany is described as a "noted author and historian" who has appeared on numerous television shows and who founded the Individualist Research Foundation in 1986 (31).

3. While Carter, like his character Talcott Garland, is clearly conservative, neither one is conservative in the outspoken way of Talcott's father, Oliver Garland. In that regard, it is at least interesting that K. Anthony Appiah's *New York Review of Books*' review of *Emperor* is set next to Jane Meyer's "True Confessions," a review of David Brock's *Blinded by the Right: The Conscience of an Ex-Conservative*, a book in which the formerly conservative African American journalist Brock recants his earlier "exposé" of Anita Hill.

Works Cited

Anderson, James D. "Race-Conscious Educational Policies Versus a 'Color-Blind Constitution': A Historical Perspective." *Educational Researcher* 36.5 (2007): 249-57. Print.

Appiah, K. Anthony. "What Garland Knew." Rev. of *The Emperor of Ocean Park*, by Stephen L. Carter. *The New York Review of Books* 27 June 2002: 4-6. Print.

Arnold, Matthew. *The Poetry and Criticism of Matthew Arnold*. Ed. A. Dwight Culler. Boston: Houghton Mifflin, 1961. Print.

Bakhtin, M.M. "Forms of Time and of the Chronotope in the Novel." *The Dialogic Imagination: Four Essays*. Ed. Michael Holquist. Trans. Caryl Emerson and Michael Holquist. Austin University of Texas Press, 1994. 84-258. Print.

Betz, Phyllis M. *Lesbian Detective Fiction: Woman as Author, Subject and Reader*. Jefferson, NC: McFarland, 2006. Print.

Black, Joseph, Leonard Conolly, Kate Flint, Isobel Grundy, Roy Liuzza, Jerome McGann, Anne Prescott, Barry Qualls, and Claire Waters, eds. *The Broadview Anthology of British Literature*, 2d ed., Vol. 5: The Victorian Era. Toronto: Broadview Press, 2012. *Google Books*. Web. 18 Aug. 2014.

Bloom, Harold. *The Book of J*. New York: Grove Weidenfeld, 1990. Print.

Carby, Hazel V. Introduction. *The Magazine Novels of Pauline Hopkins*. Ed. Henry Louis Gates, Jr., and Hazel V. Carby. New York: Oxford University Press, 1990. Print.

Carter, Stephen L. *The Emperor of Ocean Park*. New York: Knopf, 2002. Print.

———. *Jericho's Fall*. New York: Knopf, 2009. Print.

———. *New England White*. New York: Knopf, 2007. Print.

———. *Palace Council*. New York: Vintage, 2009. Print.

———. *The Violence of Peace: America's Wars in the Age of Obama*. New York: Beast Books, 2011. Kindle edition, *Amazon.com*. Electronic book.

"Carter, Stephen L. Jericho's Fall." Rev. of *Jericho's Fall*, by Stephen L. Carter. *Kirkus Reviews* 1 July 2009. *Literature Resource Center*. Web. 10 July 2010.

Chemerensky, Erwin. "The Supreme Court vs. the Justice System." *Pittsburgh Post-Gazette* 10 July 2011: B1, 4. Print.

Cordell, Sigrid Anderson. "'The Case Was Very Black Against' Her: Pauline Hopkins and the Politics of Racial Ambiguity at the *Colored American Magazine*." *American Periodicals* 16.1 (2006): 52-73. *MLA International Bibliography*. Web. 17 Jan. 2014.

Dally, Ann. "Status Lymphaticus: Sudden Death in Children from 'Visitation of God' to Cot Death." *Medical History* 41.1 (1997): 70-85. *NCBI Resources*. Web. 23 May 2014.

Donahue, Deirdre. "Author Loves to Keep His Readers Guessing." *USA Today* 23 July 2009. *Academic Search Complete*. 4 Aug. 2010. Web.

Donaldson, Will, composer. "Doo wacka doo." Perf. Paul Whiteman Orchestra. *National Jukebox*. Library of Congress. Web. 15 Aug. 2014.

Dred Scott, Plaintiff in Error v. John F.A.

Sandford. Sup. Ct. of the U.S. Dec. 1856. *The Supreme Court Collection.* Cornell Law School. Web.

E., Jeffrey. "America's Illuminati Occult Conspiracy." *Illuminati Archives: Occult Conspiracy Library and Illuminati Videos.* Illuminati Archives, 2007. Web. 10 July 2010.

Eliot, T.S. *The Complete Poems and Plays, 1909–1950.* New York: Harcourt, Brace, and World, 1971. Print.

English, Daylanne K. "The Modern in the Postmodern: Walter Mosley, Barbara Neely, and the Politics of Contemporary African-American Detective Fiction." *American Literary History* 18.4 (2006): 772–96. Print.

Fisher, Rudolph. *The Conjure-Man Dies: A Mystery Tale of Dark Harlem.* Ann Arbor: University of Michigan Press, 2000. Print.

———. "John Archer's Nose." *City of Refuge: The Collected Stories of Rudolph Fisher.* Ed. John McCluskey, Jr. Columbia: University of Missouri Press, 1987. Print.

"fizgig," *Random House Dictionary of the English Language*, unabridged edition. Ed. Jess Stein. New York: Random House, 1971. Print.

Ford, Elisabeth. "Miscounts, Loopholes, and Flashbacks: Strategic Evasions in Walter Mosley's Detective Fiction." *Callaloo* 28.4 (2005): 1074–90. Print.

Gates, Jr., Henry Louis. *The Signifying Monkey: A Theory of African-American Literary Criticism.* New York: Oxford University Press, 1989. Print.

"Goodie Mob." *Wikipedia.* The Wikimedia Foundation. Web. 4 Aug. 2010.

Gosselin, Adrienne Johnson. "The Psychology of Uncertainty: (Re)Inscribing Indeterminacy in Rudolph Fisher's *The Conjure-Man Dies.*" *Other Voices* 1.3 (1999). *Other voices.* University of Pennsylvania. 18 July 2011. Web.

———. "The World Would Do Better to Ask Why Is Frimbo Sherlock Holmes?: Investigating Liminality in Rudolph Fisher's *The Conjure-Man Dies.*" *African American Review* 32.4 (1998): 607–19. Print.

The Governor's Commission on the Los Angeles Riots. *Violence in the City: An End or a Beginning?* 2 Dec. 1965. *Doheny Electronic Resources Center.* University of Southern California. Web. 19 July 2011.

Graham, Lawrence Otis. *Our Kind of People: Inside America's Black Upper Class.* New York: Harper Perennial, 2000. Print.

Hahn, Robert C. "PW Talks with Walter Mosley: The End of Easy?" *Publishers Weekly* 31 Dec. 2007:25. *Literature Resource Center.* Web. 20 July 2011.

Harding, Anthony J. "A Brief History of Blood Transfusion." *IBMS.* Institute of Biomedical Science, April 2011. Web. 18 July 2011.

Heglar, Charles. "Rudolph Fisher and the African American Detective." *The Armchair Detective* 30.3 (1997): 300–305. Print.

Hess, Mickey. *Icons of Hip Hop: An Encyclopedia of the Movement, Music, and Culture.* New York: Greenwood, 2007. Print.

Himes, Chester. *All Shot Up.* 1960. New York: Thunder's Mouth Press, 1996. Print.

———. *The Big Gold Dream.* 1960. New York: Thunder's Mouth Press, 1996. Print.

———. *Blind Man with a Pistol.* 1969. New York: Vintage, 1989. Print.

———. *Cotton Comes to Harlem.* 1965. New York: Vintage, 1988. Print.

———. *The Crazy Kill.* 1959. New York: Vintage, 1989. Print.

———. *The Heat's On.* 1966. New York: Vintage, 1988. Print.

———. *Plan B.* Jackson: University Press of Mississippi, 1994. Print.

———. *A Rage in Harlem.* 1965. New York: Vintage, 1991. Print.

———. *The Real Cool Killers.* 1959. New York: Vintage, 1988. Print.

———. *Run Man Run.* 1966. New York: Carroll and Graf, 1995. Print.

The Holy Bible. King James Version. Nashville: Today, 1976. Print.

Hopkins, Pauline. *Hagar's Daughter: A Story of Southern Caste Prejudice. The Magazine Novels of Pauline Hopkins.* Ed. Henry Louis Gates, Jr., and Hazel V. Carby. New York: Oxford University Press, 1990. Print.

_____. "Talma Gordon." *Vintage Short Mystery Classics*. Hornpipe Vintage Publications. Web. 17 Jan. 2014.

Johnson, James Weldon. "Self-Determining Haiti: I. The American Occupation." *The Nation* 28 Aug. 1920. *Windows on Haiti*. Guy S. Antoine. Web. 23 Decn. 2014.

_____. "Self-Determining Haiti: II. What the United States Has Accomplished." *The Nation* 4 September 1920. *Windows on Haiti*. Guy S. Antoine. Web. 23 Dec. 2014.

"Junkanoo." *Dictionary of Caribbean English Usage*. Ed. Richard Allsopp. Kingston, Jamaica: University of West Indies Press, 2003. Print.

Kakutani, Michiko. "Bound by Suspicion." *NYTimes.com*, 19 Jan. 1997. The New York Times. Web. 13 July 2010.

Kaminsky, Jack. "Spencer, Herbert." *The Encyclopedia of Philosophy*. Vol. 7 and 8. New York: Macmillan, 1972. 523–27. Print.

Kaufman, Natalie Hevener, and Carol McGinnis Kay. "Grafton's Place in the Development of the Detective Novel." *The Longman Anthology of Detective Fiction*. Ed. Deane Mansfield-Kelley and Lois A. Marchino. New York: Pearson Longman, 2005. 219–228. Print.

Kendrick, Douglas B. *Blood Program in World War II*. Washington, D.C.: Department of the Army, 1964. *Office of Medical History*. U.S. Army Medical Department. Web. 18 July 2011.

Kozol, Jonathan. *Savage Inequalities: Children in America's Schools*. New York: Harper Perennial, 1992. Print.

_____. *The Shame of the Nation: The Restoration of Apartheid Schooling in America*. New York: Crown, 2005. Print.

"Late Registration." *Wikipedia*. The Wikimedia Foundation. Web. 4 Aug. 2010.

Lombardo, Paul. "Eugenics Laws Against Race Mixing." *Image Archive on the American Eugenics Movement*. Dolan DNA Learning Center, Cold Spring Harbor Laboratory. Web. 15 July 2011.

"Malindo." *The Internet Living Swahili Dictionary*. The Kamusi Project. Web. 18 July 2011.

Mason, Jr., Theodore O. "Walter Mosley's Easy Rawlins: The Detective and Afro-American Fiction." *The Kenyon Review* 14.4 (1992): 173–83. Literature Resource Center. Web. 20 July 2011.

Mayer, Jane. "Whatever It Takes: The Politics and the Man behind '24.'" *New Yorker* 19 Feb. 2007: 66–82. Print.

Mills, Alice. "Warring Ideals in Dark Bodies: Cultural Allegiances in the Work of Walter Mosley." *PALARA* 4 (2000): 23–39. Print.

Minster, Christopher. "Haiti: The U.S. Occupation, 1915–1934." *Latin American History*. About.com. Web. 23 Dec. 2014.

"Mobb Deep." *Wikipedia*. The Wikimedia Foundation. Web. 4 Aug. 2010.

Mosley, Walter. *All I Did Was Shoot My Man: A Leonid McGill Mystery*. New York: Riverhead Books, 2012. Print.

_____. *Bad Boy Brawly Brown*. Boston: Little, Brown, 2002. Print.

_____. *Black Betty*. New York: Pocket Books, 1995. Print.

_____. *Blonde Faith*. New York: Little, Brown, 2007. Print.

_____. *Cinnamon Kiss*. New York: Little, Brown, 2005. Print.

_____. *Devil in a Blue Dress*. New York: New York: Pocket Books, 1991. Print.

_____. *Gone Fishin'*. New York: Pocket Star Books, 1998. Print.

_____. *Known to Evil: A Leonid McGill Mystery*. New York: New American Library, 2011. Print.

_____. *Little Scarlet*. New York: Little, Brown, 2004. Print.

_____. *A Little Yellow Dog*. New York: Pocket Books, 1997. Print.

_____. *The Long Fall: The First Leonid McGill Mystery*. New York: New American Library, 2010. Print.

_____. *A Red Death*. New York: Pocket Books, 1992. Print.

_____. *Six Easy Pieces*. New York: Atria Books, 2003. Print.

_____. *When the Thrill Is Gone*. New York: Riverhead Books, 2011. Print.

_____. *White Butterfly*. New York: Pocket Books, 1993. Print.

Musgrave, Mariam E. "Ishmael Reed's Black Oedipus Cycle." *Obsidian* 6.3 (1980): 60–67. *MLA International Bibliography*. Web. 1 Aug. 2014.

Myers, Walter Dean. *Now Is Your Time! The African-American Struggle for Freedom.* New York: Harper Trophy, 1991. Print.

The New English Bible with the Apocrypha. Trans. Joint Committee on the New Translation of the Bible. London: Oxford University Press, 1970.

Nickel, John. "Eugenics and the Fiction of Pauline Hopkins." *American Transcendental Quarterly* 14.1 (2000): 47–60. *MLA International Bibliography.* Web. 17 Jan. 2014.

"Nkulunkulu." *Zulu-English Dictionary.* Ed. John William Colenso. Natal: P. Davis & Sons, 1884. *Google Books.* Web. 23 Dec. 2014.

Omry, Karen. "Literary Free Jazz? *Mumbo Jumbo* and *Paradise*: Language and Meaning." *African American Review* 47.1 (2007): 127–141. *MLA International Bibliography.* Web. 1 Aug. 2014.

Plessy v. Ferguson. 163U.S.537. Sup. Ct. of the U.S. 18 May 1896. *The Supreme Court Collection.* Cornell Law School. Web.

Pynchon, Thomas. "A Journey into the Mind of Watts." *Pomona Pynchon Page.* San Narciso Community College. Web. 19 July 2011.

Ravitch, Diane. *The Death and Life of the Great American School System: How Testing and Choice are Undermining Education.* New York: Basic Books, 2010. Print.

Raz, Guy. "Jay-Z: A Master of Occult Wisdom?" *All Things Considered.* NPR. National Public Radio, 20 Sept. 2009. Web. 19 July 2010.

Reddy, Maureen T. *Traces, Codes, and Clues: Reading Race in Crime Fiction.* New Brunswick: Rutgers University Press, 2003. Print.

Reed, Ishmael. *The Last Days of Louisiana Red.* 1974. Normal, IL: Dalkey Archive Press, 2000. Print.

_____. *Mumbo Jumbo.* 1972. New York: Scribner Paperback Fiction, 1996. Print.

Rodriguez, Ralph E. *Brown Gumshoes: Detective Fiction and the Search for Chicana/o Identity.* Austin: University of Texas Press, 2005. Print.

Rzepka, Charles J. *Detective Fiction.* Cambridge: Polity Press, 2005. Print.

Sacks, Oliver. *An Anthropologist on Mars: Seven Paradoxical Tales.* New York: Knopf, 1995. Print.

Saldivar, Ramon. "The Second Elevation of the Novel: Race, Form, and the Post-Race Aesthetic in Comtemporary Narrative." *Narrative* 21.1 (2013): 1–18. *MLA International Bibliography.* Web. 1 Aug. 2014.

Salvant, Shawn. "Pauline Hopkins and the End of Incest." *African American Review* 42.3-4 (2008): 659–77. *MLA International Bibliography.* Web. 17 Jan. 2014.

Selden, Steve. "Eugenics Popularization." *Image Archive on the American Eugenics Movement.* Dolan DNA Learning Center, Cold Spring Harbor Laboratory. Web. 15 July 2011.

Sengoopta, Chandak. "'Dr. Steinach Coming to Make Old Young!': Sex Glands, Vasectomy and the Quest for Rejuvenation in the Roaring Twenties." *Endeavor* 27.3 (2003): 122–26. *Elsevier.com.* Web. 18 July 2011.

Smith, Christopher Holmes and John Fiske. "Naming the Illuminati." *Music and the Racial Imagination,* ed. Ronald Radano and Philip V. Bohlman. Chicago: University of Chicago Press, 2000. Print.

Soitos, Stephen F. *The Blues Detective: A Study of African American Detective Fiction.* Amherst: University of Massachusetts Press, 1996. Print.

Strombeck, Andrew. "The Conspiracy of Masculinity in Ishmael Reed." *African American Review* 40.2 (2006): 299–311. *MLA International Bibliography.* Web. 1 Aug. 2014.

Stuart, Jan. "Fiction chronicle." Rev. of *Jericho's Fall,* by Stephen L. Carter. *The New York Times Book Review* 6 Sept. 2009: 15. *Literature Resource Center.* Web. 10 July 2010.

Sullivan, Kathleen. "What Happened to 'Brown'?" *New York Review of Books* 23 Sept. 2004:47–52. Print

Thomas, Lorenzo. "Two Crowns of Thoth: A Study of Ishmael Reed's *The Last Days of Louisiana Red.*" *Obsidian* 2.3 (1976): 5–25. *MLA International Bibliography.* Web. 1 Aug. 2014.

Tignor, Eleanor Q. "Rudolph Fisher." *Afro-American Authors from the Harlem Renaissance to 1940*. Ed. Trudier Harris-Lopez and Thadious M. Davis. *Dictionary of Literary Biography*, Vol 51. Detroit: Gale Research, 1987. *Literature Resource Center*. Web. 19 July 2011

"U.S. Invasion and Occupation of Haiti, 1915–34." *Office of the Historian*. Bureau of Public Affairs, United States Department of State. Web. 23 Dec. 2014.

Wallinger, Hanna. *Pauline E. Hopkins: A Literary Biography*. Athens: University of Georgia Press, 2005. Print.

Whall, Helen M. "Walter Mosley and the Books of Ezekiel." *Paradoxa* 16 (2001): 190–202. Print.

Whitehead, Colson. *The Intuitionist*. New York: Anchor Books, 2000. Print.

Yeats, William Butler. *The Collected Poems of W.B. Yeats*. New York: Macmillan, 1974. Print.

Young, Mary. "Walter Mosley, Detective Fiction and Black Culture." *Journal of Popular Culture* 32.1 (1998): 141–50. Print.

Index

Abram/Abraham 37–40
Achebe, Chinua 103
Albert, Prince 129, 193–194ch5n1
Alexie, Sherman 3, 19, 139
All I Did Was Shoot My Man 178
All in the Family 193ch5n3
All Shot Up 78
Al Qaeda 5
"Amber Gate" 142, 151–152, 154, 158–159
Amerika 92, 105
Amos and Andy 121, 131
Anaya, Rudolfo 14, 19, 139
Anderson, James D. 189
Anerikaz Nightmare 194ch7n1
Antigone 119, 123, 126
Appiah, K. Anthony 167, 194ch7n3
Aquinas, Saint Thomas 186
Armstrong, Louis 107
Arnold, Matthew 103
Atherton, Gertrude 58

Bad Boy Brawly Brown 138, 140, 147, 148–149, 151, 156–158
Bakhtin, M.M. 69, 114–116, 144, 145–146, 149, 150
Baudrillard, Jean 164
Beals, Jennifer 188
Beck, Glen 184
Betty Boop 109
Betz, Phyllis M. 14–16, 18–19, 41
The Big Gold Dream 80
Biggers, Earl Derr 3
Bin Laden, Osama 182
The Black Album 161
Black Betty 138, 144, 149
Blind Man with a Pistol 4, 87, 89, 90, 97, 98–103
Blonde Faith 20, 135, 143, 145, 149, 150–151, 152–153, 194ch6n1
Bloom, Harold 19, 39, 40
Blue Bloods 188

The Blues Detective: A Study of African American Detective Fiction 14, 16, 19, 35, 78–79
Body of Proof 188
Bones 8
The Book of J 39
Brand, Eleanor Taylor 139
Brown, Henry Billings 31, 32
Brown, William Wells 48
Brown Gumshoes: Detective Fiction and the Search for Chicana/o Identity 14
Brown v. Board of Education 1, 43, 81, 105, 136, 169, 179
Bruce, John Edward 14, 35
Buber, Martin 39
Buchanan, Edna 139
Bush, George H.W. 136, 162, 181
Bush, George W. 136, 162, 165, 180, 181

Cactus Blood 1, 2
The Canterbury Tales 103
Carby, Hazel V. 41–42
Carlisle Indian Industrial School 2
Carter, Charlotte 139
Carter, Stephen L. 5, 51, 69, 105, 139, 160–177, 178, 181–182, 183, 184–186
Castle 187
Chang, Leonard 139
Charlie Chan 3
Chaucer, Geoffrey 103
Chemerensky, Erwin 188–189
Chicago Code 188
Cinnamon Kiss 147, 149, 150–151, 152–153, 154, 155–156
Civil Rights Movement 105, 128, 136, 183, 184
Close to Home 8
Coel, Margaret 139
Cold Case 8
Coleman, Evelyn 139
The College Dropout 160
Colored American Magazine 21, 44, 46, 49

Conan Doyle, Arthur 55
The Conjure-Man Dies 4, 6, 53–70, 75–76, 79, 81, 184
Contending Forces 44
Cordell, Sigrid Anderson 44, 49–50
Corpi, Lucha 1, 2, 14, 18, 139
Cotton Comes to Harlem 80, 87
The Crazy Kill 81
Criminal Minds 8, 9, 188
"Crimson Stain" 154
Crossing Jordan 8
Crumb, Robert 91
CSI 8, 9, 71, 188
Cuthbert, Margaret 139

Dally, Ann 73–75
Darden, Christopher 139
Darwin, Charles 11, 79, 87, 124, 154–155, 161
Davis, Angela 175
The Death and Life of the Great American School System 180–181
Delany, Martin R. 48
DeLoach, Nora 139
Devil in a Blue Dress 3, 19, 138, 143, 145, 146, 149, 158, 184, 188
"Diamonds from Sierra Leone" 160
Dickens, Charles 5
Didion, Joan 161
Donahue, Deirdre 176–177
Donaldson, Will 109
"Doo wacka doo" 109
Doss, James D. 139
Dred Scott v. Sandford 27, 28–30, 31, 32, 34, 43, 184
Dreiser, Theodor 166
The Dresden Files 8
Du Bois, W.E.B. 2, 55

E., Jeffrey 162
Edwards, Grace 139
Eliot, T.S. 68, 103
Emancipation Proclamation 27, 144
The Emperor of Ocean Park 51, 105, 160, 164, 165, 166, 167, 171–172, 173–177
endocrinology 57–58
English, Daylanne K. 136
Ethiopianism 48
eugenics 27, 31, 33, 40, 44, 51, 81, 105, 150, 155, 184, 192–193*ch3n4*
Eulogy for a Brown Angel 3
Exhibition of the Industry of All Nations, 1853 129

Fabre, Michel 90
Fisher, Rudolph 4, 14, 53–76, 79, 105, 140, 155, 168, 171, 184

Fiske, John 163–164, 194*ch7n*1
Five Percenters 164
For Love of Imabelle 78, 79–80, 83, 86, 100
Ford, Elisabeth 158
Ford, Gerald 10
Fourteenth Amendment 27, 31, 144, 189
Freemasons 162, 164–165
Freud, Sigmund 56, 57, 58, 175
"Furnace Blasts" 49
Furutani, Dale 17, 139

Galton, Francis 33
Garcia-Aguilera, Carolina 139
Garland, Ardella 139
Gates, Henry Louis, Jr. 4, 104–107, 157
Gone Fishin' 20, 135, 138, 143, 146, 147, 149–150, 159
"Goodie Mob" 164, 194*ch7n*1
Gosselin, Adrienne Johnson 55
The Governor's Commission on the Los Angeles Riots 92–94, 141
Graduation 160
Grafton, Sue 14, 16
Graham, Lawrence Otis 167–170
Grandin, Temple 133
Grant, Madison 33
Gratz v. Bollinger 189
The Great Migration 17, 143
Greer, Robert 139
Grimes, Terris 139
Grutter v. Bollinger 189

Hagar, Jean 139
Hagar's Daughter 4, 21–44, 50–52, 184
Hahn, Robert C. 135
Haiti, US Occupation, 1915–1934 116–118
Hambly, Barbara 139
Hamlet 121
Hansen, Joseph 139
Harding, Anthony J. 56
Harlan, John Marshall 31, 43
Harlequin Romances 139
Haywood, Gar Anthony 139
"Heard 'Em Say" 160
The Heat's On 88–89
Heglar, Charles 67–68, 192*ch3n*3
Hess, Mickey 160–161
Hillerman, Tony 3, 139
Himes, Chester 4, 14, 67, 69, 77–103, 105, 140, 155, 167, 168, 171, 184, 185
Hinojosa, Rolando 139
Hirahara, Naomi 18, 139
Hopkins, Pauline 4, 14, 21–52, 81, 140, 184, 187
Hughes, Langston 174
Hurricane Katrina 13, 136

Illuminati 6, 162, 163–165, 194*ch7n*1, 194*ch7n*2
The Impeachment of Abraham Lincoln 166
Indian Killer 3, 19, 139
The Infamous 194*ch7n*1
Infamy 194*ch7n*1
The Intuitionist 4, 126–134

Jack and Jill 168, 159
Jansky, Jan 56–57
Japanese American Internment 2, 17, 18
Jay-Z 161, 163, 164, 165
The Jeffersons 193*ch5n*3
Jericho's Fall 166, 172–177
Jim Crow 105, 143
"John Archer's Nose" 70–76, 192*ch3n*1
Johnson, James Weldon 116–118
"A Journey into the Mind of Watts" 93–94, 96
"Journey of the Magi" 103
Junkanoo 111
Just War Theory 181–182, 186

Kafka, Franz 91–92, 105
Kakutani, Michiko 161, 175
Kaminsky, Jack 193*ch3n*6
Kaufman, Natalie Hevener 7, 8
Kay, Carol McGinnis 7, 8
Kendrick, Douglas B. 56
Kennedy, John F. 174
Kerry, John 162
King, Martin Luther, Jr. 2
King, Rodney 136
King, William R. 129
Kirkus Review 166
The Knight's Tale 103
Knowledge and Experience in the Philosophy of F.H. Bradley 68
Known to Evil 178, 183, 186–187
Kozol, Jonathan 136–138
Ku Klux Klan 105, 184
Kuhn, Thomas 63
Kunetka, James W. 139

Lamar, Jake 139
Landsteiner, Karl 56–57
The Last Days of Louisiana Red 4, 106, 118–126, 127, 131
The Last Thing He Wanted 161
Late Registration 160
Latour, Jose 139
"Lavender" 152
Law and Order 8, 187, 188, 191*ch1n*1
Lear, Norman 193*ch5n*3
Lee, Chang-rae 18, 139
Lee, Gus 139
Lesbian Detective Fiction 14–16

Lewis, Reginald 168
Little Green 194*ch6n*1
Little Scarlet 141–143, 145, 146, 152, 156
A Little Yellow Dog 145, 154
LL Cool J 164
Lombardo, Paul 33
The Long Fall 178, 183, 184, 186–187
Longfellow, Henry Wadsworth 27, 51
Loving v. Virginia 43, 155, 179, 184
Ludlum, Robert 166
Lukacs, Georg 144, 146, 149

Major, Clarence 14
Malcolm X 2
Manifest Destiny 18, 38
Mason, Theodore O., Jr. 135, 144, 145–146
Massachusetts Fifty-fourth Regiment 34, 192*ch2n*2
Massey, Sujata 139
Mayer, Jane 11, 12
McCone, John A. 92–94
Medium 9–10, 191*ch1n*4
Mendel, Gregor 33
The Mentalist 187
Mexican Farm Workers Strike 2, 18
Mickelbury, Penny 139
A Midsummer Night's Dream 102
Mills, Alice 157
Milton, John 165; see also Paradise Lost
Minster, Christopher 117
Mobb Deep 164, 194*ch7n*1
Monk 5, 8, 9, 10, 191*ch1n*1, 191*ch1n*2
monogenesis 48
Mosley, Walter 2, 3, 4, 5, 17, 18, 67, 69, 105, 135–159, 170, 171, 178–181, 182–187, 189
Moss, W.L. 56–57
MOVE 92, 94
Muller, Marcia 14, 16
Mulvey, Laura 85
Mumbo Jumbo 4, 104–118, 193*ch5n*1
Murphy, Jeannette Robinson 48–49
Musgrave, Mariam E. 121
My Lai Massacre 150
"My Lost Youth" 27
Myers, Walter Dean 192*ch2n*3

The National Association of Multicultural Education 139–140
Native Speaker 18, 139
NCIS 8, 188
Neely, Barbara 139
New England White 6, 105, 160, 162, 166, 167, 171, 172–177, 194*ch7n*1
Newton, Isaac 147, 148–149
Nickel, John 48
Nixon, Richard 162–163, 174

No Child Left Behind 137, 180, 181
Norton Anthology of African-American Literature 3–4
Numb3rs 8, 9, 11

Obama, Barack 5, 177, 178, 179, 181–182, 183, 186, 188
Omry, Karen 107–108, 111
Otis, Elisha 129
Our Kind of People: Inside America's Black Upper Class 167–170

Palace Council 105, 161, 162–163, 165, 167, 171, 172–177
Paradise Lost 22, 38, 165, 174
Paretsky, Sara 14, 16
The Passing of the Great Race 33
Paul Whiteman Orchestra 109
Pauline E. Hopkins: A Literary Biography 45–46, 48
Perry, Rufus L. 48
Phillips, Gary 139
The Philosophical Investigations 68
Pierce, Franklin 129
Plan B 4, 81, 89–98, 103, 140, 185
Plessy v. Ferguson 27, 30–32, 34, 43, 44, 46, 48, 105, 137, 184
Price, Hugh B. 139
A Primer of Facts: Pertaining to the Early Greatness of the African Race and the Possibilities of Restoration by Its Descendants 47–49
Pynchon, Thomas 93–94, 96

Racial Integrity Act, Virginia 33, 155
A Rage in Harlem see *For Love of Imabelle*
Raines 191–192ch1n5
Ramos, Manuel 139
Ravitch, Diane 180–181
Raz, Guy 165
Reagan, Ronald 137, 162, 181
The Real Cool Killers 81–87, 100
Reckless Eyeballing 193ch5n1
A Red Death 143, 144, 146–148, 149, 155
Reddy, Maureen T. 14, 16–18, 19–20, 85, 125
Reed, Ishmael 4, 14, 104–126, 127, 131
Rizzoli and Isles 188
Rodriguez, Ralph E. 14, 16
Rose Gold 194ch6n1
Rosencrantz and Guildenstern Are Dead 121, 131
Royce, Josiah 68
Run Man Run 77–78, 81, 87–88
"Run This Town" 164
Rzepka, Charles J. 8

Sacks, Oliver 133
Saldivar, Ramon 4, 128–131, 133
Salvant, Shawn 48
Sand Creek Massacre 2, 18
Savage Inequalities: Children in America's Schools 136–138
Seale, Bobby 123
"The Second Coming" 103
Selden, Steve 33
"Self-Determining Haiti: I. The American Occupation" 117
"Self-Determining Haiti: II. What the United States Has Accomplished" 117–118
Sengoopta, Chandak 57–59
The Shame of the Nation: The Restoration of Apartheid Schooling in America 136–138
Sheldon, Sidney 166
Sherlock Holmes 9, 35–36, 55, 61
The Signifying Monkey: A Theory of African-American Literary Criticism 4, 104–107, 157
"Silver Lining" 144, 154
Simulations 164
Six Easy Pieces 140–141, 154, 156, 158
Skinner, Robert E. 90
Smith, Christopher Holmes 163–164, 194ch7n1
Smith-Levin, Judith 139
Soitos, Stephen F. 14, 16, 19, 34, 35–36, 54, 78–79, 171
Soul Food 194ch7n1
Southern Thoughts for Northern Thinkers 48–49
Spencer, Herbert 56, 63–64, 65, 193ch3n4, 193ch3n6
Stabenow, Dana 139
"Stanzas from the Grande Chartreuse" 103
Status Lymphaticus 73–76
Steinach, Eugen 57–59, 64
Stoppard, Tom 121, 131
Strombeck, Andrew 106, 111–112, 125, 193ch5n1
The Structure of Scientific Revolutions 68
Sullivan, Kathleen 81
Sumner, Charles 31, 191ch2n2
Super Fly 120
Surnow, Joel 11

"Talma Gordon" 44–52
Tea Party 177
Theseus 102–103
Thirteenth Amendment 27, 30
Thomas, Lorenzo 122
Thomas-Graham, Pamela 139
Thurlo, Aimee 139

Thurlo, David 139
thymus, retained 58, 73–76
Tignor, Eleanor Q. 192ch3n2
Traces, Codes, and Clues: Reading Race in Crime Fiction 14, 85, 125
Trail of Tears 2, 18
Tramble, Nichelle 139
24 5 11–12, 20, 150, 176

The Use of Poetry and the Use of Criticism 68

Villatoro, Marcos McPeek 139
Violence in the City: An End or a Beginning? 92–93
The Violence of Peace: America's Wars in the Age of Obama 181–182, 185–186
Voronoff, Serge 57

Walker, Blair S. 139
Wallinger, Hanna 45–46, 48
The Walls of Jericho 192ch3n2
war in Afghanistan 5, 11, 186, 188
war in Iraq 5, 11, 186, 188
War on Terror 5, 11, 186, 188
Washington, Booker T. 2

The Waste Land 102
Watts Riots 92–94, 96, 136, 138, 141, 145, 146, 153, 156, 183
Wesley, Valerie Wilson 139
West, Chassie 139
West, Kanye 160
Whall, Helen M. 157
When the Thrill Is Gone 178, 180, 183
White Butterfly 144, 149
Whitehead, Colson 4, 126–134, 194ch5n4
William, George Washington 48
Williams, Donna 133
Wilson, Woodrow 105, 116
Wingate, Ann 139
Without a Trace 8
Wittgenstein, Ludwig 68
Woods, Paula L. 139
Wounded Knee Massacre 2, 18

The X-Files 161

Yeats, William Butler 57, 58, 103
Yellow Peril 17
Young, Mary 157

Zap Comix 91

www.ingramcontent.com/pod-product-compliance
Ingram Content Group UK Ltd.
Pitfield, Milton Keynes, MK11 3LW, UK
UKHW042006140426
5217IPUK00015B/1009